AF324346

WOMEN & OTHERS

WOMEN & OTHERS

SIGNS OF RACE

Series Editors: Phillip D. Beidler and Gary Taylor

Writing Race across the Atlantic World: Medieval to Modern, edited by Phillip D. Beidler and Gary Taylor (January 2005)

Buying Whiteness: Race, Culture, and Identity from Columbus to Hip-Hop, by Gary Taylor (January 2005)

English and Ethnicity, edited by Janina Brutt-Griffler and Catherine Evans Davies (December 2006)

Women & Others: Perspectives on Race, Gender, and Empire, edited by Celia R. Daileader, Rhoda E. Johnson, and Amilcar Shabazz (September 2007)

WOMEN & OTHERS

PERSPECTIVES ON RACE, GENDER, AND EMPIRE

Edited by

Celia R. Daileader,
Rhoda E. Johnson, and
Amilcar Shabazz

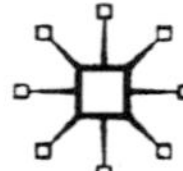

WOMEN & OTHERS

Copyright © Celia R. Daileader, Rhoda E. Johnson, and Amilcar Shabazz, 2007.

All rights reserved. No part of this book may be used or reproduced in any manner whatsoever without written permission except in the case of brief quotations embodied in critical articles or reviews.

First published in 2007 by
PALGRAVE MACMILLAN™
175 Fifth Avenue, New York, N.Y. 10010 and
Houndmills, Basingstoke, Hampshire, England RG21 6XS
Companies and representatives throughout the world.

PALGRAVE MACMILLAN is the global academic imprint of the Palgrave Macmillan division of St. Martin's Press, LLC and of Palgrave Macmillan Ltd. Macmillan® is a registered trademark in the United States, United Kingdom and other countries. Palgrave is a registered trademark in the European Union and other countries.

ISBN-13: 978–0–312–29601–8 (hardcover)
ISBN-10: 0–312–29601–0 (hardcover)
ISBN-13: 978–0–312–29602–5 (paperback)
ISBN-10: 0–312–29602–9 (paperback)

Library of Congress Cataloging-in-Publication Data is available from the Library of Congress.

A catalogue record for this book is available from the British Library.

Design by Newgen Imaging Systems (P) Ltd., Chennai, India.

First edition: September 2007

10 9 8 7 6 5 4 3 2 1

Printed in the United States of America.

*This book is dedicated to our memories
of three extraordinary women:
Sylvia Elliott (1937–2005)
Cynthia Malara (1968–2006)
Ute Brosche Winston (1939–2006)*

*For all those we love for whom tomorrow
will not be another day, we send the
sweet prayer of resting in peace.*
—Alice Randall, *The Wind Done Gone*

Contents

Part I   Literatures

Part II   Histories

SERIES EDITORS' PREFACE

I have never been to Alabama before, but it is and will forever remain seared in my memory as the place where black Americans challenged America to live up to the meaning of her creed so as not to make a mockery of her ideals.

—August Wilson (September 26, 2001)

The first thing you see when you enter the permanent exhibits at the Birmingham Civil Rights Institute is a pair of drinking fountains. Over one hangs a sign that says "White." Over the other hangs a sign that says "Colored."

As an inquiry into the cultural history of race, the series "Signs of Race" has its own obvious historical origins. It springs from a series of symposiums at the University of Alabama—the place where George Wallace made segregation's last stand. But the series finds its larger cultural and intellectual impulses in a deeper and wider history that surrounds us here. Black, brown, red, and white; African American and Afro-Caribbean; English, French, and Spanish; Celtic and Jewish; native American and northern European, creole and mestizo: such cultural categories, wherever they are found, in whatever combinations, and in whatever arrangements of historical interaction and transmission, constitute the legacy of the oceanic intercultures of race in the early modern era. In Alabama, the very landscape is steeped in such history. Twenty miles to the south of the town of Tuscaloosa, the home of the university, is a vast city of pre-Columbian mounds, the capital of a Mississippian empire that flourished at the time of the Norman Conquest and then disappeared two centuries later. The town of Tuscaloosa itself is named after a great chief of the Alabamas, known as the Black Warrior, who engaged the Spanish explorer DeSoto in the 1540 battle of Maubila, to this day thought to be the largest single combat ever fought by native Americans against Europeans. The European settlement of the Gulf Coast pitted English, French, Spanish, and American colonizers against each other well into the nineteenth century. The Revolutionary War found native tribes (their ruling families frequently intermarried with Scots-Irish traders) and allied with loyalists against American nationalists. The early nineteenth-century wars of extermination and removal against native peoples—Creeks, Choctaws, Cherokees, Chickasaws, and Seminoles—and the filling up of the rich agricultural lands thereby opened to a vast slave empire, were determining events in the southward and westward expansion of slavery eventuating in civil war.

In more recent historical memory, particular words and phrases constitute a litany of particular racial struggle: Jim Crow, Ku Klux Klan, Separate but Equal, The Scottsboro Boys, Autherine Lucy, Rosa Parks, The Schoolhouse Door. The names of major cities and towns ring forth as the Stations of the Cross of the civil rights era: Selma, Montgomery, Birmingham, Tuscaloosa. Most recently, Alabama, like much of America, finds itself newly Hispanic, with large influxes of population from Mexico and the Caribbean, South and Central America.

To the extent that every social identity is to some degree local, the meanings of race in Alabama necessarily differ, in some demographic and historical particulars, from the meanings of race in North Dakota and Northern Ireland, New York and New South Wales, Cape Town and Calcutta. But the same questions can be asked everywhere in the English-speaking world.

> How do people signal a racial identity?
> What does that racial identity signify?

This series examines the complex relationships between race, ethnicity, and culture in the English-speaking world from the early modern period (when the English language first began to move from its home island into the wider world) until the postcolonial present, when it has become the dominant language of an increasingly globalized culture. English is now the medium of a great variety of literatures, spoken and written by many ethnic groups. The racial and ethnic divisions between (and within) such groups are not only reflected in but also shaped by the language we share and contest.

Indeed, such conflicts in part determine what counts as "literature" or "culture." Every volume in the series approaches race from a global, interdisciplinary, intercultural perspective. Each volume in the series focuses on one aspect of the cross-cultural performance of race, exploring the ways in which "race" remains stubbornly local, personal, and present.

We no longer hang racial signs over drinking fountains. But the fact that the signs of race have become less obvious does not mean that they have disappeared, or that we can or do ignore them. It is the purpose of this series to make us more conscious and more critical readers of the signs that separate one group of human beings from another.

PHILIP D. BEIDLER
University of Alabama
and
GARY TAYLOR
Florida State University

Acknowledgments

The editors wish to extend sincere and heartfelt thanks to all those who made possible the symposium "Women & Others: Racial and Gender Difference in Anglo-American Literature and Culture," which took place in Tuscaloosa at the University of Alabama, in March of 2005. The symposium reflected a positive and productive collaboration of English literary studies, African American studies, and gender and women studies. Numerous institutions, academic units and individuals facilitated the coming together of our related fields of study to organize the symposium and the production of the present volume. We wish particularly to thank the University of Alabama College of Arts and Sciences, the Department of English, the Program in Creative Writing, the Bankhead Visiting Writers Series, the Hudson Strode Program in Renaissance Studies, the Women's Studies Program, the African American Studies Program, New College, the Alabama Humanities Foundation, Stillman College and the C.A. Fredd Campus of Shelton State Community College for the wonderful reception for Alice Walker, the Martin Luther King Jr. Lecture Series, the Capstone International Center, the Women's Resource Center, the Ferguson Center, Student Affairs Outreach, the University of Alabama Supply Store, the community, all the symposium participants and to Debbie Bond, Willie King, Paul Gilroy and all the fine blues artists who gave our symposium weekend a very special concert finish. We are much indebted to Scott Kopel for assistance designing the jacket, and to Trish Henley for compiling the index and being generally helpful in the final stages of production, when illness and circumstances might otherwise have slowed the team down. Finally, we would like to give a hearty hug and thanks to Cornelius Carter, who has been a great source of inspiration and support for ourselves and our students—keep on moving and teaching dancing man!

Notes on the Contributors

Celia R. Daileader is Professor of English at Florida State University and author of *Eroticism on the Renaissance Stage: Transcendence, Desire, and the Limits of the Visible* (1998); *Racism, Misogyny, and the Othello Myth: Inter-racial Couples from Shakespeare to Spike Lee* (2005); and co-editor with Gary Taylor of John Fletcher's play, *The Tamer Tamed* (2006).

Indira Ghose is professor of English Literature at the University of Fribourg. She is author of *Women Travelers in Colonial India: The Power of the Female Gaze* (Oxford: Oxford University Press, 1998) and editor of *Memsahibs Abroad: Writings by Women Travellers in Nineteenth Century India* (Oxford: Oxford University Press, 1998). She has edited two anthologies of travel writing in India for Pickering & Chatto, and in collaboration with Sara Mills has published an edition of Fanny Parkes, *Wanderings of a Pilgrim in Search of the Picturesque* (Manchester University Press, 2001).

Trudier Harris is J. Carlyle Sitterson Professor and associate chair of English and Comparative Literature at University of North Carolina, Chapel Hill. She was awarded Ohio State University's first annual Award of Distinction for the College of Humanities in 1994. Amongst her more than twenty authored and edited volumes are *Fiction and Folklore: The Novels of Toni Morrison* (Knorville: University Tennessee Press, 1991) and a memoir, *Summer Snow: Reflections from a Black Daughter of the South* (Boston: Beacon Press, 2003). She has lectured in Jamaica, Canada, France, Germany, Poland, Spain, Italy, England, Northern Ireland, and South Africa. She received the Eugene Current-Garcia Award as Alabama's Distinguished Literary Scholar in 2002. In 2005, Harris won the UNC System Board of Governors' Award for Excellence in Teaching and the John Hurt Fisher Award for Career Achievement in Letters from SAMLA.

Lawrence W. Hogue is professor of English at the University of Houston. He is the author of *Discourse and the Other: The Production* *of the Afro-American Text* (Durham: Duke University Press, 1986), *Race, Modernity, Postmodernity: A Look at the History and Literatures of People of Color Since the 1960s* (Albany: SUNY Press, 1996), *The African American Male, Writing, and Difference: A Polycentric Approach to African American Literature, Criticism and History* (Albany: SUNY Press, 2003), and the forthcoming *Postmodern American Literature and Its Other: The Euro-American Male, Woman, the African American, the Native American, the Poor, and the Global Periphery* from University of Illinois Press. Currently, he is completing two critical studies: one on re-representing the Modern American Novel and second one on African American Postmodern Fiction.

Rhoda E. Johnson is Professor of Women's Studies at the University of Alabama and author of *Women's Studies in the South* (1990). She is engaged in important research on preventative medicine for minority women and is principle investigator on NIH-funded research.

Joyce Green MacDonald is associate professor of English at the University of Kentucky, where she specializes in Shakespeare and Renaissance drama. She is the author of *Women and Race in Early Modern Texts* (Cambridge University Press, 2002) and of several articles on race, gender, and performance in Renaissance and Restoration drama.

Maxine Lavon Montgomery is associate professor of English at Florida State University where she teaches courses in African American, American Multiethnic, and women's literature. She is the author of *The Apocalypse in African American Fiction* (Gainesville: University Press of Florida; 1997) and *Conversations With Gloria Naylor* (Jackson: University Press of Mississippi, 2004). Her articles and reviews have appeared in such journals as *African American Review, The College Language Association Journal,* and *Obsidian II.* She is currently at work on a book-length manuscript on the novels of Gloria Naylor, tentatively entitled *Writing Home: Houses and Spaces of Resistance in the Fiction of Gloria Naylor.*

Patricia S. Parker is associate professor at the University of North Carolina, Chapel Hill. Her research, teaching, and community work center on issues of race, gender, class, and power in organization processes, with a central focus on girls' and women's career socialization, leadership, and empowerment. Her publications include a book on African American women's executive leadership (Florence, KY: Erlbaum, 2005), as well as several articles and book chapters appearing in edited volumes and journals such as *Communication Yearbook, Leadership Quarterly*, and *Management Communication Quarterly.*

Amilcar Shabazz is Chair of the W.E.B. Du Bois Department of Afro-American Studies at the University of Massachusetts Amherst. His *Advancing Democracy: African Americans and the Struggle for Access and Equity in Higher Education in Texas* (2004) won the T. R. Fehrenback Book Award. *The Forty Acres Documents*, a sourcebook on reparations, is among his many other published writings.

Andrea Smith is assistant professor of American Culture and Women's Studies at the University of Michigan. She is author of the forthcoming *Native Americans and Christian Right: The Gendered Politics Unlikely Alliances* (Durham: Duke University Press, 2007). She is also the author of *Conquest: Sexual Violence and American Indian Genocide* (Cambridge, MA.: South End Press, 2005). She is the coeditor of the *Color of Violence* (South End Press, 2006) and the editor of *The Revolution Will Not Be Funded: Beyond the Nonprofit Industrial Complex* (South End Press, 2007).

Vron Ware is based in London where she is a freelance writer and independent scholar. Her books include *Beyond the Pale: White Women, Racism and History* (London: Verso, 1992) and *Out of Whiteness: Color, Politics and Culture* (Chicago: University of Chicago Press, 2002). She is currently completing a study of postcolonial identity and global citizenship called *Who Cares About Britishness? A global view of the national identity debate* (London: Arcadia, 2007).

WHO IS THE OTHER WOMAN?
AN INTRODUCTION

Celia R. Daileader

> "I love you" is addressed by convention or habit to an enigma—an other. An other body, an other sex. I love you: I don't quite know who, or what. "I love" flows away, is buried, drowned, burned, lost in a void. We'll have to wait for the return of "I love." . . . Where has "I love" gone? What has become of me?
>
> —Luce Irigaray, *This Sex which is not One*

> Uh huh, listen. Really listen this time: the only voice is your own.
>
> —Gloria Naylor, *Mama Day*

I cannot speak for other women . . . but I do. When I speak as a feminist, I speak for other women. "Speak for yourself," these other women may say. And indeed, almost from its inception, feminist thought and activism has struggled with the problem of differences among women—differences of class, cultural background, sexual orientation, religious affiliation, age. Speaking anecdotally, I think of the young, African American woman who, at the first meeting of my feminist theory class, raised her hand and proudly announced, "My ambition in life is to be a soccer-mom." *Her* mother "worked her life away"; *my* mother pined for a professional life, intellectually floundering in suburban affluence and begrudging domesticity. To cite another classroom soundbyte, this one from a white woman, "But what about those women who steal other women's husbands? I mean, fuck coalition! Whatever happened to sisterhood?" Helena Michie writes:

The term "other" and "woman" form a familiar pairing. In popular culture the anxiety generated by both words is contained within a single figure: "other woman" points to and indicts the mistress. For feminists since Simone de Beauvoir, the two words are virtually synonymous, the pairing redundant: all women are in some sense other. . . . Popular culture uses the transfiguration of female otherness into the mistress to locate it outside the family; the mistress, as not-wife, becomes the locus of all that is troubling, problematic, unfamiliar about female sexuality and sexual difference.[1]

As Luce Irigaray's famous title underscores, in phallogocentric discourse, "this sex"—that of women—is not "one." Woman, in other words, is not a sex in its own right, but the negative inverse of the male, the "hole," the gap, the lack defined by Freud as the essence of femininity. This sex that is not "one" is relegated to the margins by the logic of the self-same, the (phallo)logic that defines woman as other, as not-me, as not male. How to speak, then, of women's interactions with "one another," with "one and other," with "one an(d)other"?

Perhaps the conjunction should be replaced by some form of punctuation:

an other/woman
an other-woman
an/other/woman

One is tempted to add an "m" and play on the relationship between the "other woman" and the "mother woman" in the popular discourse briefly addressed by Michie at the opening of her influential book on female relationships. In the mythology of films such as *Fatal Attraction* and *The Hand that Rocks the Cradle*, the threat to the nuclear family embodied in the mistress is most evident in her presumed nonmaternal qualities: she is foil to the Angel in the House, the destructive, sexual antimother. (That women who have affairs with married men can *also* be wives and mothers is, of course, something the mythology works to obscure.) Allow me one last bit of typographical play:

$a\frac{m}{n}$other woman

Outside the soap operatic popular discourse at issue, the term "other" appears frequently in the emphatic formulation of "a whole other." One hears it often in the context of political debate: "Candidate X opposes the death penalty, but that's a whole other subject." Imagine, however, what would happen, linguistically, if these two veins of

American colloquial speech came together. It would look like this: "I caught my husband in bed with a whole other woman!" Now, that sounds ridiculous, but let us talk—in the manner of Austin and Wittgenstein—about why. The "whole" of the "whole other" (for the moment I will resist playing on the common malapropism, "a whole nother") acts more as an intensifier than as a signifier in its own right. Like the "n" we add in English to the indefinite article when followed by a vowel (an apple, an orange, an other), the "whole" is semantically void, it is a semantic "hole" or, at most, a kind of phonic division between two proximate linguistic entities. Like the "n" that, misplaced (whether accidentally or jocularly), creates the nonword "nother," the "whole" of the "whole other" is a rhetorical flourish. Candidate Y, in naming the "whole other issue," means to say that Candidate X's position on the death penalty (or abortion, or gay marriage, or affirmative action) is a *totally* different issue. But in fact, in many of these contexts, the speaker's rhetorical gesture toward a "whole other" subject is patently disingenuous: that other issue is not "other" but related. It is Candidate X, the opponent, who is "other." The "whole" is needed to emphasize the difference between the two candidates, which might otherwise be missed—especially if (as is often the case) they are both white and male, and *especially* if they are both members of the same political party. In *still* "other" words, in American colloquial speech, the term "other" does not easily translate from the (male) field of political competition and/or intellectual debate to the (female) field of domestic relations and sexuality.

Let us go back to the ludicrous phrasing of "a whole other woman." Is this ludicrous because the term "whole" is presumed? After all, the husband may be a philanderer, but we can assume he is no Jeffrey Dahmer and no weird fetishist of nail pairings or used hygiene products. Or, on the contrary, is the phrasing ludicrous because the speaker, in her outrage, is not likely to contemplate the philosophical question of the woman's wholeness, Because the speaker is not likely to wonder whether the erring husband is attracted to the "whole" woman—personality, beauty, intelligence, culinary genius, erotic skill altogether—rather than her body alone (that Freudian "hole"), or what sexual "possession" of a body such as hers would mean to his ego? Indeed, in this scenario, more than likely, the speaker is not thinking of the other woman as a person—whole or partial, "whole" or "hole"—at all.

Is the "other woman" ever really there? Perhaps you have been in one or the other—shall we call it a "subject position"? Few of us would be so brazen as to admit to having been, in the above scenario, the "one" or the "other"—that is, the wife (and there can only be "one," legally, in the United States, as we will discuss below) or the "other woman." But, whether you have been "there" or not (and more women have than will admit), you were most likely struck just a moment ago by my jarring use of the term "subject position" in reference to an other/wise banal scenario, because the female sexual rivalry as scripted by the myth of the "other woman" is not—in the eyes of contemporary feminist theory—really a subject at all. Indeed, Michie, after opening her book with the figure of the mistress, immediately states that the discussion will go no further. Even within Michie's otherwise other-wise theorization, the "other woman" as sexual rival remains a cipher.

Yet if one disassociates the issue of adultery and the "other woman" from either the banal world of tabloid journalism or the uncomfortable possibility of personal relevance, one perceives a politically charged and urgent historical background, because in the heyday of American slavery, the (white) wife's sexual "rival" was likely to be a woman of color. By the same token, the discourses of imperialism and colonialism often (and hypocritically) invoked the Western values of monogamy and the nuclear family in denigrating "native" sexuality through the mythology of the harem—and, later, inner-city sexual mores as condemned by the discourse of "family values." Indeed, polygamy is still a hotspot in contemporary American right-wing propaganda—notwithstanding the fact that some of the most conservative Americans (those God-fearing pseudo-Mormon cultists) illegally practice it, and notwithstanding the fact that *most* Americans practice polygamy (or polyandry) *across time.*[2]

Like many popular catchphrases that pertain to female sexuality, the phrase "other woman" does not seem to have a male equivalent. Our culture is no less intrigued by stories of male sexual rivalry, but the phrase "other man" does not—even when used in a sexual context—resonate in quite the same way. Perhaps because male competition is presumed to be ubiquitous, whereas women—particularly in the discourse of Second Wave American feminism, with its Utopian notions of "sisterhood"—are presumed to be "naturally" cooperative and averse to competition. Thus, in another groundbreaking work of feminist/gender theory, Eve Kofosky Sedgwick explores at length the male homosocial—that is, the way in which heteronormativity requires a sublimated male homoeroticism, operating through male rivalry over a love-object such as Shakespeare's "dark lady" in the sonnets. But Sedgwick's *Between Men: English Literature and Male Homosocial Desire* (1985) leaves untheorized any notion of a female homosocial. By contrast, Luise Eichenbaum and Susie Orbach's *Between Women: Love, Envy and Competition in Women's Friendships* (1988) made little impact in the academy (despite—or perhaps because of—its promotion by Oprah Winfrey), while Sedgwick's paradigm went on to dominate the critical discourse for the better part of two decades.

Let us look briefly at the shadowy female figure that acts as the hinge for the love-triangle in Shakespeare's sonnets, the so-called dark lady who enters into the sequence and disrupts an idyllic homoerotic exchange between the poet-speaker and a lovely, "fair," young man. I am often surprised at the persistence of certain gendered tropes across historical periods as far removed as Shakespeare's and our own. Sedgwick's analysis of the "dark lady" sonnets elucidates the binary oppositions that associate the young man with the positive values of light and heaven and the woman with negative values of darkness and hell. Likewise, Kim F. Hall's *Things of Darkness: Economies of Race and Gender in Early Modern England* foregrounds the way figurations of a dark, sexualized, female alterity in the Renaissance "Classics" function to distinguish women from one another. "In many cases," Hall pointedly writes, "women are only fair or black in comparison with one another."[3] Though there is no "fair lady" to rival the "dark" one in Shakespeare's sonnets, his other works include a plethora of female rivalrous pairings that hinge on the trope of racial/complexional difference. One striking example that Hall addresses is *A Midsummer Night's Dream*, wherein the mutual love-object of Helen and Hermia dismisses the latter as an "Ethiop" and a "tawny Tartar" (3.2.258, 264).

This racialized language becomes even more interesting when it arises in the work of Shakespeare's female contemporaries. Thus, the first original English play authored by a woman, Elizabeth Cary, pits her heroine in *The Tragedy of Mariam, Fair Queen of Jewry* (1613) against a number of female foils, figured as lecherous, duplicitous, and dark-complected, in contrast to her own complexional and moral superiority (note the term "fair" in the title). As Kim Hall and Gwynne Kennedy observe, "The play constructs white privilege by aligning beauty, virtue, high rank, and white skin as superior qualities all signifiable by fairness." Nor is Cary alone amongst English women writers in deploying this language; as Hall and Kennedy also note, Lady Mary Wroth does the same in her romance *Urania* (1621). Later in the century, Margaret Cavendish's fantasy travel narrative *The Blazing World* (1668) imagines, in lieu of the usual early modern complexional-racial markers of "white, black, tawny, olive or ash," people with green, purple, or azure skin.[4] Cavendish's *Blazing World*, interestingly, originally appeared in print as an appendix to her *Observations on Experimental Philosophy*, which critiques Robert Boyle's theories about the etiology of skin color.[5]

No discussion of early female authors writing race would be complete without noting Aphra Behn's intervention in the discourse later in the seventeenth century. Behn's influential African love-story *Oroonoko, or, The Royal Slave* (1688) broke with racist-xenophobic precedents by glorifying not just its titular African prince, but also his beloved, "the beautiful black Venus" to his black Adonis, the princess Imoinda. Indeed, Behn's relationship to her black heroine has produced interesting commentary: some scholars hold that her romance abjects and marginalizes Imoinda, privileging the relationship between the English, female narrator and her African hero, while others find Behn's "black Venus" a rare moment of interracial woman-to-woman identification.[6] That Behn seems actually to have traveled to Surinam, the exotic locale of her novel, further complicates the dynamic between author and subject(s). Indeed, rumors that the English author actually had relations with her hero's real-life counterpart—though entirely unproven and unproveable—attest to her culture's obsession with this particular form of miscegenation, an obsession I have elsewhere dubbed "Othellophilia" and theorized at length.[7] More pertinently, though, these rumors underscore the habit of viewing white and black women as sexual rivals, rather than as sisters in patriarchal oppression.

Behn was unusual amongst Englishwomen of her time in having had the opportunity to travel, but within a century or so, British imperialism made it possible for well-to-do women to confront the *most* other of other women: non-Europeans. Thus, early in the eighteenth century, Lady Mary Wortley Montagu traveled extensively with her ambassador husband throughout Europe and the Ottoman Empire. Her letters from Constantinople provide a fascinating glimpse of cross-cultural sympathy—particularly amongst women. Indeed, a mere glance at her collected letters reveals the intensity of her attention to the dress and manners of women of different cultures. Here are a few excerpts from the 1716–18 section of the Table of Contents:

> The Hungarian ladies . . .
> Civility of the ladies . . .
> Morality of the ladies . . . Privileges of the Harem
> The fair Fatima . . .
> Turkish ladies and Grecian belles . . .
> Pleasures enjoyed by Turkish women . . .
> False notions respecting Turkish women . . .
> French and English women contrasted . . .[8]

Montagu provides exquisitely detailed descriptions of the physiques, fashions, and manners of her hostesses, even going so far as to count the 110 natural braids on the head of one Turkish lady: "I never in my life saw so many fine heads of hair," she writes, admitting without hesitation "that every beauty is more common here than with us."[9] Indeed, she seems to fall in love with the Sultana Fatima. Of the latter she writes:

> I have seen, all that has been called lovely in England or Germany, and [I] must own that I never saw anything so gloriously beautiful, nor can I recollect a face that would have been taken notice of near hers. . . . I confess . . . I was so struck with admiration, that I could not for some time speak to her, being wholly taken up in gazing. That surprising harmony of features! . . . that lovely bloom of complexion unsullied by art! The unutterable enchantment of her smile!—But her eyes!—large and black, with all the soft languishment of the blue![10]

A bit farther down she excuses herself for the extravagance (and perhaps, subliminally, the homoeroticism) of her description: "I think I have read somewhere that women always speak in rapture when they speak of beauty, but . . . I rather think it [a] virtue to be able to admire without any mixture of desire or envy."[11]

Montagu's remarks strike me as fairly generous in contrast to the racist-xenophobic rhetoric of her Renaissance predecessors and the racism of her modern successors. It is true that these Turkish beauties measure up to the standards that Hall ascribes to the European cult of fairness: Montagu makes a point of praising their "shiningly white"[12] skin along with their black hair and eyes. Yet her fascination with skin color does *not* participate in the *moral* aspect of the discourse critiqued by Hall—a discourse that seeks to align fairness with both pale skin and a particularly Anglo, class-specific ideal of female chastity. On the contrary, Montagu comments on the sexual habits of foreign women (and men) in markedly neutral tones. For instance, in Vienna she observes dryly that "'tis the established custom for every lady to have two husbands, one that bears the name, and another that performs the duties,"[13] in a letter that ends with a gesture of striking moral relativism ("gallantry and good-breeding are as different, in different climates, as morality and religion"[14]). Another example of this leniency is her observation that the "perpetual masquerade" of Turkish women's attire gives them not *less* freedom than European women, but *more*, for "'Tis impossible for the most jealous husband to know his wife when he meets her" in the street on her way to a tryst with her lover. She concludes, "You may easily imagine the number of faithful wives very small in a country where they have nothing to fear from a lover's indiscretion," observing how often her own compatriates commit adultery despite "all the threatened punishment of" the Christian afterlife. She goes on to make a subtle but devastating point about Turkish women's property rights versus the absolute dearth of such rights in England: "Neither have they much to apprehend from the resentment of their Husbands, those Ladys that are rich having all their money in their own hands, which they take with 'em upon a divorce with an addition which he is oblig'd to give 'em."[15] Montagu's claim has been confirmed by Islamic scholars: Turkish marriage contracts at the time involved a financial gift from the groom to the bride, paid in part at the wedding and the remainder in the event of divorce. Unlike English women, who forewent all rights to their property upon marriage, Turkish women maintained control of their assets despite marital status.[16]

These counterstereotypical maneuvers earned Montagu the admiration of a number of twentieth-century feminist critics; writing in 1979, Katharine Rogers appreciates Montagu's "wicked comment on the Englishman's complacent assumption that England was 'the paradise of wives.'" On the other hand, Rogers was also clearly uncomfortable with the implications of this moral stance: she writes, "it is upsetting to note that she defined women's liberty in terms of spending money and carrying on adulterous affairs with impunity."[17] But "impunity" is an ill-chosen term: Montagu's main target in her reflections on Turkish versus English morality is the sexual double-standard and its appalling perpetuation in eighteenth-century British law. These inequities were more than evident in contemporary divorce cases such as that of the notorious philanderer William Yonge and his estranged wife Mary, whom Montagu defended in her poem "Epistle from Mrs. Y[onge] to her Husband."[18]

Not surprisingly, Montagu's discussions of the habits and freedoms of Turkish women often focus on the question of attire. Thus she relates a visit to the baths when her hostesses tried to convince her to undress and join them. She writes:

> They being all so earnest in persuading me, I was at last forced to open
> my shirt, and shew them my stays . . . they believed I was so locked up
> in that machine, that it was not my own power to open it, which
> contrivance they attributed to my husband . . . [One of the women]
> cried out to the other ladies in the bath: "Come hither and see how
> cruelly the poor English ladies are used by their husbands. You need
> boast indeed of the superior liberties allowed you, when they lock you
> thus up in a box."[19]

In fact, Montagu soon adopted the Turkish habit for convenience and anonymity. She was painted in Turkish attire—minus the veil—as early as 1722.

Montagu's reactions to women in Turkey might appear either liberal-minded and protoglobal, or patronizing and Orientalist, depending upon your point of view—indeed, a glance at criticism of her Turkish embassy letters proves, as one critic puts it, that "the verdict is not yet in."[20] As for the question of her feminist sympathies, we can applaud her for her poems such as the above-mentioned epistle on the Yonge divorce, as well as her scathing (and hilarious) satirical response to Alexander Pope's nauseously misogynistic "The Lady's Dressing-Table." That Montagu's class status enabled her travels and thus her friendly gestures toward Turkish women is as relevant or irrelevant as the fact that class privilege enabled her feminism—a perhaps insurmountable paradox that we educated, first-world feminists are bound continually to run into. I close with one vital historical fact: Montagu introduced to Western medicine the practice of inoculation against smallpox, which she learned of from an elderly female healer in Turkey.[21] In our calculus of her credentials as a feminist, an activist, and a conduit between cultures, this achievement deserves at least as much attention as the question of the "Orientalism" or "Counter-Orientalism" of her letters. Montagu gave credence to an old and probably poor Turkish woman practicing folk medicine and as a result saved innumerable lives. On this question, then, the verdict is in.

*　*　*　*　*

Not all female travelers to the Orient (or to Africa, or to the Americas, for that matter) exhibited the open-mindedness and cultural fluency evident in Montagu's letters—or even in her portrait in Turkish attire. A century or so later, as Indira Ghose points out, Englishwomen in India—obsessed with their roles as representatives of their ("superior") culture—scorned the silk native habits and insisted on braving the tropical heat in English garb weighing four pounds or more without shoes. Nor did the *Memsahibs* follow Montagu's lead in their judgment of English versus native female freedom. As Ghose explains in her chapter in this volume, "Even in the case of women who were engaged in social reform, for instance in the field of female education, their self-definition was constructed against the foil of Indian women as less emancipated than they were."

Ghose's observations about colonial India strike a disturbingly contemporary note, given the cynical pseudofeminist gestures toward Muslim women that have become part and parcel of the Bush administration's neoimperialist discourse. As Vron Ware writes in her chapter, "Feminism has long been concerned with the ways in which some ideas about women—their rights, wrongs, entitlements and essences—can be mobilized to inflame patriotism and nationalist fervor, to support and glorify war and to justify domination." And indeed, Montagu's reflections on Turkish women's "disguise" place contemporary Western invocations of the *burqa* in a weird, new light— just as her Turkish hostesses' distress at the sight of her corset resonates oddly with Ghose's observation about Englishwomen's stifling fashions in colonial India. I confess that the mere sight of a *burqa* makes me physically ill—I think of a funeral shroud and imagine life inside it as death-in-life—but I also take seriously Sonali Kolhatkar's statement that "We need to begin treating Afghan women with dignity and not reduce them to a piece of clothing" (quoted in Ware). In my "liberated" Western democracy, perfectly healthy women feel compelled to cut open their breasts in order to "look good" in the revealing garments we consider symbols of emancipation. Clearly the issue of female sartorial and physical freedom is more complex than that.

That Christian fundamentalism in the West and Muslim fundamentalism in the east are cut from the same cloth has become a truism in contemporary leftist political discourse. I note again the conjunction between Muslim polygamy and that associated with American Mormon cultists—the latter arguably the *other* among Christian fundamentalist sects. At the same time, as Andrea Smith points out in her chapter, the evangelical feminist movement in America co-opts the language of its liberal counterpart, so that groups such as Concerned Women for America simultaneously attack "feminism" and claim that "their members . . . are the women carrying on the true legacy of Susan B. Anthony." Could this get any more confusing? Yes, it does. Also according to Smith, running parallel to, but not intersecting with, the evangelical feminist movement, the "race reconciliation movement" has attempted to bring African Americans back to the evangelical fold—though not with much success.

Christianity's role in black history is, of course, an ambivalent one. On the one hand, black churches (and a few white ones too) provided the organizational and polemical backbone of the civil rights movement; on the other hand, the traditionalist, conservative collective mentality represented by "good churchgoing folks" can function as the primary engine for black-on-black othering. Thus, scholars of African American literature such as Trudier Harris and Maxine Montgomery note the ambivalence of community, family, and church in fiction by black authors. In this volume, Harris and Montgomery both discuss the struggle for communal and familial acceptance on the part of black homosexual characters in novels by Randall Kenan and Gloria Naylor, respectively. As Montgomery notes, "Naylor complicates the issue of identity politics" by portraying (for instance) a black, lesbian character who first objects to her community's homophobia ("Black people were all in the same boat . . . and if they didn't row together, they would sink together") but then goes on "to 'other' 'others' who are 'othered'" by way of epithets such as "wierdos" and "fags." Likewise, Harris traces Kenan's protagonist's descent into madness and suicide as he internalizes homophobia—hallucinating a scene in his church wherein he is collectively shamed, abused, and abjected.

A more positive vision of black community arises in Patricia S. Parker's chapter in which she argues that black women's tradition of "creative resistance and community building"—a tradition that arose "during the era of slavery"—can provide positive models of black female leadership and self-realization. Admitting that "tradition is a complicated and often politically charged concept" that "can be highly oppressive," Parker nonetheless holds that "positive cultural continuity in Black women's history" offers "one way to counter historical and contemporary discourses that devalue Black women." To return to African American fiction for a moment, one finds examples of this in the matriarchal heroines of Toni Morrison and even Naylor herself in a novel such as *Mama Day* (a novel that I cannot resist teaching as a countertext to Shakespeare's protoimperialist, patriarchal *The Tempest*). Parker's challenge in her chapter is poignant: "If the postmodern world is marked by fragmentation and indeterminacy, is it possible to even imagine a Black women's tradition of leadership that is based on a collective history?"

Perhaps what makes this possible is our ability to critique that very notion of the "postmodern," in its theoretical complicity with white male privilege. Lawrence W. Hogue's chapter thus takes up a white, male author whose programmatic postmodernity leads him to assault the modern truisms of the unitary self and instrumental reason—only to fall back upon tired, old, masculinist, Eurocentric fantasies of the black female as sexualized, primal Other. Paul Auster, whose *New York Trilogy* is the subject of Hogue's critique, makes the astute observation that "no one can cross the boundary into another—for the simple reason that no one can gain access to himself" (quoted in Hogue). Ironically, this self-opacity leads his white, male protagonist (who at one point in the trilogy *becomes* his authorial self, "Paul Auster") to view black women as mammies and whores, and to view white women (even prostitutes!) as their essentially sexless foils.

Hogue's critique, in exposing the retrograde racial and gender politics in so recent and intellectually "hip" a work of fiction, explodes postmodern elitist masculinist pretension along with any residual humanism we postmoderns might betray in looking for evidence of linear social progress in the source materials for this eclectic collection. Thus Auster's fever-dream of "an enormous black woman . . . washing her cunt" resonates strangely with early modern associations between a feminized, racial blackness and moral/sexual filth (one thinks of the common figuration of "washing the Ethiope"—a trope for fruitless labor). Moreover, the racist sexual adventurism of Auster's male characters harks back to the de facto prostitution of women of color in the New World, an institution Joyce Green MacDonald rightly compares to contemporary "sex tourism." Auster may even be—paradoxically—*less* racially liberal than his eighteenth-century predecessors. MacDonald's chapter on George Colman's 1787 comic opera *Inkle and Yarico* may surprise readers unfamiliar with what was then a popular theatrical piece. Colman harnesses minstrel conventions in the service of a stunningly pro-miscegenation reverse-Othello, complete with a photonegative of Shakespeare's interracial couple and a happy ending. The hero sings, "With jealousy I ne'er shall burst, / Who'd steal my bone of bone-a? / A white Othello, I can trust / A dingy Desdemona" (quoted in MacDonald). And although this is the most backhanded of backhanded compliments (he can trust her sexually because no other man would want a "dingy" lover), it nonetheless strikes at the heart of Othellophilia in exposing racist-masculinist hypocrisy over white men's sexual predation upon women of color.

I began with two student quotations—one from an African American woman with aspirations to happy domesticity, one from a white woman worried about "those women who steal other women's husbands" (the latter comment no more misguided about feminism than it is demeaning of the "stolen" husbands). The racial encoding of these two statements (not uttered in the same classroom) gives pause in light of the painful history wherein racist-masculinist hegemony has deployed the ideology of domesticity, marriage, and the nuclear family to keep women divided along race and class lines. This is the legacy of the plantation, wherein women of color were denied the material comforts and respect promised women by domestic ideology (despite their performing the most taxing of domestic and reproductive chores for their white masters), while white women, cognizant of their servants' erotic availability in the eyes of their husbands, let jealousy poison their enjoyment of those same envied social and material privileges. That the racial and class encoding of this history can now be reversed also deserves note. In an utterly believable episode in Spike Lee's *Jungle Fever*, the African American hero's otherwise genteel wife responds to news of his interracial fling with unmitigated rage against the "low-class white bitch" he "boned" (a term Lee, in character as the husband's best friend, uses) after hours in the office.

Perhaps this is why Michie's otherwise compendious discussion of what she terms "sororophobia" shies away from theorizing female sexual rivalry as written in the figure of "the mistress"—because in the discourse of popular culture, these tales so often descend to the tone of Spike Lee's character, describing the transgressive sexual exchange in the crude terminology of "boning." The crudeness is not the director's, of course, and indeed I believe his film to be one of the most nuanced and complicated explorations of the miscegenation taboo in American mainstream cinema.[22] At the same time, in punishing the interracial lovers, Lee's vision does not depart widely from the Shakespearean, tragic precedent, given the drastically contrasting historical and social context. Indeed, depictions of nonmonogamous and even miscegenous sexuality need not be so predictable. Alice Randall's *The Wind Done Gone* (2000) constitutes a programmatic (if artfully parodic) response to that viciously racist "classic" of Southern antebellum nostalgia, Margaret Mitchell's *Gone with the Wind* (1935). In contradistinction to Mitchell, who sweeps the historical reality of miscegenation under a very romantic rug, Randall confronts the legacy directly, granting Scarlett O'Hara a "mulatta" half-sister, Cynara, the love-child of mammy and Gerald. In a beautifully appropriate reversal, Cynara—who also competes with her half-sister for the love of Rhett—speaks of Scarlett as "Other," rather than using her Christian name.

Can feminists speak for other women? Or can we speak only for ourselves? Linda Alcoff critiques what she calls "the 'retreat' response" among feminists who claim only to speak for themselves: "in some cases certain political effects can be garnered in no other way" than by "speaking for others."[23] The concept behind the symposium that gave rise to this volume—held at the University of Alabama March 17–19, 2005—germinated when I began pondering the relevance of American poststructuralist gender theory to feminist antiracist activism and hooked up with my collaborators Rhoda E. Johnson and Amilcar Shabazz in putting together an eclectic, interdisciplinary, and culturally diverse group of speakers on the theme. If, we asked in our initial call for papers, feminists are to take seriously Judith Butler's deconstruction of the category "woman," how can we claim to speak as (never mind speaking *for*) women? On a certain level, of course, "we" cannot—and do not—that is to say, Second Wave generalizations about "Woman" as transcendent of racial, ethnic, demographic, sexual, and class categories (in other words, the assumption that "Woman" is white, Anglophone, and middle-class) have become anathema in the language of self-identified feminists, black and white. And the notion of coalition versus identity politics has gained widespread support in the academy (outside the academy, in the sphere of feminist activism, coalition has always been presumed, if not always practiced). But there is still a lingering unease about the question of representation, an unease Butler's discussion in the Preface of *Gender Trouble* famously foregrounds.[24] Unlike Butler, I prefer *not* to scare-quote or question the noun "women," but the preposition (speaking "for," speaking "as"). But her caveat remains relevant. Thus, the original symposium blurb ended wondering, "What other way to speak?"

The problem may be, however, neither the noun nor the preposition, but the verb, as Vron Ware has helped us realize. In response to the wording of the initial call for papers (composed before the event we still call 9/11 and the subsequent wars in Afghanistan and Iraq), Ware's chapter speaks of feminism in the global north as needing an "other way to *listen*" to women of other cultures. There have been good historical reasons for feminism's preoccupation with the right to speak out, but speech is pointless in a context where no one listens.[25] And perhaps women's socialized gift for perception, pacifism, communication, diplomacy, and empathy is something feminists should cultivate at this historical juncture, with the odious fruits of phallic aggression, blind patriotism, and political zero-sums staring a terrified world in the face. Perhaps it is time—now that we have spent a good two or three decades "deconstructing" these traditionally "feminine values"—to *celebrate* women's role as peacemakers, rather than sweeping it under the poststructuralist theoretical rug, along with all those other nasty essentialisms such as "maternal instinct" and (God forbid) "penis envy." After all, as Diana Fuss points out, essentialism *is* what essentialism *does*.[26]

> Nothing they can do can separate I and I.
>
> —Bob Marley

"Woman," Irigaray writes, "always remains several, but is kept from dispersion because the other is already within her . . ."[27] I do not think I agree with Irigaray's suggestion that the plurality ("neither one nor two") of the female sexual organs essentially alters our self-perception, and I am not a lesbian, so I can neither endorse nor critique the gorgeously poetic, homo(theo)rotics of her essay "When our lips speak together." Nonetheless the problem of "other women" with which we have been grappling calls for resolution in Irigaray's paradigm for intragender interaction, in her rhetorical and theoretical dissolution of the self/other binary, and in her metaphor of, not speaking *for* and not even speaking *as*, but speaking *together*.

"We're not speaking." This banality conjures images of turned backs and squared shoulders—and it is gendered. It is women who are taught "If you can't say anything nice, don't say anything at all." In general, men will talk whether or not they have something "nice" to say. The expression, however, is a functional oxymoron: the person saying she is "not speaking" quite patently is doing just that. What she means is "we're not speaking to one another" or "to each other": the English translation of Irigaray's title is not idiomatic, and there's a reason. "Together" is too close for comfort for two women speaking. There must be a preposition, a space, and an "other." Or better yet, leave the prepositional phrase implicit; let the "other" dissolve into silence. "We're not speaking," period—no need for an ellipsis.

Popular culture is rife with instances of woman-on-woman othering. Indeed, one is hard-pressed to find a romantic comedy, melodrama, or even an "action flik" that does *not* feature a mother-in-law/daughter-in-law tiff, a stiletto-heel-in-the-eye "cat fight" between romantic rivals, or a battle of "dirty looks" between the uptight disapproving Ice Queen and some loveable Mary Jane (often played by Jennifer Aniston). "Are you Catherine [Zeta-Jones] or Jennifer?" *Cosmopolitan* perkily asks its readers. As if a woman could only identify with one of these two actresses—the jilted or the "home-breaker," the nice girl or the vamp. There is nothing new here, as Virginia Woolf has told us; masculinist culture, in conceiving of women *only* as sexual partners of men, distorts and flattens the complexity of female intragender interaction. Citing Shakespeare's *Antony and Cleopatra*, she observes, "Cleopatra's only feeling about Octavia is one of jealousy. Is she taller than I am? How does she do her hair? The play, perhaps, required no more. But how interesting it would have been if the relationship between the two women had been more complicated." Woolf then observes how seldom in literature "two women are represented as friends."[28] Toni Morrison notes the threat posed by so simple a concept: "I went someplace to talk about *Sula* and there were some genuinely terrified men in the audience. . . . They said, 'Friendship between women?' Aghast. Really terrified."[29]

Morrison's *Sula* is, indeed, a radical work of art in mapping out the terrain of a relationship between two apparently heterosexual women, Nell and Sula, that I would describe as a sort of spiritual marriage. This friendship falls apart when Nell catches her husband and Sula making love. As predictable a plot twist as that seems, Morrison's subtlety in etching out the psychological aftermath on both women is nothing short of groundbreaking. Nell fails in properly grieving the end of either relationship (her husband, Jude, simply puts on his pants and says, "I'll be back for my things"). Morrison uses the image of a "little gray ball" to encapsulate Nell's repressed grief:

> She spent a whole summer with the gray ball, the little ball of fur and string and hair always floating in the light near her but which she did not see because she never looked. But that was the terrible part, the effort it took not to look. But it was there anyhow, just to the right of her head.[30]

I think most readers recognize the gray ball—certainly anyone who has practiced denial will respond powerfully to the passage. The gray ball is also, however, a fitting metaphor for the other—that presence that shadows us but that we cannot bear to look in the face, to the extent that our avoidance of it begins to dictate our every motion. In this way the other defines the self, as the effort of othering becomes the self's raison d'etre. Nell and Sula finally speak again years later when Sula is on her deathbed. Nell confronts Sula about the fling with Jude and receives this response: "What you mean take him away? I didn't kill him, I just fucked him. If we were such good friends, how come you couldn't get over it?"[31] Nell's epiphany comes over Sula's grave. Here is how the book ends:

> A soft ball of fur broke and scattered like dandelion spores in the breeze.
>
> "All that time, all that time, I thought I was missing Jude." And the loss pressed down on her chest and came up into her throat. "We was girls

together," she said as though explaining something. "O Lord, Sula,"
she cried, "girl, girl, girlgirlgirl."
It was a fine cry—loud and long—but it had no bottom and it had no
top, just circles and circles of sorrow.[32]

This is the cost of recognizing the other: the realization of the other
in the self, and hence, the danger of the loss of self. "We was girls
together." The grammatical "error" supplied by Nell's vernacular
subtly underscores the elision of "I" and "you": I was, you were, "we
was." "We was . . . *together.*"

In a conversation with Gloria Naylor, Morrison highlighted the
radical potential of the kind of love between women portrayed in
Sula: "You see, if all women behaved like those two . . . everything
would just crumble—hard. If it's not about fidelity and possession
and my pain versus yours, then how can you manipulate, how can you
threaten, how can you assert power?" Naylor concurred, adding, "We
do share our men. We may not like it very much, but there's a silent
consensus about that and it hasn't really torn us apart as women." The
"us" here, however, is racial; Naylor is speaking specifically of
African American women.[33] And there is a widespread accord in black
feminist thought that a tradition of love between women—whether
familial, sexual, or Platonic—has granted women of color a special
strength in the face of poverty and oppression. These bonds do not
always fall within the usual rubrics and call for special coinages such as
the term "othermother," indicating a woman who shares childrearing
responsibilities in an extended family.[34] One wonders whether white
women's relative affluence has not been both a blessing and a curse, in
breeding—along with the ideology of the nuclear family—complacency,
competition, and isolation, where there might be community and
interdependence.

Yet white women also "share our men"—and share them with
women of color. In white southern American culture there is a term
for the wife or ex-wife of one's husband or ex-husband: "wife-in-law."
Wives-in-law are expected to be civil, even friendly to one another
(not to do so would be, as a native Alabamian explained to me,
"tacky")—but the potential for real homosocial bonding rarely goes
beyond that. In the same way that African American culture generally
is more frank about sexuality (take, for example, the lyrics of Hip-hop
music), authors such as Randall, Naylor, and Morrison have been
pioneers in exploring the erotic possibilities and realities belied by
white hypocrisy, homophobia, and the cult of the nuclear family. (Had
I more space in this chapter, I might have broadened the discussion to

include the eroticism of James Baldwin's fiction.) Adultery, bisexuality, same-sex love, romantic friendships, and communal childrearing—these things *do happen*, in life, in literature, and in history. Rather than treating such practices as embarrassing secrets—or theorizing them into abstraction—feminist discourse might look to them for emancipatory potential. In Alice Walker's *The Color Purple* (1970), the heroine falls in love with her abusive husband's mistress, and this shared love of a third party ultimately transforms their relationship and ends the abuse. Tuzyline Jita Allan argues that Walker's novel—widely criticized for its unflattering depictions of African American men—in fact exposes *both sides* of racial/gender oppression, portraying woman-on-woman othering as equally brutal, psychologically if not physically.[35] Yet Walker manages to deliver this critique in the course of a novel that ends with all parties having reconciled—and believably so. Likewise, Randall's *Wind Done Gone* ends when Cynara (having walked out on her white sugar-daddy) gives her love-child with a black congressman to his beautiful, black, barren wife. Cynara goes on to forgive her white half-sister (and through her, I believe, the dead white female author who created her): "A lifetime of hating Other has made me fit for an eternity of loving her."[36]

At basis loving the other is really about loving oneself. In his reading of *Sula* and *The Color Purple*, Kevin Everod Quashie observes, "This love of the other . . . is a love that manifests for an/other woman who is the self—an identification with and as the other woman. *With* and *as* identifications also employ disidentification, represented by the progression to repeating moments when there really is no other woman . . . except one's ability to be that other woman."[37] As Irigaray observes in the epigraph for this introduction, when the words "I love" are lost in a void—directed at an other conceived as "an enigma"—one ultimately winds up wondering "what has become of me?" Who is the other woman? Nobody: everybody. You yourself.

*   *   *   *   *

When Alice Walker speaks, people listen.

In planning Walker's keynote lecture for the Alabama Symposium, we were told, "Be sure to check the microphone. She's wonderful—but soft-spoken." A first-rate sound-system was a given: we expected standing-room audiences in Morgan Auditorium, and indeed the crowds started arriving hours before her talk. Events in Alabama on the week of March 17, 2005 only drove home the urgency of our theme and the appropriateness of the speaker. Alabama state representative Gerald Allen shocked the university community by proposing a ban on all books including gay characters or representing homosexuality as a viable lifestyle. Walker's *The Color Purple*—along with much of the Western literary canon—would be thrown (in Allen's phrasing) in a "great big hole" and buried. Unbeknownst to Walker, students at the University of Alabama chose the day of her visit to campus for their demonstration against the gay-book ban. They did not expect her to participate—nor did they recognize the petite and soft-spoken author until she signed the petition.

When Walker spoke that evening, the auditorium was packed—aisles, balconies, and lobby earshot space crowded with warm bodies sitting (or standing) utterly rapt, *utterly silent.* Standing backstage with Walker's companion and my collaborator Rhoda E. Johnson, I craned my neck and listened. I think all three of us were practically holding our breath. Walker spoke of the war in Iraq. Walker spoke of her books. She spoke as a woman, she spoke for women, she spoke to women (and men). Most courageously of all, Walker spoke of that afternoon's demonstration against the gay-book ban. In reference to Allen's homophobic bill, Walker said, "Do not go backward, Alabama." Soft-spoken as she was, everyone heard. There, at the University of Alabama, site of that infamous and tragic stand against black civil rights, Walker said, "Do not go backward, Alabama. There's nothing back there but an incredible amount of pain and an incredible amount of confusion. Don't let them push you back, because all of us must live." Two days later, Allen relented on putting the gay-book ban forward. In other words, Alabama listened.

The American South—let us not forget—is the subaltern of America, and by extension of the global north. So it seems now Alabama has something to tell America, through voices such as Walker's and our own, in the pages of this book. Do not go back.

So, listen. Really listen this time, because maybe, just maybe, the one talking here is you.

NOTES

1. Helena Michie, *Sororophobia: Differences among Women in Literature and Culture* (Oxford: Oxford University Press, 1992), 3.
2. I am grateful to Mormon feminist Brandie Siegfried for correcting my earlier impression that polygamous cults such as Warren Jeffs's are representative of, or even doctrinally compatible with, mainstream Mormonism.
3. Kim F. Hall, *Things of Darkness: Economies of Race and Gender in Early Modern England* (Ithaca, NY: Cornell University Press, 1995), 100.

4. Kim Hall and Gwynne Kennedy, "Early Modern Women Writing Race," *Teaching Tudor and Stuart Women Writers* (New York: MLA, 2000), 238–39.

5. See Gary Taylor, *Buying Whiteness: Race, Culture, and Identity from Columbus to Hip-Hop* (New York: Palgrave, 2005), 386; for Taylor's discussion of Enlightenment theories of complexional "whiteness" see 258–302.

6. See, for instance, Margaret W. Ferguson, "Juggling the Categories of Race, Class, and Gender: Aphra Behn's *Oroonoko*," in *Women, Race and Writing in the Early Modern Period*, ed. Margo Hendricks and Patricia S. Parker (New York: Routledge, 1994), 209–24; and Jane Spencer, *The Rise of the Woman Novelist: Fom Aphra Behn to Jane Austen* (Oxford: Blackwell, 1986).

7. See Celia R. Daileader, *Racism, Misogyny, and the Othello Myth: Interracial Couples from Shakespeare to Spike Lee* (Cambridge University Press, 2005).

8. Lady Mary Wortley Montagu, *The Letters and Works of Lady Mary Wortley Montagu, Edited by her Great-Grandson, Lord Wharncliffe* (New York: AMS Press, 1971), xii–xiv.

9. Ibid., 298.

10. Ibid., 317–18.

11. Ibid., 318.

12. Ibid., 285.

13. Ibid., 244–45.

14. Ibid., 246.

15. Ibid., 299.

16. See, for instance, Joseph Schacht, *Introduction to Islamic Law* (Oxford: Clarendon, 1964), 161–174.

17. Katharine Rogers, *Before Their Time: Six Women Writers of the Eighteenth Century* (New York: Frederick Unger, 1979), x.

18. Montagu writes, "Are we not form'd with Passions like your own? . . . For Wives ill-us'd no remedy remains, / To daily Racks condemn'd and to eternal Chains." See *Essays and Poems, and Simplicity, A Comedy*, ed. Robert Halsband and Isobel Grundy (Oxford: Clarendon, 1977), 230–32. Elsewhere in the Embassy Letters, Montagu mitigates somewhat the sunny picture she paints of life as a woman in Turkey when she recounts a woman's brutal and mysterious murder, but this material is deemphasized, as Cynthia Lowenthal demonstrates. See Lowenthal, "The Veil of Romance: Lady Mary's Embassy Letters," *Eighteenth-Century Life* 14.1 (1990): 66–82.

19. Montagu, *Letters and Works*, 286.

20. Devoney Looser, "Scolding Lady Mary Wortley Montagu? The Problematics of Sisterhood in Feminist Criticism," in *Feminist Nightmares: Women at Odds: Feminism and the Problem of Sisterhood*, ed. Susan Ostrov Weisser and Jennifer Fleishner (New York: New York University Press, 1994), 45. For readings of Montagu as Orientalist see

Kader Konuk, "Ethnomasquerade in Ottoman-European Encounters: Reenacting Lady Mary Wortley Montagu," *Criticism* 46.3 (Summer 2004): 393–414, and Maria Koundura, "Between Orientalism and Philhellenism: Lady Mary Wortley's 'Real' Greeks," *The Eighteenth Century: Theory and Interpretation* 45.3 (Fall 2004): 249–64. Konuk argues that Montagu's ethnomasquerade is a "short-lived fantasy of embodying the Other . . . that keeps her Englishness intact" (394). In sharp contrast, Joseph W. Lew declares her "counter-orientalist" as well as progressive in her stance toward English patriarchy ("Lady Mary's Portable Seraglio," *Eighteenth-Century Studies* 24.4 [Summer 1991]: 432–50). Elizabeth A. Bohls states that "The Letters' treatment of Turkish women is thoroughly ambivalent, doubtless tangled up with Montagu's ambivalence about women's status in her own culture" ("Aesthetics and Orientalism in Lady Mary Wortley's Letters," *Studies in Eighteenth-Century Culture* 23 (1994); 179–205; 196.

21. Isabel Grundy, "Lady Mary Wortley Montagu," *Oxford Dictionary of National Biography* online (2004). http://www.oxfordnb.com.proxy. lib.fsu.edu

22. A film that inverts Othellophilia by depicting a love affair between a white man and an African American woman came out in 2006, as this essay was in its final stages. *Something New* was directed by a woman of color, Sanaa Hamri; unlike *Jungle Fever*, the film ends happily.

23. Linda Alcoff, "The Problem of Speaking for Others," *Feminist Nightmares*, 269–309; 296.

24. Judith Butler, *Gender Trouble: Feminism and the Subversion of Identity* (New York: Routledge, 1990), 1–6.

25. Gayatri Chakravorty Spivak critiques the "self-abnegating intellectual pose" of white, male theorists who refuse to "speak for" the other; in Spivak's view the notion of "listening to" is equally problematic, as it mystifies the socially constructed positions of oppressor and oppressed. See Spivak, "Can the Subaltern Speak?" *Marxism and the Interpretation of Culture*, ed. Cary Nelson and Lawrence Grossberg (Urbana: University of Illinois Press, 1988).

26. Diana Fuss, *Essentially Speaking: Feminism, Nature & Difference* (New York: Routledge, 1989).

27. Luce Irigaray, *This Sex Which Is Not One*, trans. Catherine Porter (Ithaca, NY: Cornell University Press, 1985), 31.

28. Virginia Woolf, *A Room of One's Own* (New York: Harcourt, 1929, 1981), 82.

29. Quoted in "A Conversation: Gloria Naylor and Toni Morrison/ 1985" in *Conversations with Gloria Naylor*, ed. Maxine Lavon Montgomery (Jackson: University of Mississippi Press, 2004), 22.

30. Toni Morrison, *Sula* (New York: Penguin, 1973), 109.

31. Ibid., 145.

32. Ibid., 174.

33. Quoted in "A Conversation," 21–22.

34. See, for instance, Patricia Hill Collins, *Black Feminist Thought: Knowledge, Consciousness, the Politics of Empowerment* (New York: Routledge, 1991), 119–23, and Rosalie Riegle Troester, "Turbulence and Tenderness: Mothers, Daughters, and 'Othermothers' in Paule Marshall's *Brown Girl, Brownstones*," *Sage: A Scholarly Journal on Black Women* 1.2 (1984): 13–16.

35. Tuzyline Jita Allan, "Womanism Revisited: Women and the (Ab)use of Power," in *The Color Purple*, "*Feminist Nightmares*, 88–105.

36. Alice Randall, *The Wind Done Gone* (Boston: Houghton Mifflin, 2001), 206.

37. Kevin Everod Quashie, "The Other Dancer as Self: Girlfriend Selfhood in Toni Morrison's *Sula* and Alice Walker's *The Color Purple*," *Meridians: Feminism, Race, Transnationalism* 2.1 (2001): 187–217; 195.

Part I
Literatures

1

Miscegenation as Consolation in George Colman's *Inkle and Yarico*

Joyce Green MacDonald

The second half of the eighteenth century was "a difficult time for European imperialism," perhaps especially as that international system was supported by slave labor in the New World.[1] Communities of escaped slaves harassed their Dutch rulers in Surinam from the 1770s onward; slave rebellions periodically rumbled across Jamaica for most of the century, including a plot uncovered in 1769 in which a group of Kingston slaves allegedly planned to burn the city and kill all the white inhabitants; and most sensationally, in 1791, slaves in Haiti began a revolt that culminated in the overthrow of French rule and the establishment of the world's first independent black republic.

For the purposes of my discussion here of the economic context of class and racial representation in George Colman's 1787 comic opera *Inkle and Yarico*, these imperial crises must also include the American Revolution. The revolution disrupted the global triangle trade that had shipped slaves from London to the Caribbean and U.S. ports and sent rum and sugar from the Caribbean islands to U.S. mainland and back to London; it shattered the Caribbean economy.[2] With virtually all the islands' arable land devoted to raising sugar cane, the West Indies were dependent on British North America for most of their necessities, from grain, lumber, and livestock to butter and soap and candles. And as the political conflict between the North American colonies and England intensified after mid-century, the economic position of the islands grew increasingly tenuous. Such actions as London's closing of the port of Boston may have been intended as a punitive political response to increasing North American demands for greater independence in trade, but it also inevitably threatened the Caribbean colonies' survival. The international dimensions of the conflict, in which the French navy and American privateers challenged British naval dominance and interfered with shipping between England and the Caribbean (where France maintained its own sugar colonies), added additional pressure, causing severe inflation as well as starvation among slaves in islands such as Barbados, the setting for Colman's play. The revolutionary war so damaged the plantation system in the islands—closing markets and stifling the flow of goods and human chattel—that it never recovered.[3]

The contexts of Colman's *Inkle and Yarico*—immediately understood by its late eighteenth-century audience as an antislavery play[4]— thus include this realization of slavery's loss of profitability (Barbados was particularly hard hit) and the increasing sense of slavery's political illegitimacy in an age of revolution.[5] With knowledge of the profits, social impact, and moral consequences of slavery resonating from the New World across the Atlantic to Europe and back again, the play stands as a document of the eighteenth-century transatlantic history, tracing lines in a web of economic collapse and social shame. Yet, turning from this grim social history to Colman's play and to the long literary tradition of which it is part, one is immediately struck by the contrast between such tragic knowledge and the tone of the dominant genre in which the *Inkle and Yarico* story was retold for eighteenth-century consumption.[6] Overwhelmingly—with the glaring exception of the first place the *Inkle and Yarico* story appears in, as we shall see—the authors of new versions of *Inkle and Yarico* chose to retell it as a sentimentalized love story primarily illustrating faithless men's betrayal of the innocent women who love them.[7]

Mary Louise Pratt points us toward the ideological functionality of sentimentalism as a way of comprehending Britain's experience with the lands and nonwhite peoples of Asia, Africa, and the Americas, particularly after the trauma of the Haitian Revolution, whose violence shocked and challenged antislavery sympathies across western Europe.[8] In this chapter, I will maintain that the sentimental triumph of true love over commercial instinct that Colman's play celebrates is powerfully inflected by the realization that the economic juggernaut that was the Barbadian sugar industry would soon grind to an almost complete halt. The emergence of sensitive feeling in a character who enters the play as an unfeeling capitalist enables the textual invocation of "conjugal love as an alternative to enslavement and colonial domination."[9] That the love affairs in Colman's *Inkle and Yarico* are miscegenous as well as merely romantic—Inkle falls for the Indian maiden Yarico, while his servingman Trudge claims her black maid-servant Wowski—works, I argue, to reproduce British control in its Caribbean possessions in sexual and racial terms. The emotional susceptibility and racial transgressiveness that distinguish Colman's two heroes become the hallmarks of a new kind of triumph that is moral and personal rather than financial and national, in colonial encounter.

The first widely circulated sentimental version of the *Inkle and Yarico* story appeared in the March 1711 volume of *The Spectator*. There, Mr. Spectator attends the salon hosted by Arietta, a lady of taste and feeling who "is visited by all persons of both sexes, who have any pretence to wit and gallantry."[10] One day, he observes Arietta maintain her composure as she listens to "a common-place talker"[11] who holds forth on the timeworn topic of female inconstancy in love. When it is her turn to speak, she rises to the defense of her sex with her account of the story of Inkle and Yarico, for which she gives a proper bibliographical reference and which she upholds as deriving "from plain people" who lack either the "ambition or capacity to embellish their narrations with any beauties of imagination."[12] For Arietta, natural sympathy is what draws the young couple together; once they overcome the "first surprize" of their meeting, they realize quickly that they are "mutually agreeable to each other." Opposites attract. Inkle is as "highly charmed with the limbs, features, and wild graces of the naked *American*" as Yarico is fascinated by "the dress, complexion, and shape of an *European*, covered from head to foot."[13] After a tender sojourn of several months' duration hidden in a cave away from Yarico's people, Inkle eventually reawakens to commercial considerations of "his loss of time, and . . . how many days interest of his money he had lost during his stay with Yarico." Even though she has already told him she is pregnant with their child, Inkle sells her to a Barbadian merchant; his knowledge of her pregnancy only makes him drive a harder bargain with the purchaser. Mr. Spectator reports that he was so moved by Arietta's account that he "left the room with tears in my eyes," and the tears, he is sure, are more validating to a woman of Arietta's "good sense"[14] than any verbal expressions of his approval he could make.

The Spectator understands the Inkle and Yarico story's significance to be in its ability to cut through the social noise of cultural and rhetorical sophistication and reach what it regards as a more emotion-ally authentic place. While it retains many of *The Spectator*'s tropes of description and characterization, Colman's version is finally radically different in tone from the journalistic account, as he adds dialect and early blackface humor, dancing, and songs set to popular tunes of the day.[15] But both *The Spectator* and Colman are just as different from the first recorded appearance of the story that Arietta cites, Richard Ligon's account in his 1657 *History of the Island of Barbados*. The prevailing tone of Ligon's much briefer original is one of sardonic detachment as he describes how, after the Indian girl Yarico helped a young English seaman hide himself from her marauding countrymen, the Englishman promptly "forgot the kindness of the poor maid, that had ventured her life for his safety, and sold her for a slave, who was as free born as he: And so poor *Yarico* for her love, lost her liberty."[16]

Despite initiating a tradition that will culminate in Colman 130 years later, Ligon demonstrates none of *The Spectator*'s emotionalism.[17] I would also suggest that his account posits a very different notion of audience and rhetorical purpose. *The Spectator* invoked a new urban and bourgeois public sphere, drawing on principles of politeness, respectability, and sociability as it fashioned a way of showing the modern city to itself.[18] Ligon's interests, however, are more truly transatlantic rather than urban in scope, as he devotes the bulk of his *History* to explicating the potential benefits and wonders of colonial trade for a domestic audience. His description quickly enough skips over the unfortunate event of the planter selling Yarico into slavery, in favor of a lengthy description of the skills and initiative of the island's large planters; for him, Yarico's sale is clearly only what must be expected in a society such as Barbados and is finally insignificant to the story he wants to tell his English audience about the island's history. Much of his *History* is taken up with description of Barbados's geography, flora and fauna, its foods and drinks, the structure of its society—including the relative standing of slaves and the island's white "servants"—and the new technologies enabling the manufacture of sugar. He holds the great planters he calls the "masters" of the island in high esteem. These men are, in his view, "men of great abilities and parts, otherwise they could not go through, with such great works as they undertake; the managing of one of their Plantations, being a work of such a latitude, as will require a very good head-peece, to put in order, and continue it so."[19] He is full of admiration for the way they can feed 200 mouths daily, keep order among slaves and indentured servants, manage and organize their agricultural labor, and mechanically maintain the cane presses, among other responsibilities: he asserts,

> If anything in the Rollers, as the Goudges, Sockets, Sweeps, Cogs, or Braytrees, be at fault, the whole work stands still; or in the Boyling-house, if the Frame which holds the Coppers, (and is made of Clinkers,

fastned with plaister of *Paris)* if by the violence of the heat from the
Furnaces, these Frames crack or break, there is a stop in the work, till
that be mended.[20] . . . [L]et us consider how many things there are to
be thought on, that go to the actuating this great work, and how many
cares to prevent the mischances, that are incident to the retarding, if
not the frustrating of the whole work; and you will find them wise and
provident men, that go on and prosper in a work, that depends upon so
many contingents.

Ligon's repetition of the word "work" here seems to strive for an
almost incantatory power, as he marvels over the powers of conception, organization, and supervision that distinguish the great planters.
Their economic risk-taking eclipses anything to be found in the
capital. Ligon provides his account of the planters' energy "to stop
those men's mouths, that lie here at home, and expect great profit in
their adventures, and never consider, through what difficulty, industry
and pains it is acquired."[21]

None of the post-Ligon treatments of the Inkle and Yarico story
approaches the activity of maintaining the sugar plantations of
Barbados with anything like his reverence and admiration. If Ligon's
protoindustrial consciousness rapidly drops out of the tradition, however, Colman achieves a distinction of his own: his play is the first document in the tradition to seriously acknowledge and attempt to
reconcile the effects of racial identity and difference in its colonial
setting. Even before the advent of the abolitionist movement in the
second half of the eighteenth century, Mr. Spectator's tears suggest a
kind of protoabolitionist sensibility, as constructed and circulated for
metropolitan consumption.[22] Colman's *Inkle and Yarico* makes this
connection explicit, as it rejects the profit motive that so fascinates
Ligon in favor of an extraordinary doubly miscenegous happy ending.
The play's two great love affairs, finely graded across class as well as
racial difference, catch Colman in the act of imagining a new world in
which Ligon's infatuation with new technologies and new mentalities
becomes irrelevant. Not just the marketplace but also the sensibilities
it generates will be rolled back.

It would be simple enough to assign Colman's divergence from his
narrative tradition to the fact that his play was produced during a
period when British moral revulsion against the slave trade was
becoming strongly established; abolition and emancipation lay less
than 50 years in the future after his play's premiere. But the play's
rejection of the profit motive and apparent embrace of race-mixing are
phenomena with an economic as well as affective matrix. The time
between Ligon's slightly sardonic anecdote, which occupies so little

space in his whole *History*, and its celebratory undoing in Colman marks the distance between the time of the founding of the great Barbadian sugar fortunes in the middle of the seventeenth century, an economic process Ligon observed firsthand, and the collapse of the sugar trade after the American Revolution. Writing in the decade of the collapse, Colman articulates his reproduction of the boom time through romance and moral awakening instead of through the making—and eventual loss—of great fortunes. *Inkle and Yarico* overwrites the ugly facts of life in slave society and of economic failure with an uplifting account of a more successful international and cross-cultural speculation. As it mystifies its economic context and switches nimbly between high- and low-cultural registers, Colman's *Inkle and Yarico* wishfully disestablishes the grounds of economic disaster.

Ligon traveled to Barbados and wrote his *History* at mid–seventeenth century, when Barbados was completing its rapid conversion from its unsuccessful concentration on tobacco as a cash crop to cotton and indigo and finally to sugar.[23] By 1680, the biggest Barbadian planters were apparently the richest men in British America (although no one can say exactly how rich, since they were careful to keep exact tallies of how much sugar was produced or exported a secret from authorities in London). They may have been responsible for as much as 70 percent of the sugar shipped from the West Indies to England in the 1670s, and even by the end of the century, when Jamaican sugar had begun to catch up, the value of the sugar shipped from Barbados annually was still more than the value of goods exported from all of North America.[24] Ligon's *History* was reprinted in the 1670s, by which time travelers were beginning to write home about Barbados's beauty and prosperity. The anonymous author of *Great Newes from the Barbados* (1676) doubted that the "Sumptuous Houses, Cloaths, and Liberall Entertainment" of the richest planters could "be Exceeded by . . . their Mother Kingdome it self."[25]

The move from tobacco to sugar, which underwrote this conspicuous success and whose potential Ligon recognized before the Restoration, was, of course, supported by slave labor. The census of 1680 indicates that African slaves in Barbados outnumbered white indentured servants by a ratio of seventeen to one; while the population of whites on the island steadily declined through the seventeenth century, the number of slaves rose, so that by 1684 there were more than 46,000 slaves and fewer than 20,000 white inhabitants.[26] The island was rife with rumors of planned slave revolts from the 1680s onward. A particularly lurid alleged plot uncovered in 1692 was reported to have aimed at killing all the Christian men on the island.

The plot's leaders intended "to have taken up the Sirnames and Offices of the Principal Planters and men in the Island, to have Enslaved all the Black men and Women to them, and to have taken the White Women for their Wives."[27] Strains in the Barbadian social fabric also resulted from the increasing problem presented by the island's white indentured servants. It had been an article of their indenture since the first decade of British settlement in 1630 that servants were to receive a small plot of farmland after the end of their period of service. But as smallholdings were engrossed into the larger holdings that made cane growing more practical, less and less land remained on the open market to be used as land grants to servants at the end of their indenture. Many became vagrants. Since many of the indentured servants were Irish Catholics, some of whom had been transported from Ireland after the Commonwealth's victory at Drogheda in 1649, religious and political prejudice added to the island's social unease. Irish house servants were regarded as being much less reliable than African slaves, and an alleged plot for a slave revolt uncovered in 1686 was supposed to have turned on slaves conspiring with disaffected Irish servants to rise up against their mutual English masters.[28]

The contrast between slave and free and the class disparity among white Barbadians were not the only manifestations of violence and dispossession on the island. The Amerindian tribes who migrated eastward to Barbados from the Orinoco basin in South America as early as the seventh century had been largely wiped out on the island by the early sixteenth century, mostly falling victim to slaving raids by Spanish colonists from Hispaniola. The absence of natives helps to explain why the first English colonists arriving with Henry Powell in 1627 found the island relatively easy to settle. On the way to discovering the potential of sugarcane as a cash crop, within twenty years of their arrival, the English settlers had burned away most of the rainforest that originally covered Barbados.[29] The Caribbean, with seventeenth century Barbados as its hub, served as a kind of world laboratory for any number of institutions more frequently associated with the eighteenth and even the nineteenth century: a plantation system supported by slavery, colonialism, a mechanized factory system (in this case, the one that turned cane juice into sugar), an international shipping and transportation system, the development of an international commodity market. It hosted a racially and socially complex society, with rich and rigid gradations of skin color and caste, and the economic success of its main cash crop was enabled by the ecological destruction of native species and habitats. With its precocious modernity, Barbados was also the earliest to arouse revulsion for the human slavery that drove its economic engine. In 1684, Thomas Tryon, a self-educated tradesman who lived in Barbados for five years, denounced slavery as the work of "Flint-hearted Tyrants" who drove their slaves like animals, or even worse than animals.[30] For Tryon, the sweet commodity to whose cultivation and manufacture the slaves' lives were sacrificed was contaminated by its origins in the cruelties of slave labor. Slaves were "crush[ed] to pieces" in the trying works Ligon so admires, or they died horribly when, exhausted from toil, they fell into cauldrons of "fierce boyling Syrups."[31]

Writing at the end of sugar's ascendancy and at a historical moment when the contradiction between chattel slavery and the desire for human liberty in European political discourse had become too sharp to ignore, Colman completely devalues the economic activity with which the Ligon source materials are so fascinated. While none of the eighteenth-century treatments of the Inkle and Yarico story between Ligon and Colman pays money much attention, Colman is noteworthy for the scorn with which he treats the colonial profit motive. When we first meet his young Inkle, he is virtually an abacus with legs, indifferent to the wonders and dangers of the "American Forest" where the play's first scene is set: "Do you think I travel merely for motion? What, would you have a man of business come abroad, scamper extravagantly here and there and every where, then return home, and have nothing to tell, but that he has been here and every-where? . . . Travelling, uncle, was always intended for improvement; and improvement is an advantage; and advantage is profit, and profit is gain."[32] More than merely caricaturing the capitalist mentality Ligon praises, Colman also condemns the corrosive effects of the drive to acquire what *The Spectator* characterizes as the natural "sympathy" that maintains between races in a state of unimproved nature. The two miscegenous passions Colman depicts, Inkle for Yarico and Trudge for Wowski, finely graded as they are across class as well as racial difference, catch Colman in the act of imagining a new world in which Ligon's infatuation with new technologies and new mentalities will not be allowed to stand. Not just the marketplace but modernity itself will be rolled back.

A certain imperial nostalgia, I would suggest, thus distinguishes Colman's *Inkle and Yarico* as a love story. Love and sentiment are deployed in two ways here: to rarefy the well-known account of Barbadian economic collapse of its capacity to inspire dread and shame, and perhaps especially to mollify the fears of white racial era-sure that accompanied the successes of colonial adventure virtually from their beginnings. As early as 1657, 30 years after the first English settlements took hold, Ligon notes that many planters' houses were built to resemble "Fortifications," with "Lines, Bulwarks, and Bastions to defend themselves, in case there should be any uproar or commotion in the Island, either by the Christian servants, or *Negro* slaves." These dwellings often enclosed their own water supplies, not only "for drink whilst they are besieged; as also, to throw down upon the naked bodies of the *Negroes*, scalding hot,"[33] in case of an attack. Barbados passed its first comprehensive "Act for the better ordering and governing of Negroes" in 1661, a law that was reformulated with increasingly severe provisions of punishment through 1688 and provided one of the first models for the surveillance and control of slaves in the English-speaking world.[34] The account of the 1692 slave rebellion plot, whose aim was said to have been the ringleaders' usurpation of the planters' names and wives, whether true or not, is a clear expression of racial and sexual anxiety, if not actual fear. Colman's recasting the nature of the Barbadian adventure as the story of a young protocapitalist awakening to true love defuses such increasingly feverish outbreaks of racial panic. In the late eighteenth-century space of imperial loss created by economic collapse and revolution, Colman's opera—itself a hybrid of elite and popular forms and thus aesthetically suggestive of the process of breaking and remaking political and economic circumstance—works toward clearing new ground for asserting cultural dominance. The scientific indifference to everything except profit with which Inkle begins the play gives way, in the face of emergency, to a recognition of higher emotional and sensual claims that, in their turn, become the badges of a new kind of colonial hero.

Colman's play simplifies both Barbados's sobering economic history and the racial and sexual controls that drove it. Ligon, for example, is aware of the island's complex racial makeup. It contains white planters and indentured servants, large numbers of African slaves, and Indians who were first brought from the South African mainland because of their familiarity with the food crops that could grow in the region and were eventually also enslaved themselves. Racial and cultural crossings between Africans, Europeans, and Indians were facts of Antillean life, another one of those New World colonial inventions that was to resonate powerfully in later times.[35] In many cases, of course, this intermixture was sexual, whether coerced or consensual. Ligon himself, for example, is powerfully interested in the African women he meets when he first arrives in the Caribbean. He describes the clothing of the "black Mistress" of the governor of St. Jago in great and approving detail, but for him, "her eyes were her richest

Jewels, for they were the largest, and most oriental that I have ever seen."[36] According to the *OED*, "oriental" in this usage refers to the brilliance and lustre of the woman's eyes, a sensual description that links her physical allure to that of the exotic "green Taffaty"[37] turban, elaborate pendant earrings, and long black shoulder ribbon she wears as ornaments. The very teeth of this "rarest black Swan" are like "rows of pearls, so clean, white, orient, and wel shaped, as *Neptunes* Court was never pav'd with such as these."[38] On the way to refill their ship's water casks, Ligon's party encounters "many pretty young *Negro* virgins, playing about the Well."[39] He is careful to identify these "free *Negroes*" as somehow not African in appearance. They are unlike "those that dwel near the River of *Gambia*, who are thick lipt, short nos'd, and commonly low foreheads."[40] Adorned with more chandelier earrings and "bracelets of Counterfeit pearls," they are dressed so as to "lay open to the view, their breast round, firm, and beautifully shaped."[41] Compared to the mature beauty of the governor's mistress, whose "State and Majesty" command homage, these "young beauties force, and so commit rapes upon our affections."[42]

While Hulme remarks on Ligon's constant readiness "to add to his collection of native breasts, of which he was a tireless admirer,"[43] more than idle lust seems to be going on here. Ligon's association between these women's bodies and valuable jewels participates in the common Renaissance association of female sexuality with colonial treasure.[44] His attraction and detailed ethnographic descriptions are also clearly indexed to these women's status in island society; the governor's mistress, who belongs to one man, and the free young girls, who belong to no one, meet with his enthusiastic approval. Later in his *History*, Ligon will ascribe grotesque physical excess to the bodies of enslaved African women; their proportions are faulty, he writes, and when they have borne several children, "their breasts hang down below their Navels, so that when they stoop at their common work of weeding, they hang down almost to the ground, that at a distance, you would think they had six legs."[45] Increasingly identified as reproductive machines for the slave economy that is becoming more and more of an uncomfortable subject in the period under study here, black women's bodies barely achieve early modern dramatic representation.[46] The abjection of slave women's bodies in such description as Ligon's projects white unease with the sexual commodification of these bodies in slavery as well as points to the need to define the bodies of members of other races in terms of their resemblance to or distance from white bodies as a function of racial and colonial domination.[47] Finally, Ligon's comparison of the effect of the young girls' beauty on him with rape displaces the sexual predation to which women of color were vulnerable onto the women themselves, at the same time as it might imply that all cross-racial sexual transactions in colonial society were innocently playful seductions. He posits interracial sexual contact as normal and perhaps inevitable, at the same time as he portrays even adolescent girls as potential rapists. His colonial eye is curiously and finally passive.

Colman's play markedly simplifies this multiracial (and multiply-motived) society. Apart from a group of undifferentiated "Blacks" (1.2., s.d.) who chase Inkle and Trudge and who may or may not be slaves, we see only one particular African—Wowski, about whom more later—and one Indian, Yarico. For Ligon, Indian women were much less physically distasteful than African women; they had "very small breasts, and have more of the shape of the *Europeans*, than the *Negroes*."[48] The European appearance he gives them signifies what Peter Hulme calls "the unmarked centrality of imperial whiteness."[49] That is to say, Yarico's near-white appearance, and the standard English she speaks, close the racial gap between her and Inkle, enabling the miscegenation that recuperates the possibility of colonial success.

Flattening out Barbadian racial differences, Colman instead organizes his play around two kinds of discursive and social performance to make sense out of the bewildering jumble of possibilities introduced by the project of initiating global trade and colonial bonds. The first of these aesthetic resources is pastoral, or rather perhaps more accurately savagism, so strongly represented here by the innocent Yarico's appeals to the idealized values and relations maintaining in her Caribbean Eden. I would argue that the play's discourse of precivilization is particularly useful as an alternative setting to the no-longer applicable portrait of the island as a beehive of trade and industry. Peter Hulme has called our attention to the Golden Age trope so prevalent in early modern descriptions of the New World, particularly those focusing on the Caribbean.[50] The natives of these regions "are the most content, the happiest, the least vicious, the most sociable, the least deformed, and the least afflicted by disease in the world," wrote Jean-Baptiste DuTertre about the Antilles.[51] The trope appears in Colman's text, too. On first seeing Yarico, Inkle calls her "wild and beautiful"; she vows to bring him "food by day, and then lead you to our unfrequented groves by moonlight, to listen to the nightingale."[52] Later fearful that he does indeed intend to sell her, Yarico seeks to remind him of their love with "tales about our old grot," bidding him to "remember our palm-tree near the brook, where in the shade you often stretched yourself, while I would take your head upon my lap, and sing you to sleep." "Our grotto was the sweetest place," she sings, "The bending boughs, with fragrance blowing, / Would check the brook's impetuous pace, / Which murmur'd to be stopped from flowing."[53] Inkle's love for her returns him to a state of nature, the time before commerce or profit or the prudent marriage he had planned to contract with the colonial governor's daughter. Set in the undifferentiated wilds of "An American Forest," Inkle and Yarico's love story looks backward from economic failure to a time before the end of the venture had become known, and in so doing, it fashions a new set of origins for the enterprise. The pleasure *Inkle and Yarico* takes in the triumph of sentimental affect is perhaps its post-crash rendition of the admiration Richard Ligon felt in 1657 for the habits and characters of the men he calls the island's "Masters": after the fall, grottoes and streams replace counting house and boiling house as scenes of morally charged industry. Romantic love becomes newly culturally productive work.

The second of the aesthetic and social resources I meant when I spoke about Colman's habit of yoking together unlike kinds in order to rewrite his colonial history of boom and crash in Barbados is the social performance of class mobility by Inkle's man Trudge. If, as I have suggested, Colman's *Inkle and Yarico* calls on pastoral to invoke an idealized premodern past, it also calls on Trudge's social flexibility— something looked on with suspicion and disdain in London itself—in order to perform a kind of hocus-pocus on the notions of racial difference that undergirded life in eighteenth-century Barbados and in the metropolis.[54] Colman, as did Ligon before him, pays close attention to racial difference, not only that between his two heroes and the two women they find on the island, but also that between Yarico and Wowski. Ligon is frankly intrigued by the African women he finds on Barbados.

Colman's Trudge, the working-class hero of the comic plot, evaluates color by an imaginatively new set of standards. He describes Yarico's complexion as "quite dark, but very elegant— like a Wedgwood tea-pot,"[55] a comparison that locates her among other goods aimed for domestic consumption and appreciation.[56] In Trudge's commercial counter-narrative of skin color, racial difference is commodified and traded on in order to build new social and moral capital for Englishmen, while avoiding the brutal realities of Barbados's active slave trade altogether. Indeed, he uses the same adjective to describe his black love Wowski as one of Colman's planters uses to describe a heavily laden ship full of trade goods bearing down on Bridgetown's harbor. The word is "tight."[57] With Yarico's skin the color of an earthenware teapot and Wowski's voluptuous body linked to a profit-making merchant ship, race as it is marked by color enters the marketplace without any of the "Indignity" ascribed to the awful necessity of buying slaves by one seventeenth-century planter: "[O]ne of the great Burdens of our Lives is the going to buy *Negroes*. But we must have them; we cannot be without them, and the best Men in those Countries must in their own Persons submit to the Indignity."[58]

While both Inkle and Trudge recognize the debt they owe the women for having saved their lives, only Trudge challenges the role of color in the English decision-making process: refusing to sell "Wows," his "poor, dear, dingy wife," Trudge rebukes a planter who has trouble believing he actually plans "to live here with a black." He "may feel a little queer, perhaps, at showing her face," he tells the planter, "but damme if ever I do anything to make me ashamed of showing my own,"[59] and adds that if the trader's "head and heart were to change places, I've a notion you'd be as black in the face as an ink bottle."[60] To regard skin color as primarily metaphorical rather than material locates this Barbadian narrative firmly in the symbolic realm and thus liberates its imagination of the conjunction of white and black bodies from social disapprobation as well as from knowledge of how black bodies were sexualized and sold in Barbados.

One sign of this entry into fantasy may be read in Trudge's song at the end of Act 3, scene 1, which locates his liaison with Wowski among the kind of imitation of their betters of which young serving men were always being accused; in a London theatre lobby outfitted in his high boots, he was considered by the English girls to be "quite the kick," but once he sailed to America, he became even more successful as he boldly ratcheted up his search for high fashion:

> On English belles I turn'd my back,
> Diddle, daddle, deedle:
> And got a foreign fair, quite black,
> O twaddle, twaddle, tweedle![61]

London belles may be vain of their pouting under lips, he sings, but his "Wows,"[62] whose upper lip pouts twice as much, would beat a hundred such. Ligon's description of enslaved African women's bodies makes them seem repellent, but here in Colman's symbolic revaluation of miscegenous bonds, the bodily excess iconographically assigned to African women becomes instead a sign of Trudge's class mobility and sexual appetite and initiative. Trudge's song celebrates the fact that he has been bold enough to acquire a woman who explodes Eurocentric standards of what constitutes a sexy mouth. He boasts of his ability to master Wowski's excessive body. (She is, for example, much more sexualized than Yarico, having confessed to several *white* lovers in the past.)

The last verse of the song triumphantly rewrites the sexual and racial panic that undergirded so many eighteenth-century productions of Shakespeare's *Othello*:

> Rings I'll buy to deck her toes,
> Jemmy linkum feedle;
> A feather fine shall grace her nose,
> Waving sidle seedle.
> With jealousy I ne'er shall burst,
> Who'd steal my bone of bone-a?
> A white Othello, I can trust
> A dingy Desdemona.[63]

A white Moor of Venice cast adrift among blacks, Trudge will retain his racial authority and identity. Man enough to handle Wowski, he also needs to have no fear of anyone trying to seduce away the girl he calls his "dingy Desdemona." Joan Hamilton reads this line as a racist reflection on Wowski's supposed physical grotesqueness—Trudge need not worry because no other man would want her—but the context of my discussion here suggests that the line may be as much about Trudge's capacity to keep what he has won as a new kind of New World venturer. While Colman's Inkle ultimately sets aside financial interest in the name of true love, his opera also and as significantly purifies colonial venture of the fear of racial erasure. Such fears were aroused by stories—true or exaggerated—of slave rebellion beginning to filter back from Barbados and the Indies before the end of the seventeenth century and figured so prominently in a whole series of increasingly racially paranoid eighteenth- and nineteenth-century *Othello*s. In William Macready's early Victorian production, Desdemona's murder took place behind the closed bedcurtains. Only after the struggles and screams quietened down did Macready—in dark makeup—thrust his face out from between the white curtains. The effect was so sensational that at least one woman in the audience was reported to have fainted.[64] Trudge's exultant public claiming of Wowski enacts a kind of early sex tourism, performing the pleasurable results of his trip to the islands for the audience's enjoyment. His song re-enacts such perilous colonial voyages as Ligon's by purifying them of risk, celebrating only the potential rewards and radically compressing the nature of those rewards into the sexual. As did European explorers before the imperial crisis of the second half of the eighteenth century, Trudge and Colman classify, organize, and master knowledge of the unknown world.[65] In *Inkle and Yarico*'s case, however, Colman gives his public all the exotic pleasure and power of foreign possession without any of the danger, reassuringly reinscribing heterosexual masculinity as well as whiteness into the identity of his new colonial actors.

The end of Colman's opera, with mistaken identities revealed and true love rewarded, accompanies its celebration of Inkle and Yarico's affection with a song and dance bringing all the main characters together onstage. Patty, the governor's daughter's maid and a former flame of Trudge's, raises the lone voice of objection to the theatrical play and pleasure of the scene—surely a rational audience in "an age like this" cannot approve "Thus taking black for white."[66] Applause dissolves all dissension, of course, and Colman sends his audience home humming familiar tunes and laughing at Wowski's fluent pidgin. His play takes the geopolitical crisis of the loss of Britain's American colonies and the collapse of British sugar and salvages success from it. The price of sugar in London soared after the crash, marking the price of a New World economic paradise lost, but Colman's *Inkle and Yarico* works hard to restore and rearticulate the pleasure of colonial adventure, routing it firmly through the sexual possession of nonwhite women's "tight" bodies.

Notes

1. Mary Louise Pratt, *Imperial Eyes: Travel Writing and Transculturation* (London: Routledge, 1992), 72.
2. Eric Williams, *Capitalism and Slavery* (Chapel Hill: University of North Carolina Press, 1944; rpt. 1994), was the first extended economic analysis of the end of slavery in the Caribbean. While not rejecting Williams' conclusions about the economic factors driving amelioration and abolition, later historians such as David Brion Davis, *The Problem of Slavery in the Age of Revolution, 1776–1823* (Ithaca, NY: Cornell University Press, 1975) and Robin Blackburn, *The Overthrow of Colonial Slavery, 1776–1848* (London: Verso, 1988) have pressed interpretations that more strongly advance the role of ideas about race, abolition, and British and American politics in the slavery crisis at the turn of the nineteenth century.
3. On the West Indies' economic dependence on the American mainland, see Selwyn H. H. Carrington, "The American Revolution and the British

West Indies' Economy," *Journal of Interdisciplinary History* 17 (1987): 823–50.

4. Joan Hamilton, "*Inkle and Yarico* and the Discourse of Slavery," *RECTR* 9.1 (1994): 17–33.

5. The classic account of eighteenth-century British responses to slavery and the development of abolitionist sentiment is Wylie Sypher, *Guinea's Captive Kings: British Anti-slavery Literature of the XVIII Century* (Chapel Hill: University of North Carolina Press, 1942), 25–100.

6. Lawrence Marsden Price's *Inkle and Yarico Album* (Berkeley: University of California Press, 1937) was the first collection of known versions of the story. Also see Frank Felsenstein, *English Trader, Indian Maid: Representing Gender, Race, and Slavery in the New World: An Inkle and Yarico Reader* (Baltimore: Johns Hopkins University Press, 1999); and Sypher's review of Inkle and Yarico texts, 122–44.

7. Martin Wechselblatt, "Gender and Race in Yarico's Epistles to Inkle: Voicing the Feminine/Slave," *SECC* 19 (1989): 197–223; Moira Ferguson, *Subject to Others: British Women Writers and Colonial Slavery, 1670–1834* (London: Routledge, 1992), 69–90.

8. Pratt, *Imperial Eyes*, 74–84.

9. Ibid., 86.

10. I cite the modernized edition of *The Spectator*'s story included in Felsenstein, *English Trader, Indian Maid*, 82.

11. Quoted in Felsenstein, *English Trader, Indian Maid*, 83.

12. Ibid., 86.

13. Ibid., 87.

14. Ibid., 88.

15. Felsenstein discusses the performance history of Colman's play, *English Trader, Indian Maid*, 20–21 and 167–70.

16. I cite the second edition of Richard Ligon, *A True and Exact History of the Island of Barbados* (London: 1673), which reproduces the 1657 text without additions or changes. Here, 55.

17. Peter Hulme, *Colonial Encounters: Europe and the Native Caribbean 1492–1797* (London: Methuen, 1986), 233–40, compares Ligon and *The Spectator*.

18. Scott Black, "Social and Literary Form in *The Spectator*," *ECS* 33 (1999): 21–42.

19. Ligon, *History*, 55.

20. Ibid., 56.

21. Ibid., 57. On the early planters, see Larry Gragg, *Englishmen Transplanted: The Early Colonization of Barbados, 1627–1660* (Oxford: Oxford University Press, 2003).

22. Here, see Julie Ellison, "Race and Sensibility in the Early Republic: Ann Eliza Bleecker and Sara Wentworth Morton," *American Literature* 65 (1993): 446. Julie Ellison's "Cato's Tears," *ELH* 63 (1996): 571–601,

also discusses the connections between male tears and political and racial discourse.

23. On the early history of the English in Barbados, from the arrival of the first settlers in the 1620s to the turn to large-scale sugar cultivation and the dominance of slave labor, see Gary A. Puckrein, *Little England: Plantation Society and Anglo-Barbadian Politics, 1627–1700* (New York: New York University Press, 1987), 22–72.

24. Richard S. Dunn, "The Barbados Census of 1680: Profile of the Richest Colony in English America," *William and Mary Quarterly* 26 (1969): 3–30.

25. Quoted in Dunn, "The Barbados Census," 5.

26. Dunn, "The Barbados Census," 7–8.

27. Anon, *A Brief, but Most True Relation of the Late Barbarous and Bloody Plot of the Negro's in the Island of Barbados* (London, 1693), n.p.

28. Hilary McD. Beckles, "'A Riotous and Unruly Lot': Irish Indentured Servants and Freemen in the English West Indies, 1644–1713," *William and Mary Quarterly* 47 (1990): 503–22. Also see his *A History of Barbados: From Amerindian Settlement to Nation-State* (Cambridge: Cambridge University Press, 1990), 35–40.

29. Beckles, *History*, 1–6; Philip D. Morgan, "The Caribbean Islands in Atlantic Context, 1500–1800," in *The Global Eighteenth Century*, ed. Felicity Nussbaum (Baltimore: Johns Hopkins University Press, 2003), 52–64.

30. Thomas Tryon, *Friendly Advice to the Gentlemen-Planters of the East and West Indies* (London: 1684), 88.

31. Tryon, *Friendly Advice*, 89. On the association abolitionist rhetoric made between sugar and the blood of the suffering slaves who manufactured it, to the point where eating sugar became rhetorically and sometimes literally associated with eating human flesh, see Charlotte Sussman, "Women and the Politics of Sugar, 1792," *Representations* 48 (1994): 49–58. On Tryon's use of the cannibalism trope, see Daniel Carey, "Sugar, Colonialism, and the Critique of Slavery: Thomas Tryon in Barbados," *SVEC* 9 (2004): 310–16.

32. I cite George Colman, *Inkle and Yarico an Opera. In Three Acts. As Performed at the Theatre-Royal in the Hay-Market* (Dublin: 1787); here, s.d., 3 and 6.

33. Ligon, *History*, 29.

34. On the slave code, see Gragg, *Englishmen Transplanted*, 129–31 and 159–60.

35. Peter Hulme, "Black, Yellow and White on St. Vincent: Moreau de Jonnès' Carib Ethnography," in *The Global Eighteenth Century*, ed. Felicity A. Nussbaum (Baltimore, MD: John Hopkins University Press, 2003), 182–94.

36. Colman, *Inkle and Yariko*, 12.

37. Ibid., 2.

38. Ibid., 13.

39. Ibid., 15.

40. Ibid., 15–16.

41. Ibid., 16.

42. Ibid., 17.

43. Hulme, *Colonial Encounters*, 237.

44. See, for example, Shankar Raman, "Can't Buy Me Love: Money, Gender, and Colonialism in Donne's Erotic Verse," *Criticism* 43 (2001): 135–68.

45. Ligon, *History*, 51.

46. On this paucity of representation, see Joyce Green MacDonald, "The Disappearing African Woman: Imoinda in *Oroonoko* after Behn," *ELH* 66 (1999): 71–86. Felicity Nussbaum, *The Limits of the Human: Fictions of Anomaly, Race, and Gender in the Long Eighteenth Century* (Cambridge: Cambridge University Press, 2003), links this absence from representation to black women's role as helping to define and articulate white English identities, both male and female, 151–88.

47. On the distortion ascribed to slave women's bodies by European observers in the period, see Jennifer L. Morgan, "'Some Could Suckle over Their Shoulder': Male Travelers, Female Bodies, and the Gendering of Racial Ideology, 1500–1700," *William and Mary Quarterly* 54 (1997): 167–92.

48. Colman, *Inkle and Yarico*, 54.

49. Hulme, "Carib Ethnography," 194.

50. Hulme, *Colonial Encounters*, 229–33.

51. Quoted in Hulme, *Colonial Encounters*, 230.

52. Colman, *Inkle and Yarico*, 16.

53. Ibid., 37.

54. Daniel O'Quinn, "Mercantile Deformities: George Colman's *Inkle and Yarico* and the Racialization of Class Relations," *Theatre Journal* 54 (2002): 389–409; Linda V. Troost, "Social Reform in Comic Opera," *SVEC* 305 (1992): 1427–29.

55. Colman, *Inkle and Yarico*, 49.

56. Nandini Bhattacharya, "Family Jewels: George Colman's *Inkle and Yarico* and Connoisseurship," *ECS* 34 (2001): 207–26.

57. Colman, *Inkle and Yarico*, 21, 22.

58. Edward Littleton, *The Groans of the Plantations: Or a True Account of Their Extreme Sufferings by the Heavy Impositions Upon Sugar and Other Hardships* (London: 1689), 6.

59. Colman, *Inkle and Yarico*, 33.

60. Ibid., 34.

61. Ibid., 51.

62. Ibid., 52.

63. Ibid., 52.

64. Michael Neill, "Unproper Beds: Race, Adultery and the Hideous in *Othello*," *SQ* 40 (1989): 385–90.

65. Joseph Roach, "The Enchanted Island: Vicarious Tourism in Restoration Adaptations of *The Tempest*," in '*The Tempest*' *and Its Travels*, ed. Peter Hulme and William Sherman (Philadelphia: University of Pennsylvania Press, 2000), 60–70. I thank Gary Taylor for recommending Roach's article to me.

66. Colman, *Inkle and Yarico*, 68.

2

Fear of Family, Fear of Self: Black Southern "Othering" in Randall Kenan's *A Visitation of Spirits*

Trudier Harris

A careful perusal of African American literature reveals that most of the writers include representations of southern U.S. territory at some point in their work.[1] Writers as diverse as James Baldwin, Edward P. Jones, Tayari Jones, William Melvin Kelley, Randall Kenan, Yusef Komunyakaa, Toni Morrison, Phyllis Alesia Perry, Alice Walker, Margaret Walker, Richard Wright, and a host of others imaginatively engage the South in fiction, drama, poetry, and essays. African American writers, whether born in Idaho, New York, and Massachusetts, or Alabama and Georgia, do not seem to be able to claim themselves as African American writers until they have allowed the South to dominate their imaginations. Perhaps because of the collective history of slavery, or the southern soil that shapes so much of the interpretive power of African American life and culture, black writers traverse southern soil in identifying with the totality of African American experience. It could reasonably be argued that no writer of African descent born on American soil can consider himself or herself an African American writer until he or she has made peace—or attempted to do so—with what the South means to him or her in particular and to black people in general.

There is no better example of this than James Baldwin. In *Just Above My Head* (1979), narrator Hall Montana observes: "Look at a map, and scare yourself half to death. On the northern edge of Virginia, on the Washington border, catty-corner to Maryland, is

Richmond, Virginia. Two-thirds across the map is Birmingham, Alabama, surrounded by Mississippi, Tennessee, and Georgia." To actually travel those states and to go along the roads observed on the map "can be far more frightening than the frightening map."[2] Hall makes this observation as his brother Arthur, a member of a singing quartet, is preparing to make a trip to the South. For Baldwin, the South is an enigma, an engulfing space specially designed to destroy young black men. He uses *Just Above My Head* to highlight the physical violence, both imagined and real, that can be done to black men and the psychological violence that other black men suffer as a result of it.

He does this initially by allowing Hall's fears to become reality. While the quartet from Harlem is singing in a small southern town, one of their members, Peanut, on a trip to the outhouse behind the church, simply disappears. No amount of searching uncovers Peanut's whereabouts. No amount of searching locates his body. He just disappears. It is that fear of disappearance on southern territory that informs the notion of a scary Mason-Dixon Line. The fear of castration is tangible and psychologically destructive enough, but imagine the greater fear of actually having a body lost and never finding it, indeed never learning a single fact about how it disappears or where it might have ended up. In that mental space of the possibility *for* and the knowledge *of* disappearance is where James Baldwin and many other nonsouthern black writers reside when they think of the South. Your body can be destroyed. You can disappear. You will be lost and not found.

As fearful to Baldwin as the black body disappearing is the black body hanging on southern territory. There is no more vivid example than his depiction of the lynching in the flashback in *Going to Meet the Man* (1965). The lynched black man, accused of the age-old crime of impropriety toward a white woman, is the image that fuels racism and repression. The white sheriff in the story, who remembers his father taking him to the lynching, castrating, and burning of a black man, conjures up that image to gather the scattered pieces of his manhood when he is confronted with young black demonstrators in an unnamed southern town. By recalling the lynching and imagining that as the "rightful" place for black men who step out of line, Jesse the sheriff can collect his nerves sufficiently to confront the demonstrators and can bolster his sexuality sufficiently to make love to his wife "like a nigger."

Lynching black men but desiring the very sexuality that has presumably led to the lynching, Baldwin posits, is the natural position of white men in the South and the natural reason for black men to be fearful of the South. Indeed, it is almost impossible in a Baldwin work to be a black *man* in the South. The two states are irrevocably oppositional. Yet another way that Baldwin exhibits fear of the South in his work, therefore, is that of the psychological loss of manhood. While this fear might accompany the physical loss of the ability to do the things usually associated with being a man, such as going where one wants, holding a job, or providing for one's family, what Baldwin finds most distasteful is the breaking down of the black male mind, of the ability to think of one's self in a masculine vein.

Baldwin's fears of the South, like those of many northern as well as southern black writers, center upon the legacies of slavery as well as the tradition of white supremacy. It is an understandably *reactive* posture assumed in relation to a terrible enemy. Again and again for Baldwin, the mere knowledge of entering southern territory created in him—as it does in his characters—the sense that his very body was threatened. Baldwin's fears are almost always manifested in the psychosexual dimensions of interactions between black males and white males. However, other black writers exhibit various fears of the South in other ways. What happens, for example, when the fears that arise come most immediately from *within* black communities rather than from the outside? How can black fictional characters themselves contribute to a notion of a scary Mason-Dixon Line? In what ways can they exhibit traits of the southern monster that Baldwin envisions?

Randall Kenan is one of the black writers who presents situations in which black people instilling fear in other black people on southern territory is the *primary* concern. Kenan focuses on small town eastern North Carolina, where the legacies of slavery are somewhat quietly in the background, but where a sense of black family tradition has become so all-consuming that it is perhaps worse than slavery. In *A Visitation of Spirits* (1989), his first novel, Kenan created the fictional soil of Tims Creek, a mythical territory to which he returns for the short stories contained in *Let the Dead Bury Their Dead* (1992). Tims Creek is small town United States, tobacco-growing and hog-killing country. It is a southern village where everybody knows everybody, where family means everything, where churchgoing is as expected as breathing, and where deviation from whatever the established norm is designated to be is at best stupid and at worst suicidal.

In Tims Creek, whites are on the fringes of black lives; it is mainly the well-established black Cross family that provides the frame for evaluating other blacks. The novel centers upon sixteen-year-old Horace Cross, named after his great-grandfather. A precocious young man who has read more than most college students, Horace is an

A student who turns renegade during the course of the novel. As a senior in high school, having experienced in a very short period of time what he perceives to be the debauchery of sexual experimentation with males and then complete indulgence in that sexuality, Horace realizes that he is an "abomination" in the eyes of his church and his family. He determines that the only way to escape his fate is to perform an act of sorcery that will transform him into a red-tailed hawk and thus enable him to fly away from his destiny.

In a classic dark night of the soul, Horace performs the ceremony that will conjure up the demon that can transform him; he realizes that the demon he has conjured cannot be controlled and is instead controlling him and, at the demands of the demon and his accompanying ghoulish host, wanders the territory of his life and the town of Tims Creek before he blows his brains out early the next morning in front of his cousin Jimmy, a pathetic minister-turned-principal who has been more successful in denying his homosexual tendencies than Horace. What leads Horace to this fate is fear of family, fear of Christianity (that is, the church and rules as practiced by his family, friends, and neighbors), and fear of himself as a result of internalizing the rules in spite of his desire *not* to abide by them.

One of the mistakes cultural observers frequently make is assuming that black communities are monolithic, that they all adhere to certain beliefs and follow in certain paths. What cultural watchers often forget is that black communities can be just as controlling of what they perceive to be deviance as other communities. For Horace, that control begins when his relatives believe he has sinned against family. Now, of course, we could argue that families everywhere put pressure on their young members. In the small town South, however, that pressure has unique qualities, and it comes with a history.

Most black folks who survived slavery never received forty acres and a mule. Set adrift without skills or resources, blacks wandered here and there, tried to locate relatives, and often settled in haphazard ways or in unanticipated locations. For the Cross family of Tims Creek, North Carolina, however, no such haphazardness prevails. As early as the first few years of Reconstruction, the patriarch, Ezra Cross, managed—through legal means or otherwise—to acquire hundreds of acres of land in eastern North Carolina. That acquisition gave status and independence to his family. The Crosses became Tims Creek's version of the black elite comparable to early middle-class enclaves in Atlanta, Chicago, and Richmond. For a formerly enslaved black man to have succeeded so exceptionally well is prestige beyond prestige.

For the five generations leading up to Horace, therefore, the Crosses have borne the burden of black family success and black family history. Kenan assigns their surname to reflect their at-times troubled position in the community as well as the high standards they have imposed upon themselves. Small blots on the record, such as drunkenness or promiscuity, do not ultimately stain the name. The overall family tradition continued, and descendants always kept the land in the family. Even when Horace's father impregnated a girl of whom his family did not approve, his grandfather Ezekiel and his wife Aretha simply took that child, Horace, and raised him as their own. Upon his grandmother's death, when he is ten, Horace finds himself in the hands of his great aunt Jonnie Mae, his grandfather Zeke, Jonnie Mae's daughters Rebecca, Rachel, and Ruthester (teachers all), and—as the tradition goes—a host of relatives and friends. All of them have high hopes for Horace, for, as one of Horace's classmates points out, "But don't you know it yet, Horace? You the Chosen Nigger."[3]

For a young man of sixteen, an only child, to live up to five generations of expectations is formidable indeed. However, Horace succeeds admirably well from a purely academic standpoint. With his straight A's and his intention to become a scientist/inventor, Horace is on track to do more than anyone in his family has done (teachers, preachers, and lawyers are the dominant nonfarming professions thus far). That bright future is hampered by a lingering awakening: Horace is increasingly apprehensive about and finally irrevocably convinced that, in terms of sexuality, he prefers men to women. One of his final reveries in the text makes clear how long that attraction has existed. Horace comments:

> I remember watching men, even as a little boy. I remember feeling strange and good and nasty. I remember doing it anyway, looking, and feeling that way. I remember not being able to stop and worrying and then stopping worrying. I remember the sight of men's naked waists. I remember the abdomen that look sculptured and the sinews' definition. Solid. The way the dark hair would crawl from the pants and up the stomach toward the chest. I remember looking at arms, firm arms, with large biceps like ripe fruit . . . I remember the way my neck would prickle and my breath would come shallow.[4]

These thoughts are from a young man whose family is aggressively heterosexual, whose patriarchs surreptitiously applaud their erring sons for loving "pussy"[5] and who themselves commit adultery, and whose relatives plan futures for individuals that are acceptable to the entire family. Horace cannot possibly thrive in such a directive environment. In fact, he labels his sexual preferences a "disease" against which he does not know how to "fight"[6] sufficiently to return to health.

Thus the burden of family: how can a young black man, in the small town South, knowing that relatives have raised him when his father and mother proved unable or unwilling to do so, escape the guilt he must feel upon recognition that he is not "normal," not what they think he is—or should be? If that family history were truncated, perhaps it would be easy to be an aberration. If his father had not been weak and his mother not inadequate, it might have been possible for him to be unusual. But Horace owes too much to the people who have raised him and to the family history that those people represent for him to ever be content with the early sexual awakenings that he feels. Even after he acts upon those feelings, the burden of guilt always follows the sexual pleasure.

Horace moves toward transformation and escape from himself when he realizes that he has failed the people who have held such high hopes for him. On the fateful Thanksgiving Day of his senior year, his family makes clear how they feel about any man who would have sexual preferences for another man. To show solidarity with his recently acquired group of young white male friends, Horace pierces one of his ears and inserts an earring. Late for the traditional meal and wearing the earring, Horace finds himself the center of vocal and unrelenting family disapproval. All the people who have cared for him appear in this scene to reject him totally and completely. They refuse to allow him to explain his decision. The simple fact that he is wearing an earring places him beyond their notion of family and history. The fact that he calls young white men his friends is tantamount to betrayal. His great aunt Jonnie Mae asks Horace if he has "lost" his mind, his grandfather Zeke concludes that Horace is "crazy," and his elderly cousin Rebecca—usually his defender—avows that he "ain't got a lick of sense." Horace can only stammer out "I" and "But" before they insist that he remove the earring. When Horace is finally allowed to try to explain that "all the guys . . . ," his family then jumps on him for being stupid enough, as Jonnie Mae asserts, to do what "them white fools do." It is she, whom Horace holds in special esteem, who pronounces benediction on the violation. "He *just* pierced his ear," she says in response to her daughter Ruthester's suggestion that that is all Horace has done. "Like some little girl. Like one of them perverts."[7] The conclusion to this scene is that Zeke maintains that Horace has "forfeited" his Thanksgiving dinner and orders him to leave the table.

This scene is crucial for making family influence clear in a couple of other ways, both of which involve adult males in the family. Horace is able to witness how Lester, Jonnie Mae's son, is treated and how Jimmy, the preacher, has little if any influence in the family—or little desire to have any influence. Lester's name already marks his difference from his siblings. All of his sisters have "R" names—Rachel, Rebecca, Ruthester, and Rose. He is thus nominally an aberration. Secondly, though his sisters have much to say about Horace's earring, Lester simply is not allowed a voice in the family discussion. When he tries to defend Horace by tentatively positing, "Well, I kind of like it, my—," his sister Rachel responds, "Shut up, Lester." When he comments, "It reminds me of—," his sister Rebecca offers, "Hush, Lester." Finally, after Jonnie Mae's pronouncement of Horace's betrayal, Lester tries again: "Well, I think . . . ," to which his mother Jonnie Mae replies, "Eat your dinner, Lester,"[8] which effectively ends the conversation.

Lester's silencing by his female relatives is parallel to Jimmy's cramping by the same figures. While Jimmy might have more words in the conversation, indeed offering that many young boys pierce their ears and that he will "talk with" Horace, his place is barely more secure than Lester's. In fact, Jimmy provides a pathetic example of adult male development throughout the text. His lack of aggression in pursuing his wife Anne (he is her companion for months without making a single pass at her) and his inability to make love to her when she finally invites him into her bed lead her to ask, "Are you sure you're not a faggot?"[9] and to refer to him as a "little boy" who is too romantic for the situation in which they find themselves. When he discovers her unfaithfulness and does nothing, Anne calls Jimmy a "Goddamn pussy!"[10] From his encounters with Anne, to his inability to sort out a fight between Zeke and Ruth, to his pathetic efforts at ministering, Jimmy has shadows hanging over his manhood. As with Lester, he ultimately cannot deal effectively with the women in his family, even the ninety-two-year-old Ruth.

This lack of traditional—perhaps even stereotypical—male effectiveness raises questions about the focus on homosexuality in the novel. The text perhaps inadvertently supports the misguided assumptions put forth historically that excessively strong females might have forced certain males into homosexuality. While that might not be Kenan's intention, it could certainly be argued that Jimmy and Lester, as failed male role models whose failures are shaped by the women in their lives, are counterparts in male weakness to Horace's perception of his aberration that he names homosexuality. Such an analysis places these black female characters on the side of castrating matriarchs who align themselves with white men in emasculating black men. The good intentions that might be inherent in keeping black men in line for fear of white violence nonetheless simultaneously contribute to their loss of visible manifestations of manhood.

On the other hand, what Jimmy and Lester offer could be perceived as the family-molded male images from which Horace should run for his life. From this perspective, his movement toward homosexuality is at least a movement away from the silencing and confinement that characterizes the males in his family who are closer to his generation. Why should he uphold family tradition, if all he can do is end up like Lester and Jimmy? Lester wins no family approval; Jimmy does so only by slotting himself into the role of minister that his grandmother Jonnie Mae has carved out for him. Although he offers to "talk with" Horace about his earring, Jimmy ultimately has as little clue as Horace about how to fit himself into a demanding family obsessed with history and tradition. His witnessing of the verbal assault upon Horace at the Thanksgiving dinner enables him to see the rejection that he himself has missed by hiding behind respectability.

It could be argued that Horace never recovers from this rejection. It occurs in November; he dies before graduation the following year. What Horace encounters is a wall of family tradition, the harsh attempt to keep him in line. After all, Horace's father dropped out of the family notion of success. Horace cannot be allowed to do so. His collective family pressure is not unlike that which Mama Lena Younger places on Beneatha in *A Raisin in the Sun* when she forces her to assert, "In my mother's house there is still God."[11] The difference here is the burden made possible by *black* southern family history. For this family to have achieved so much and then to witness it being threatened by Horace befriending and identifying with the very forces that have oppressed them historically, makes the family see red. If Horace can be policed only through rejection, then they will reject him.

One of the greatest ironies of the text—and indeed of black middle-class life in the South—is its modeling of success on those same forces that have oppressed black people, an observation the Cross family can apply to Horace but fails to see in its own patriarchal legacy. Ezra Cross and his descendants model whiteness and white success even as they echo the patriarchs of the Old Testaments "begats." Black people emerged from slavery with clear senses of where power and success lay. If they could be like whites in acquiring property and making those acquisitions work for them, then perhaps their descendants would not suffer as they had. They claimed white models as quickly as they rejected what white people represented in terms of violence and repression.[12] It was a fine line to walk, that is, to take the shell without the substance, and few of them managed that balancing act. Ezra and his descendants inadvertently adopt some of the values of the people whose pattern they emulate. Family moral purity (at least superficially so) and family respectability are two of those values. In their desire to value reputation and success, however, the Cross family runs the risk of devaluing blood. The fear of loss of reputation is almost as tangible as the fear of loss of property.

Inherent in the family's actions at the Thanksgiving dinner, therefore, is a fear that Horace will embarrass them, that he will do something even more egregious than his father in placing a blot on the Cross family name. As with Beneatha, Horace therefore cannot be *allowed* to be deviant. He must be kept in place even as whites kept blacks in place during slavery and after. The problem for Horace is that he cannot ultimately fall in line with his family's expectations. This is clear from a conversation he has with his cousin Jimmy one Sunday after church. Horace builds up the nerve to speak with Jimmy about his homosexual urges. To his comment that he thinks he is "a homosexual," Jimmy's response is condescendingly dismissive:

> *Jimmy (smiling, puts his hand on Horace's shoulder)*: Horace, we've all done a little . . . you know . . . experimenting. It's a part of growing up. It's . . . well, it's kind of important to—
> *Horace*: But it's not experimenting. I like men. I don't like women. There's something wrong with me.
> *Jimmy*: Horace, really. I have reason to believe it's just a phase. I went through a period where I . . . you know, experimented.
> *Horace*: Did you enjoy it?
> *Jimmy*: (*slightly stunned*): En . . . Enjoy it? Well . . . I . . . you know. Well, the physical pleasure was . . . I guess pleasant. I really don't remember.
> *Horace*: Did you ever fall in love with a man?
> *Jimmy*: Fall in love? No. (*Laughs.*) Oh, Horace. Don't be so somber. Really. I think this is something that will pass. I've known you all your life. You're perfectly normal.[13]

But when Horace suggests that he might not be normal and wonders if it is okay to be as he is, Jimmy falls back on the Bible and lets Horace conclude that the Bible says "it's wrong." Jimmy insists that Horace will change, but Horace keeps asking, "But what if I can't change?" Jimmy has no adequate answer to that question. Unable to change, but recognizing that "the possibilities of being a homosexual frightened him beyond reason,"[14] Horace is a set adrift in a familial world of sexual expectations that he can never fulfill.

It is ironic that the questing young Horace seeks advice from his cousin Jimmy, for James Malachi Greene is an ineffectual minister and one of the most inadequate human beings in the text. Jimmy is a card-carrying conformist, a born mediator who will take whatever course provides the least resistance. Zeke believes Jimmy is too deferential to Ruth, and it is clear that he is totally incapable of managing her, Zeke, or the arguments in which the two of them engage constantly. Jimmy is too unsteady in his position as a minister to dare chastise an ailing parishioner who deliberately drinks a can of beer in his presence, and he declares to another, "ain't no harm," though it is a blatant deviation from the local brand of Christianity. Jimmy then contemplates the rules that have placed him in this predicament: "I don't want to be a watchdog of sin, an inquisitor who binds his people with rules and regulations and thou shalts and thou shalt nots."[15] Yet he reverts to the rules when Horace seeks advice from him. In spite of his own homosexual tendencies, Jimmy pushes Horace toward the traditional familial and church views on the subject. Search your heart, he advises Horace, and ask God for guidance, which to a troubled teenager is probably about as helpful as suggesting that he consult an oracle.

In the last few weeks of his life, Horace discovers, as his father did, that he cannot live by family rules. His quest to turn himself into a red-tailed hawk is couched in terms of escaping human, familial, and societal rules:

> But now he was buoyed by the realization that he knew how he would spend the rest of his appointed time on this earth. Not as a tortured human, but as a bird free to swoop and dive, to dip and swerve over the cornfields and tobacco patches he had slaved in for what already seemed decades to his sixteen years. No longer would he be bound by human laws and human rules that he had constantly tripped over and frowned at.[16]

How can a powerless teenager find freedom from "acceptable" tyranny? In Horace's world, that feat can be accomplished only through imagination and/or a willful surrender of sanity, for the rules will not bend for him.

Horace's father Sammy was a wild young man who similarly sought to escape the rules. He would often stay out later than his father Zeke thought appropriate. On two occasions, Zeke laid down the law to his son. "There are rules to this house," Zeke says to Sammy when he comes in late one night, "If you live here, you live by them."[17] When

Sammy continues to resist and comes in one morning at 3 a.m., Zeke announces, "Boy, this is my house and if you think you too grown to abide by my rules, then I spect you better get up and go."[18] Sammy's departure from the premises can only be surmised as Zeke's wishes being fulfilled. For Horace, the rules are equally too much, and he has no more success than his father in abiding by them. He can remain in his grandfather's house only as long as he hides who he really is.

What finally breaks Horace's will to live is his knowledge of the fact that he has shamed his family. By shaming the present generation, he has essentially broken with the past, with his now-dead great-aunt Jonnie Mae (who cared about him in spite of her refusal to approve his wearing an earring), as well as with the four generations of Crosses who made sacrifices to enable Horace to be where he currently is. Horace "suspected his family might object to his action [piercing his ear]. But he had no idea they would pronounce treason and declare war. From top to bottom, uniformly, they condemned him. It was not the piercing of his ear, it was what it represented, they said."[19] To Zeke, the issue seems to be that Horace is more influenced by his white friends than he is by his family: "By Jesus, you'd 'just kill somebody' if one of them white boys asked you to. Wouldn't you? Wouldn't you? It shames me right much, boy. Shames me to see you come to this. We come this far for this. I'm glad your grandmother ain't around to see it. Shamed."[20]

Horace's family renders him "Other" by finally making him feel worse than a stranger. They would embrace and feed a stranger. They cannot, will not, embrace the homosexual Horace. Indeed, they consistently and adamantly refuse to see that Horace has a different sexual preference. Jimmy simply files the conversation he has with Horace away in some Paul D-like tobacco tin that will never be opened. In one reflective moment following the fateful Thanksgiving dinner, however, Jimmy seems to understand the destructive impact of family on the impressionable Horace:

> That is what finally got to Horace, isn't it? I keep asking myself. He, just like me, had been created by this society. He was a son of the community, more than most. His reason for existing, it would seem, was for the salvation of his people. But he was flawed as far as the community was concerned. First, he loved men; a simple, normal deviation, but a deviation this community would never accept.[21]

These are Jimmy's thoughts. There is no indication anywhere in the text that he shares them with anyone or that he acts in any understanding way toward Horace as a result of his analysis of the family's or the larger community's expectations of Horace. Jimmy remains just as silent on the issue of homosexuality as the Cross women force Lester to be quiet about Horace's earring.

Zeke completely refuses to reflect upon Horace's suicide or the reasons for it; there is absolutely no mention, anywhere in the text, that Zeke even remotely suspects that Horace might prefer males to females. Perhaps to do so would be to consider his own less-than-exemplary sexual life, for he cheated on his wife with several women and has at least two grown sons born out of wedlock. Horace's great-aunt Ruth suggests that the Cross family and what it represents have led to Horace's death, but it is not quite clear that she understands the true nature of Horace's demise. In response to Zeke's accusation—a year and a half after Horace's death—that Ruth drove his brother, Jethro, who was also Ruth's husband, to drinking, Ruth's response is: "'Well, you'll see yourself one day, Ezekiel Cross. See what you and your family, your evil family have wrought. And it wont just on Jethro. It's on Lester. It's on this boy here [Jimmy]. It was on your grandboy. You all is something else.'"[22] Even without naming homosexuality, Ruth knows that the family's lack of understanding for and sympathy toward Horace have played significant roles in Horace's death. She refers to Zeke's wife as "the Royal Miz Jonnie Mae Cross Greene" who has made a "slave"[23] of her son Lester; that negative influence undoubtedly descended down to Horace.

Inherent in this lack of understanding is black people's stereotypical refusal to name suicide, yet another sin that Horace commits. To take one's own life can only entail silence about the act. Like the hogkilling so vividly portrayed at the beginning of the text and the requiem for tobacco with which it ends, Horace passes through the Cross family line without making a perceptible dent in its reputation or presaging change for its future.

It is obvious that Kenan intended multiple connotations in assigning the name "Cross" to his protagonist family. They not only burden their members and force them to make tremendous sacrifices—such as taking land from Jethro, not forgiving Rose for having children out of wedlock, forcing Jimmy to become a preacher,[24] and treating Ruth as an outsider instead of an in-law—but they do so under the ironic banner of Christian goodwill. The largest cross they construct, however, they plop onto Horace's shoulders. He will be "the One," in that tradition of choosing black leadership and success to which Ernest J. Gaines refers in *The Autobiography of Miss Jane Pittman* (1971). The Cross family's externally imposed cross and the one that

Horace bears because he knows the depths of hell to which his family and community will consign him for being homosexual make burden-bearing in the text approximate biblical proportions. This conjoining of the secular and the sacred will never yield a peaceful resolution for Horace in this life.

The irony is that Horace's sin, as he himself perceives it, cannot be forgiven, whereas the text is rife with sinners who self-righteously continue on their paths of presumed forgiveness. The difference between those sinners and Horace is that they engaged in *sanctioned* sins, whereas Horace's sin is *unsanctioned*. Adultery is a known practice in Tims Creek, so those persons who may be privy to Zeke's infidelity to Aretha do not consider that the end of a way of life. The most vivid example of this is the scene in which Jimmy comes home early one day and finds his wife Anne in bed with another man. He simply turns from the bedroom, goes out to the front porch stoop, and stares into space; later, he ends up puking all over the guestroom bed. However, neither his world nor his marriage ends as a result of this infidelity. The same is true for persons who drink excessively. Ruth's husband Jethro neglected her and their children during his drinking sprees, but he was not cut off from his family because of it, and he was not deemed to have "shamed" them. Thus the line between traditionally "acceptable" sins and the unknown, unconsidered abominations such as homosexuality is sharply and irrevocably drawn in Tims Creek. It is Horace's misfortune that he falls on the wrong side of that line.

Though family is perhaps the primary source of fear for Horace, the more intense fear is the one that originates in the Bible and the practitioners of Christianity in Tims Creek. Horace, like most black youngsters bred on small town southern soil, has church in his pores. From his earliest memories to his death, church and church activities have saturated his existence. It is understandable, therefore—and exactly what his family and community would have desired—that Horace sees himself through the eyes of Christianity as practiced by Reverend Barden, Reverend Jimmy Greene, and other members of his family and community. Their brand of Christianity is an exacting one in which the God of the Old Testament is much more prevalent than the forgiving Jesus of the New Testament. Hellfire and brimstone are the watchwords for these small town black southerners, and anyone who does not follow the straight and narrow path is in danger of eternal damnation.

Biblical language, therefore, dominates the text and dominates Horace's references to himself and his condition. He has been in the church for so long that, like a good baptized believer, he carries its strictures around in his head. Even if others did not condemn Horace for his same-sex preferences, he would effectively condemn himself, for he knows what is "right" and "wrong" as well as they do. It is that double burden—the external admonitions to do right combined with equally dominant internal injunctions—that leads Horace to suicide. Horace might have been able to survive if he had not believed so fervently in what he had been taught. He is thus, in the words of his fellow believers, condemned out of his own mouth.

During Horace's dark night of the soul, one of the places he visits is his church. The church is crowded with a scene from his youth, and he sees a young Horace sitting in a pew while the Reverend Barden delivers a condemnatory sermon on same-sex relationships. There is absolutely nothing normal about such a condition, Reverend Barden repeatedly iterates. It will send one to hell, and deservedly so. The same fear and trembling, then, with which one comes before God and confesses one's sins before being saved is the fear and trembling with which one is sent to hell for deviating from what God has designated normal sexual activity. Again at issue is sanctioned and unsanctioned sins, for numerous are the tales of so-called believers in Horace's community committing "regular" sins, which presumably would land them in hellfire as effectively as other sins.

What Horace hears from Reverend Barden is what has guided his attitude toward his own sexuality: "Unclean. That's what it is. Unclean. And you knows it."[25] The demon orders Horace to kill the Reverend as he is praying, but Horace, unable to respond, can only watch as one of the harpies accompanying him lops off the reverend's head, with the word "unclean" emitting from his re-dying lips. Horace sits briefly in the pulpits and hears—or imagines—the voices that represent his grandfather's brand of religion.

> The voices started, first from this corner, then from that, from overhead, then from below.
> Wicked. Wicked.
> Abomination.
> Man lover!
> Child molester!
> Sissy!
> Greyboy!
> Old men, little girls, widows and workers, he saw no faces, knew no names, but the voices, the voices . . .
> Unclean bastard!
> Be ashamed of yourself!
> Filthy knob polisher! . . .

Cocksucker.
Oreo. . . .
Homo-suck-shual!
Ashamed. Be ashamed.
Faggot![26]

With these monstrous accusations in his head, Horace has essentially "Othered" himself. As with his religious belief, there is no reason to have family or neighbors calling out derogatory names. He has internalized the names and therefore internalized his own rejection and ultimate suicide.

Fear of God is a primary directive in Christianity. To approach God otherwise is to run the risk of blasphemy, to border on committing the sin that Nathaniel Hawthorne's Ethan Brand commits when he goes looking, aggressively, for a sin that God will be unable to forgive. Such boldness is the epitome of rejecting fear, which no sane person in Horace's community would do. "Fear God, and keep his commandments," so one ecclesiastical injunction goes, "for this *is* the whole *duty* of man."[27] And preachers from Jonathan Edwards to T. D. Jakes have reiterated that directive.

Fearing God is one thing and arguably acceptable in the tradition of Christian belief. Fearing the *people* who profess belief in God is a layered dimension that the text embroiders to indict almost all of those who make such claims. To be fearful of those who would invite one into the fold of Christianity is a paradoxical position in which to find one's self, for the standard declaration is that God is love. God's people, as they are represented in *A Visitation of Spirits*, are not loving or lovable. They are small-minded and selfish, judgmental and insistent upon their narrow interpretations of the Bible. Their imaginations are limited by the strictures they place upon themselves as well as upon others. They are not tolerant. They are not forgiving. They attempt to confine God to their smallness and use him to beat down all opposition, including their own flesh and blood. Kenan indicts them again in "The Foundations of the Earth," one of the stories in *Let the Dead Bury Their Dead*.[28]

With this judgmental variety of belief, then, it is no wonder that Horace fears not only God but also his family and his community. Through the prism of the Christianity that he has been taught, Horace recognizes his family as being as willing to consign him to hell as the Old Testament God would be. While Kenan does not give us extended interactions between Horace and his relatives, we see them sufficiently to know that their serious-mindedness about religion does not allow for even miniscule lapses. For Horace to have lapsed so titillatingly into the pleasures of the flesh is something they could never condone. And because they have taught him well and he has believed their teachings, Horace realizes that he is finally, utterly, alone and that the beckoning grave may as well be inviting because he cannot undo what has been done, to garner either forgiveness or love from his family. The tears he sheds in his final few hours of life, tears that his family would have considered cleansing signs of repentance, when Horace graduated from the mourners' bench, are now the benediction sealing his fate. He cries for himself as well as for what he can never be. He cries for what he has lost in the way of family. And he cries because he is alone, with not a single Christian soul to offer him comfort. "Suddenly life beneath the ground had a certain appeal it had never had before. It was becoming attractive in a macabre way. No more, no more ghosts, no more sin, no more, no more."[29] Echoing a spiritual "Many Thousand Gone," which repeats the refrain "No more" and which contains the line "No more auction block for me,"[30] Horace's determination to commit suicide is as much a release from the slavery of religion as it is a release from life.

Horace fails his family much more dramatically than his father Sammy, but the difference is one of degree, not one of kind. Both have been subjected to rules by which they could not finally consent to live. When Horace confronts Jimmy at sunrise, just before he kills himself, and Jimmy asks why he is doing what he is doing, Horace's— or the demon's—response is "too many fucking rules."[31] As a part of his final reverie just before this scene, Horace comments: "Then I remember the day I realized that I was probably not going to go home to heaven, cause the rules were too hard for me to keep. That I was too weak."[32] Perhaps it is less a matter of Horace's weakness than of the inability of the family and community that have nurtured him to make a place for him. Implicit in the text is the argument that there ought to be a place in the small town South where black Horace Cross, sixteen years old, could be homosexual *and* live. Nonetheless, the community, with its warped rules and values, has won, for once again Horace condemns himself out of his own mouth, a condemnation that his family and community have taught him well.

What is left for Horace to fear beyond family and church is the self that has been shaped by those forces. Indeed, it is reasonable to suggest that there is very little of Horace beyond family and church— except school, and even there he experiences more than his share of rejection, even as he dishes out rejection to Gideon, the first young man with whom he has sex. Given the state of his mind throughout the text, Horace would be hard put to say who/what he is. He names himself repulsive, unclean, faggot. He names himself descendant of one of the most famous and powerful black families in the area. And he names himself "brilliant,"[33] a designation that serves only to achieve his escape from the first two designations.

In America, it is difficult to be an impressionable teenager under almost any circumstances. But Kenan suggests that it is particularly difficult when one is surrounded, as Horace is, by sanctimonious relatives and neighbors who scoff at and reject the very budding identity that Horace is attempting to shape. It is difficult to make friends when the classmates with whom one most identifies are not of one's own race and even more difficult to feel the reverse rejection by black friends who assume that one has first rejected them. Underneath the calmness of the pretty boy, good boy, well-mannered, straight-A-student exterior, therefore, Horace is a building volcano of such intense emotions and so severely truncated identity formation that his hurt and fear could well occupy several teenagers instead of a single individual.

What Horace has to fear most about himself are his mind and his hands—the mind that indicts his very existence, the mind that concocts the spell of escape, the mind that brings the demon forth or is itself transformed into a demon, the hands that he uses to masturbate into violent spasms of uncontrolled pleasure, the hands that gather the spell-casting ingredients, the hands that carry the shotgun throughout his long, miserable night. Horace's final night on earth is a night of war within his mind or between his mind and his body. Having condemned his body for its participation in illicit pleasure, his deranged or possessed mind carries him to the point of suicide and through that act. He reaches various points during the evening when it is clear that he cannot trust himself, cannot trust his perception of the world around him or his own feelings and analyses, but there is no one else upon whom he can depend.[34] In his agony, his self is transformed, abused, chided, derided, and violated, both psychologically and physically. His body becomes the enemy, the prison, from which he must escape. And escape he does.

Sadly, even Horace's escape is modeled on his Christian upbringing. Above all else, during his evening of searching, questioning, and revisiting his earlier life, Horace is looking for salvation (he is also perhaps looking for validation and/or exoneration). When the conjured demon orders Horace to march, he complies, and "he was happy, O so happy, as he cradled the gun in his hand like a cool phallus, happy for the first time in so, so many months, for he knew the voice would take care of him and teach him and save him." When the hellish crew shouts "profanity and blasphemies," "he smiled and joined in for this was his salvation, the way to final peace, and . . . he marched along aware of the gun that he held tight in his hand, glad to be free, if free was a word to describe what he felt."[35]

Concocting the idea of turning himself into a red-tailed hawk allows Horace to escape from the judging eyes of people and the unrelenting attractions of the flesh. Returning to church, school, and the theater where he worked one summer are similarly desperate attempts to find something that will inspire him to want to remain on earth—or perhaps something that will spur him on to remove himself from earth. Either would be a salvation that has not previously been available to him. Unfortunately, there is no kindly reverend waiting to welcome him from the mourners' bench, no smiling Jesus waiting to lift the burden of homosexuality off his back, no motherly, nurturing church sisters to embrace him as he emerges from the waters of a new baptism. He is completely alone.

In that aloneness, the fragile self that has had such difficulty in forming essentially dissolves. The shotgun blast to the brain is but the culmination of the dissolution that has already occurred. After his grandfather expresses "shame" toward Horace, the narrator ponders: "What does a young man replace the world with, when the world is denied to him?" The narrator comments further: "His loneliness led him into careless and loveless liaisons with men who cared only for his youth, and though he pretended not to care, he worried more and more for his soul, and his increasing confusion took on a harsher guilt and self-loathing."[36] By the time Horace casts his spell, calls forth his demon, and makes his final journey through Tims Creek, he is already dead to everything that matters to him and to everything that he wanted so desperately to cling to and in which he wanted to be affirmed.

In the final analysis, Horace discovers that he has no living mirrors. Persons around him, especially his family members, only reflect distortions back to him. It is appropriate, therefore, that on the night when he wanders back through his life and the theater in which he worked, he encounters an image of himself seated before a large mirror.[37] That image is busily applying layers of thick white pasty makeup to the other Horace—obviously a reference to the duplicitous roles Horace has been forced to play. When the image forces Horace to confront the mirror, which reveals him madly making love with one of the visiting actors, which in turn leads to another series of memories, Horace shoots the image of himself: "There on the ground he lay, himself, a gory red gash through his chest."[38] His efforts to convince himself that he has only killed a ghost or something that was not real do not suffice; he finally takes a permanent vacation from his own mind and succumbs to the call of life underground.

In effect, Horace "disappears" himself. There are no white men with dogs chasing him through a marshy swamp. No threats of lynching. No violent mob waiting for him to make a trip to an outhouse. Only Horace has the power to make Horace disappear. By the time he meets Jimmy at school on the morning of his death, "Horace did not know it was Jimmy. Horace was no longer there."[39] The disappearance is the culmination of so many assaults upon his very being that Horace finally gives in and voluntarily disappears into insanity and suicide. The fragmented self from which so many people demanded so much simply crumbles under the load of expectations. The disappearance of the mind is but the prelude to the disappearance of the body, and perhaps it is merciful that Horace's mind goes before his body. The war between mind and body thus ends violently, but, paradoxically, it also ends peacefully. Like Pecola Breedlove in Toni Morrison's *The Bluest Eye* (1970), *A Visitation of Spirits* essentially posits that there is no viable alternative for Horace.

Certainly it could be argued that a young man declaring his sexual preference for other males is a difficult process any place in the United States. While that might be an undeniable truth, it is also undeniable that southern manifestations of such sexuality can be more acutely problematic in particular kinds of communities, especially in small southern black communities whose ability to name themselves respectable is so tenuous. Anyone who threatens that respectability is expendable. Blood may be thicker than water, but sexuality that is deemed to be perverse can break even the bonds of blood. Horace finds those bonds broken without anyone in his family ever having named him homosexual to his face; they simply let the innuendoes hang in the air long enough for him to receive the strong message of rejection that leads to him killing himself.

Fascinatingly, Kenan does not depict Horace's funeral (though he does depict the funeral of Horace's great-aunt Jonnie Mae). Such a depiction would perhaps have forced family members into discussion about the nature of Horace's death, and it would perhaps have unveiled the silence surrounding his homosexuality. In this instance, therefore, the text conspires with Horace's relatives and with small town southern morality in keeping homosexuality the unspoken (perhaps open) secret that leads to suicide instead of acceptance. If no one can even broach the subject, or if broaching the subject yields the kind of reaction that Horace received from Jimmy, then it is no wonder that such small town southern black environments induce a fear that can chill—or stop—the blood.

NOTES

1. I am currently pursuing this observation in a book-length exploration that I have entitled "The Scary Mason-Dixon Line: African American Writers and the South," which is under contract with LSU Press.
2. James Baldwin, *Just Above My Head* (New York: Dell, 1979), 399, 400.
3. Randall Kenan, *A Visitation of Spirits* (New York: Grove, 1989), 13.
4. Ibid., 248.
5. Ibid., 55.
6. Ibid., 160.
7. Ibid., 183, 184.
8. Ibid., 183, 184, 188.
9. Ibid., 176.
10. Ibid., 180.
11. Lorraine Hansberry, *A Raisin in the Sun* (1959; rpt. New York: Signet, 1988), 51.
12. Richard Wright explores the same phenomenon in his presentation of the character Silas in "Long Black Song." Silas acquires acres of land and tries desperately to emulate white success, but it all ends tragically when he is caught in a web of racism that undermines completely any hope he had for success. See Richard Wright, *Uncle Tom's Children* (New York: Harper&Row, 1940).
13. Kenan, *Visitation*, 112, 113.
14. Ibid., 156.
15. Ibid., 109, 110.
16. Ibid., 12.
17. Ibid., 56.
18. Ibid., 64.
19. Ibid., 238.
20. Ibid., 239. There are echoes of Walter Lee Younger's "five generations of sharecroppers" speech in Zeke's speech. If a black family that was not generally expected to achieve very much has nonetheless beaten the odds and arrived at a kind of success, then how can one of its own members forget his pride and do something stupid? See *Raisin*, 147–48.
21. Kenan, *Visitation*, 188.
22. Ibid., 197.
23. Ibid., 137.
24. It is striking in one instance when Jimmy forgets his "calling" and begins to eat before he has blessed the food. To Zeke and Ruth, that borders on the criminal. See 194. The scene makes clear that Jimmy's inspiration to preach is more other-inspired than internally inspired. He is also

"unrepentant" about refusing to forgive his mother Rose for having left him with his grandparents (121). Such resistance to forgiveness is certainly not the high road of Christianity.

25. Kenan, *Visitation*, 79.
26. Ibid., 86–87.
27. *The Bible*, King James version, Ecclesiastes 12:13.
28. For my discussion of this Kenan story, see Trudier Harris-Lopez, *South of Tradition: Essays on African American Literature* (Athens: University of Georgia Press, 2002), 160–74.
29. Kenan, *Visitation*, 231.
30. See one version of the song in *Call and Response: The Riverside Anthology of the African American Literary Tradition*, ed. Patricia L. Hill, Bernard W. Bell, Trudier Harris, William J. Harris, R. Baxter Miller, Sondra A. O'Neale, and Horace A. Porter (Boston: Houghton Mifflin, 1998), 238.
31. Kenan, *Visitation*, 252.
32. Ibid., 251.
33. Ibid., 225.
34. Toni Morrison's Sula comes to a similar conclusion—that she can depend upon no one but her self—but she, like Horace, finds that the self cannot ultimately be counted on either. See Morrison, *Sula* (New York: Knopf, 1974), 118–19.
35. Kenan, *Visitation*, 28.
36. Ibid., 239, 240.
37. Ibid., 219–20.
38. Ibid., 235.
39. Ibid., 241.

3

Looking for Love in All the Wrong Places: Same-Sex Relations in the Fiction of Gloria Naylor

Maxine Lavon Montgomery

Gloria Naylor, arguably one of the most talented authors on the contemporary literary scene, has never shied away from addressing taboo subjects in her fiction. Her treatment of same-sex relations offers an example of her willingness not only to confront delicate social and interpersonal issues, but to also handle them with deftness and sensitivity. A reading of her expanding canon reveals an ongoing authorial concern with the triumph and tragedy, joy and, more often, sorrow of those who dare to defy heterosexual norms. Naylor is, of course, not the first or only African American woman writer to explore gay/lesbian relations. Alice Walker, Gayl Jones, Ntozake Shange, and Audre Lorde, among others, have navigated this territory as well. But the forbidden love that imperils many of Naylor's characters is a continuing emphasis in the author's works, even as it serves as a locus for the interrogation of space.

It is Naylor who makes the association between self and space when she comments regarding her second novel, *Linden Hills*, that she used space deliberately, as a metaphor for the middle-class woman's existence.[1] Successive generations of Nedeed wives find themselves isolated from the social mainstream, confined to a restrictive domestic sphere despite their husbands' entry into the realms of power, privilege, and authority. Each woman is eventually consigned to the basement of the expansive Nedeed home, and it is in this subterranean locus of exile that the women draw strength from the ties of sisterhood sustaining black women in America. Bourgeois ideology, with its emphasis on patriarchal privilege and the pursuit of material success, is responsible for the collective oppression that the wives experience. Rather than being a welcoming, maternal space, the home is thus the site of the centuries-old subjugation that the Nedeed wives endure.[2]

The line of demarcation separating private and public spheres is rigidly drawn and is evident everywhere in Naylor's canon, with the domestic arena figuring as the exclusive purview of women and the larger society—the marketplace—under the dominion of males. Naylor's treatment of same-sex love complicates the politics involved in the construction of a gender-specific space, however, as she fictionalizes the efforts on the part of gays/lesbians to transverse the boundaries between male and female, self and other. Indeed, gays/lesbians in Naylor's canon refuse allegiance to any one particular sphere, preferring instead the fluidity associated with life outside fixed bounds. Those practicing same-sex love hover on the unexplored margins of society, forever displaced, always in search of an idealized arena that is free of imposed restraint. In her rendering of the collective plight of those to whom Homi Bhabha would refer as the "unhomely," Naylor thus brings into sharp focus the myriad ways that a white, patriarchal, bourgeois society engages in the troubling practice of "othering."[3] Individuals who fail to fit into a prescribed role are ignored, ostracized, vilified, and, in some cases, violently victimized as a result of society's contempt for anyone who transgresses the bounds of a heterosexual norm.

Naylor directs attention to the many places that have served a historic role as sanctuaries or protected arenas in black America. Whether it is the home, church, barbershop, beauty parlor, or lodge, the many institutions in which blacks have operated assume center stage in the author's treatment of gay/lesbian relations. Such places can offer a necessary buffer against the psychic and physical violence associated with life in the white world, as Patricia Hill Collins outlines in her discussion of safe spaces:

> These institutional sites where Black women construct independent self-definitions reflect the dialectical nature of oppression and activism. Institutions controlled by the dominant group such as schools, the media, and literature, and popular culture are the initial source of externally defined, controlling images. African-American women have traditionally used Black families and community institutions as places where they could develop a Black women's culture of resistance.[4]

While Collins refers specifically to the culture of resistance among black women, her comments are relevant to Naylor's portrait of the gay/lesbian community and its move toward self-definition. But those who practice same-sex love in Naylor's fiction must define themselves *both* within *and* against the institutional spaces present in African American life. Of the many settings figuring in Naylor's fictional landscape, three of them feature same-sex relations: Brewster Place, Linden Hills, and Bailey's Café. Indeed, Brewster Place might have continued in its predictable pattern of social relations had it not been for the unwelcome intrusion of people who are, as the Bible-thumping moralist Miss Sophie puts it, "*that* way."[5] Site of narrative action in Naylor's first and fifth novels, the squalid postwar urban community reveals the social dynamics that lay the groundwork for the author's treatment of same-sex love. Naylor is careful to distinguish Theresa, who is dark-skinned, pretty, short, and has "too much behind," from Lorraine, the lighter, skinny one.[6] Nevertheless, they acquire the designation "The Two," as if to suggest the anonymity occurring once the women enter an arena that is defined in terms of a heterosexual norm.[7] Theresa and Lorraine, no less industrious, no less civic-minded than the other residents, inhabit a yet unnamed discursive space—one that, like Brewster itself, is not geographically demarcated or linguistically coded, for that matter. In this borderland, as Gloria Anzaldua would label it, or more precisely, borderland within a borderland, all sorts of strange, unnatural behavior and secret rituals take place.[8] So perverse are the couple's acts that even the gossip-monger Sophie, who is hardly ever without commentary on other people's affairs, cannot find the words to express what the women do behind closed doors.

Theresa's rural roots do little to bridge the gulf between her and other displaced southern migrants. Brewster's colored daughters could care less that Theresa is a sister who hails from down home. Neither are they inclined to ignore her lesbianism just because she is black. Lorraine, who wages a losing battle for acceptance, ponders the way in which sexual orientation trumps racial solidarity and calls into question the foundation underlying the black nationalism that community activists Kiswana Brown and Abshu Ben Jamal espouse: "Why should she feel different from the people she lived around? Black people were all in the same boat—she'd come to realize this even more since they had moved to Brewster—and if they didn't row together, they would sink together."[9]

Meditations on aspects of difference predominate in "The Two." By far the more aggressive partner in the lesbian duo, Theresa remains

undaunted in her belief that she will never be accepted, and her asser-
tions evolve out of lived experiences, with her "been there" and "done
that" attitude. Having migrated from one community to the next—
including the upper-middle-class Linden Hills—she faces constant
rejection and comes to terms with her marginal status. Theresa,
worldlier than Lorraine, has had sexual relations with both men and
women before reaching the realization that she is meant to be a lesbian. She explains, "You can take a chocolate chip cookie and put
holes in it and attach it to your ears and call it an earring, or hang it
around your neck on a silver chain and pretend it's a necklace—but
it's still a cookie."[10] No matter how hard Theresa tries to redefine herself, she is still gay and therefore unable to escape who she really is.
Nor is she able to remove the stigma that a homophobic society would
impose. So Theresa willingly accepts the role Brewster's residents
confer upon her.

Marilyn Farwell is accurate in the assertion that Naylor intends the
relationship between girlfriends Mattie and Etta to be a counterpoint
to the relationship between Theresa and Lorraine.[11] Naylor employs
binary opposites in her texts as a means of deconstructing established
ideologies, and her authorial engagement with same-sex love is no
exception. Mattie Michael, who has nurtured women in the community through various crises, tests, and trials, informs her best friend
Etta Mae Johnson that there is no real difference between lesbianism
and the affection Brewster's colored daughters display:

> "But I've loved some women deeper than I ever loved any man,"
> Mattie was pondering. "And there been some women who loved me
> more and did more for me than any man ever did."
>
> "Yeah." Etta thought for a moment. "I can second that, but it's still
> different, Mattie. I can't exactly put my finger on it, but . . ."
>
> "Maybe it's not so different," Mattie said almost to herself. "Maybe
> that's why some women get so riled up about it, 'cause they know deep
> down it's not so different after all."[12]

If the relationship between Mattie and Etta Mae is a counterpoint
to that between Theresa and Lorraine, then it is Lorraine who enters
the medial site allowing Naylor to test communal tolerance for forbidden love. Same-sex bonds are, as Anzaldua suggests, a willful trans-
gression of fixed heterosexual bounds.[13] Lorraine detaches herself
from her companion in an effort to find the safe space that has proven
elusive. With the account of the bond between the kindly janitor Ben
and Lorraine, Naylor reinscribes the father-daughter relationship—one

that is fraught with tension in the author's canon. The two outcasts share a oneness that emanates from the trauma associated with society's attempt to proscribe the homosexual self. Ben, a tenant farmer, is unable to provide for his family or protect his daughter from the sexual advances of wealthy landowner Mr. Clyde, who exerts hegemonic control reminiscent of that of the white slavemaster. Ben is emasculated within the context of the rural southern economy. His wife Elvira's relentless tirades rob him of his masculinity by linking manhood with economic ability: "If you was half a man, you coulda given me more babies and we woulda had some help workin' this land instead of a half-grown woman we gotta carry the load for. And if you was even quarter a man, we wouldn't be a bunch of miserable sharecroppers on someone else's land—but we is, Ben."[14] Because Ben's daughter is unable to work in the fields, she is then compelled to serve as a domestic in the master's house of patriarchal privilege. As someone who acquires commodity status in the context of a capitalist system where she is bartered in exchange for extra land, Ben's nameless daughter later moves to Memphis. She likely begins a life of prostitution in an attempt to control the terms of her sexuality, an act of defiance heralding the practice among Eve's misfit boarders in *Bailey's Café*.

Whereas Ben's nameless daughter voluntarily severs ties with home, Lorraine's father, like the wrathful Old Testament God, banishes her after discovering a letter from one of her female lovers. Her father mandates that she leave behind everything he has provided for her. Lorraine writes home in an attempt to maintain contact with him, but he refuses to acknowledge her efforts. Both women experience a peculiar sisterhood based upon attempts to proscribe female sexuality. Only in the recesses of Ben's darkened, dingy basement, trope for the Dante-esque underworld Naylor's subaltern figures are forced to frequent, does the troubled Lorraine experience the kind of unconditional love and acceptance her family withholds from her. In what is perhaps the greatest irony of Lorraine's situation, as a consequence of her relationship with the fatherly janitor, she becomes not only more assertive but also increasingly critical of individuals who, like her, choose to define sexuality on their own terms. Indeed, Naylor complicates the issue of identity politics with the tendency on the young woman's part to "other" "others" who are "othered." Lorraine refers to those at the gay bar as being "coarse," "bitter," "weirdoes," even "fags."[15] She thus becomes as critical of gays/ lesbians as Miss Sophie is. After a brief emotional breakdown on Theresa's part, Lorraine, once the more passive partner, comforts Theresa in a reversal of roles.

Nurturing, which is integral to the black community's social dynamics involving care networks and mutual-aid societies, is a central practice among Brewster's displaced colored daughters whose shared friendship has been a sustaining influence. Naylor points out that "Women only had each other in our history. Around the kitchen table or at the laundromat, they would go to other women with their problems about children, about the men in their lives, about their jobs. And they would share that in places that were unimportant to the outside world, gaining strength from each other in quiet ways."[16] But the nurturing impulse fails Lorraine.[17] The bonding that occurs in Lucielia Louise Turner when Mattie bathes the grief-stricken Ciel does not take place with Lorraine, who remains distant from the female networks that comprise the novel's emotional center. Mattie bathes Ciel, in a reinscription of the mother-daughter bond, and the two bereaved mothers are one with a community of dispossessed mothers. Because of Mattie's maternal influence, Ciel survives the grief associated with the loss of her daughter Serena. There is no such redemption for Lorraine, however. Instead, Lorraine, raped en route to the gay bar, is relegated to the margins of society, a nonparticipant in the women's collective effort to dismantle Brewster's restrictive brick wall, an artificial, imposed boundary that symbolizes the limitations owing to race and gender.[18]

Despite valiant efforts on the part of Brewster's displaced, colored daughters to recreate home within the urban community's environs, the dilapidated housing project is far from being a welcoming, maternal space for Theresa, Lorraine, or the troubled Greasy either. Greasy, who is introduced in *The Men of Brewster Place*, is, of course, not "tragically gay," to borrow Barbara Smith's term.[19] Greasy is not gay at all, or even bisexual, for that matter. But he is, like Ben, entrapped within prescribed notions of masculinity, as he attempts to cope with cocaine-addiction and the attendant loss of his job and family. Although Greasy plays a minor role in Naylor's fifth novel, *The Men of Brewster Place*, his dilemma typifies that faced by black men in the city. The so-called brothers who frequent the local barbershop, Max's Place, the masculine equivalent of the female coffee klatch, fail to recreate the kind of support network prevalent among Brewster's colored daughters. In other words, with all of the good-natured conversation and joviality, the male sanctuary at Max's Place fails to offer men a safe space against the onslaught of urban chaos. Much of the trauma that invades the lives of Brewster's women finds its way into the tenuous network that the brotherhood comprises. Brewster's male residents do not provide the caring that Eve gives to the lesbian, heroin-addicted Jesse Bell in *Bailey's Cafe*. The feisty, working-class Jesse Bell turns to drugs when her marriage to the wealthy Sugar Hill King family ends in a bitter divorce. When Jesse arrives at Eve's place, the divorcee has reached the lowest point in her life. But as a result of Eve's unconventional healing method, Jesse is cured in less than a month. In response to his trials, however, Greasy commits suicide by slitting his wrists, declaring, "I'm a man."[20]

Written in response to the death of her father and the Million Man March, Naylor's fifth text examines the impact of gay lifestyle on African American men.[14] Issues of difference manifesting themselves in private conversation among Brewster's colored daughters are, among the community's men, sublimated in the psychological and emotional turmoil that Eugene experiences. A guilt-ridden Eugene finds himself enmeshed in relationships with other men as pressures of dealing with work and marriage become increasingly overwhelming. Eugene displaces his anger toward white society onto his wife Ciel, whom he blames for the couple's plight. Ciel tries to be the model wife in an effort to keep her wayward, verbally abusive husband pacified, unaware of the motive underlying his instability. As a bisexual, Eugene partakes of forbidden love reluctantly with men who, like him, appear to be straight. Foreman on the docks, Bruce is Eugene's new companion—one conforming to socially constructed notions of manliness: he is a Lakers' fan, built like a football player, and can trash talk with the best. Lucielia's wandering husband describes him in precise terms: "big, dark, and mean."[21] There is nothing about Bruce that would hint at his sexual orientation. As if to signify their athletic prowess—their manliness—the two men play one-on-one basketball.

But much of Naylor's rendering of the transgressive sexuality that entraps African American men involves a careful deconstruction of the veneer of machismo that prevents men from realizing their full potential as husbands, fathers, and lovers. Eugene and Bruce find themselves at the Purple Cock, a gay bar that offers temporary refuge from the hostility of the outside world in a manner reminiscent of Ben's darkened basement. Those who frequent the Purple Cock—the working-class men—are no less persistent in their pursuit of fulfillment than patrons at The Bull and Roses, where "Brooks Brothers meets the leather trade."[22] In this arena, individuals are free of all inhibitions and can define themselves on their own terms. Although Eugene refers to Bruce as a godfather, the burly foreman's role more closely resembles that of Dante's Virgil as a guide through the gay underworld—a dark world of secrets, masquerades, and lies. Just as Virgil guides Dante but must leave once Dante is in purgatory, so, too, does Bruce lead a reluctant Eugene into the macabre side of gay life. There is no mention of Bruce as Eugene gains confidence in navigating his way through the gay world.

It is Chino, a Latino drag queen/king and prostitute, who executes the ritual of penance that is to liberate a contrite Eugene from an emotional and psychological hell. The transgender male, who prefers the rough atmosphere of the Purple Cock, stops short of becoming a woman and is an embodiment of the bitter, coarse, prancing people Lorraine decries. Existing in the medial space between genders, neither male nor female, not only does Chino reveal how fluid the boundaries demarcating genders are, but also his lifestyle encourages a rethinking of the fixed ideological perspective underlying society's insistent homophobia. In other words, Chino carries out the process of developing a counterhegemonic discourse—one that is in opposition to the limiting script to which society would consign him.[23] Therefore, instead of being a site of limitation and enclosure, the marginal space that Chino inhabits becomes a place of liberation—a locus for exploring the infinite possibility at the heart of Naylor's expanding canon:

> He grew up believing that he loved men because he was meant to be a woman. It's a long process to change your sex—the battery of psychological tests, the hormone injections, and then finally a series of operations. Coming down to the finish line, he faced the truth that he didn't really want to be a woman. It was just easier to handle the world's contempt—as well as his own—to think of himself as a woman loving men than as a man loving men. But they had already castrated him when he stopped the operations. And there was no going back. So he moved forward, caught in limbo, and left to define himself.[24]

Theresa's lament in *The Women of Brewster Place* that society has no words to describe the dynamics of forbidden love thus finds its answer in the multiple and, at times, competing subject positions Chino adopts. A figure reminiscent of *Bailey's Café*'s Miss Maple, Chino defies reductive, essentialist notions of identity. As if to signify his liberation from the narrow space within which society would limit him, he refers to himself in the third-person:

> It's called the third person. I speak of myself in the third person. Isn't it obvious that there's just too much beauty here for one person?" I looked to Bruce for help, but he'd suddenly become interested in watching people walk past the window out on the street. "I mean," Chino continued, "how can one person—*one person*—be me?"[25]

Chino thus demonstrates the polyphony that Mae Henderson attributes to texts by African American women.[26] He appropriates a multiplicity of selves, a myriad of voices, thereby disrupting the single, solitary authoritative text of a strictly masculine identity. By introducing such a character, Naylor heralds a disruption of the master narrative embedded in a heterosexual norm.

Naylor's rendering of the Chino-Eugene encounter, arguably the most disturbing scene in the novel, is telling in its emphasis not so much on the raw physical aspect of sex, but the psychological turmoil that Eugene experiences. Overwhelmed with guilt and grief, unable to come to terms with his bisexuality, Eugene is already suffering immensely. In a ritual of sadomasochism that is laced ironically with religious overtones of penance, absolution, and purgatory, Chino uses a leather whip to punish the contrite Eugene who, like the pilgrim Dante, must descend before ascending to new life.

With Eugene, who makes an attempt to atone for his past wrongs, there is the possibility of redemption, despite his failure to acknowledge the fact of his bisexuality. The reader is to assume that, as with Eugene's grieving wife Luciela, his suffering will end and he will be able to move forward in life. There is no such sympathy for *Linden Hills'* Winston Alcott, however, who allows his quest for acceptance within corporate America to subsume his eight-year relationship with his lover David. Upon receiving a letter disclosing his son's gay lifestyle, Winston's father coerces his son into marrying Cassandra. Winston's father serves as an agent for the forced heterosexuality that prevails in the upper-middle-class community. Marriage is the sine qua non for social progress, according to the bourgeois code successive generations of Nedeed men uphold. On the eve of the marriage, Luther tells David that "No one's been able to make it down to Tupelo Drive without a stable life and family."[27] Same-sex marriages are not only illegal, they are an anathema in a society governed by male privilege. It is as if Winston has no choice in his own future. Rather, his destiny is under the control of others. Public knowledge of his gay lifestyle would derail a promising career. Not only is the young man's reputation at stake, his financial security would be in jeopardy if he chooses to persist in his relationship with David. Marrying Cassandra will therefore result in a severing of ties between the two men.

Whereas Theresa mentions Linden Hills as one of the places to which she and Lorraine have fled, only in Naylor's second novel, Linden Hills, does the author reveal the social dynamics that made life unbearable for the two young women. Naylor indicts bourgeois society, with its rigid definitions of marriage and family, for the role that it plays in proscribing individual sexuality. Nowhere is this more evident than in the relationship between Lester Tilson and Willie K. Mason. While the two young, aspiring poets are not gay, they share a kindred spirit with other Naylor characters whose sexuality exceeds fixed bounds. Willie, whose name is a masculine rendering of Willa, current Nedeed wife, is closely associated with the female character, and he and Willa are "two sides of the same coin."[28] In much the same way that the Nedeed wives are rendered nameless, faceless, and invisible, so, too, does Willie entertain fears of a loss of self. He dreams of being without a face and is afraid to view his reflection in a department store mirror. When a disheveled Willa ascends from her basement prison, she and Willie gaze upon her visage in a mirror.

Much of the homoeroticism that critics have noted in their analysis of the novel has to do with the authorial attempt to dismantle established conceptions of masculine and feminine, self and other.[29] Lester and Willie uphold the same code of machismo that Bruce espouses when they lie about sexual conquests of the girls at Wayne Junior High School. Willie confesses that he has erotic dreams about Ruth Anderson. Lester, fearful of being labeled "a fruit or something" if others learn of his poetic interests, is quick to refer to Xavier McDonald as a "fruit" and calls Winston Alcott a "fag."[30]

Even though Willie feels sickened when he recognizes the depth of David's love for Winston, both he and Lester have an attraction to men that is equally compelling. Lester enjoys gazing at Hank Aaron's strong, muscular body. Willie has a sexual stirring while looking at the body of a basketball player: "And once he had gotten the same crazy feelings from staring at the thighs of a Knicks center that he got from touching pretty Janie Benson."[31]

Perhaps the most telling incident pointing to the attraction that the two young men share occurs on the eve of the wedding between Winston and Cassandra. While David struggles to break ties with the groom-to-be, Lester and Willie attempt to disentangle themselves from a close embrace. The pair sleeps together and Lester awakens to find Willie hugging him. Later, on Christmas Eve, Willie continues to be troubled as a result of his experiences in Linden Hills, and he ponders the existence of Willa Nedeed, his feminine counterpart: "But she was waiting for him, he felt that in his guts; he just had to fall asleep. Willie shuddered. Christ, now he really was turning into a woman—he sounded like somebody's superstitious old aunt."[32]

With the novel's emphasis on the close, almost transcendent nature of the gay/lesbian bond, however, Naylor elevates same-sex relations beyond a mere physical plane. This kind of emphasis makes the severing of ties between Winston and David, who is best man at the impending wedding, all the more disappointing. The author moves beyond a portrayal of the nurturing relationship gays/lesbians share and suggests that such bonds involve a spiritual union:

> Winston looked down into his hands again. No, that's not what they were talking about. And they weren't even talking about remaining lovers; they had moved beyond that years ago. Because when two people still held on like he and David, after all the illusions had died, and accepted the other's lacks and ugliness and irritating rhythms—when they had known the joys of a communion that far outstripped the flesh—they could hardly just be lovers. No, this man gave him his center, but the world had given him no words—and ultimately no way—with which to cherish that. He smiled bitterly and looked up. "Don't you see what I'm up against? How am I going to live with you when they haven't even made up the right words for what we are to each other?[33]

Winston's comments concerning society's unwillingness or inability to articulate the nature of forbidden love recalls a similar discussion between Theresa and Lorraine. Whereas the two young women continue in their association, at least until Lorraine is raped, David breaks ties with Winston, preferring independence over the subordinate role he would play once Winston and Cassandra are married. Naylor reserves her strongest censure for Winston, who turns his back on his closest friend, however. After a wedding ceremony laced with irony, Luther gives Winston a thousand-year mortgage for a house on Tupelo Drive.

Because of his adherence to the code of success that middle-class society prescribes, Winston, like the others in Linden Hills, is thus entrapped in a bourgeois hell. That the aspiring corporate lawyer is relegated to the lowest rung of hell, a site reserved in Dante's *Inferno* for those who betray country, kin, and hospitality, is a criticism of the home under bourgeois domination. At the novel's end, only poets Willie K. Mason and Lester Tilson—"brothers" whose bond remains inviolable—scale the fence hand-in-hand and escape the holocaust.

Last in a tetralogy, *Bailey's Café* arrives at a more complex, if not ambiguous, rendering of same-sex relations than any of Naylor's novels. Miss Maple, Stanford graduate turned housekeeper/bouncer, willfully transgresses prescribed bounds owing to gender with his appropriation of female dress. Although he is quick to inform the reader that he is not gay, he is as much a victim of society's homophobia as is the heroin-addicted Jesse Bell. Much of the novel has to do with Naylor's critique of the virgin-whore dichotomy and the ways in which the label "whore" is used to proscribe the female self.[19] She is equally concerned with the ways in which individuals use the Bible as a means of "othering" because of race and gender. Jesse Bell, who refuses to allow anyone to dictate her actions, maintains a bond with "her" throughout a troubled marriage into the wealthy King clan. She is quite brazen in her relationship, ignoring strident criticism from the likes of Sister Carrie who, like Miss Sophie, condemns the lesbian lifestyle because of its flagrant opposition to scripture. Jesse finds her way to Eve's place after being incarcerated in a woman's detention center, and she reaches the lowest point in her life as a result of public disclosure of her lesbianism. Miss Maple's foray into same-sex love, by contrast, is confined to a solitary encounter while in prison: "He was six-feet-two, as broad as he was tall, as ugly as he was mean, a repeat offender serving for three counts of murder with nothing left to lose. And he wasn't a homosexual either. He wasn't anything but something that could only gauge it was alive by watching other things die."[34]

"Miss Maple's Blues," the longest and most complicated story included in "The Jam," emphasizes the importance of defining the self apart from fixed labels. Not only that, but his story also points to the vast fluidity associated with postmodern identity, and in this regard, Miss Maple's lifestyle heralds a possible resolution to many of the problems confronting Naylor's gay/lesbian characters. Of all the patrons whose mournful tales Naylor recounts, it is Miss Maple who best defies reductive definitions of self, with his ethnically diverse ancestry and empowered masculinity. He adopts feminine dress, appropriating emblems of women's identity, in response to the absurdity of America's race and gender politics. Yet he redefines those emblems according to a radically different persona he fashions. Naylor lends her approval to Miss Maple's performance of womanhood when she describes the housekeeper/bouncer as "the manliest man she has ever written about."[35] As a counterpoint to the chauvinistic Bailey, who tends to objectify women, such as his reticent wife Nadine and the alluring Peaches, Miss Maple is free from the limitations associated with the adoption of a masculine gaze. Both Bailey and Sugar Man see Peaches in sexual terms, as an object that they can possess. But as someone who lacks the tendency to "other" "others," Miss Maple negotiates a self that is as fluid as the elusive café itself. Moreover, by virtue of his willingness to move outside of socially constructed notions of race, ethnicity, and gender, he becomes a locus for the critique of the narrow perspective of the racist whites who attempt to pigeonhole him.

Intermarriage figures prominently in Miss Maple's family past, and his story is situated within the larger historic context of border tension between Mexico, Texas, and California. His mother is the youngest child of a fugitive Texan slave and a Mexican rancher, and he informs the reader that he has "aunts of all assortments." Despite the diversity represented by his past—Hispanic, Native American, and African—society engages in reductive labeling in its assessment of him: "The Americans had no problems with our identities, though; they imported one six-letter word to cut through all that Yuma-Irish-Mexican-African tangle in our heritage."[36]

Compounding Miss Maple's dilemma is his well-intentioned father's insistence on adhering to a rigid code defining manhood. Miss Maple's father wants his son to be educated, cultured, refined, and thus capable of realizing his place in society. The encounter with the Gatlins, a group of racist whites, is ironically the bouncer/housekeeper's first introduction to the kind of society that sets the terms for Miss Maple's existence. While at the freighting office, preparing to ship volumes of Shakespeare's plays, the father-son pair have an altercation with the Gatlins, and that conflict results in the father's near castration. That Miss Maple and his father escape from a storeroom dressed in a crinoline and corset—all the while fighting their opponent—reveals the father's creative adaptation to his situation.

Unwittingly, the father serves as a model for the empowered masculinity that Miss Maple later exhibits. The housekeeper/bouncer ignores Jesse Bell's "other-ing" when she refers to him as a faggot watchdog. While at Eve's boardinghouse/bordello, a medial site outside of fixed geographic bounds, Miss Maple transforms the once oppressive domestic space into a thriving business enterprise. The lines separating public and private spheres cease to exist at Eve's place, and Miss Maple plays a key role in this process. His award-winning jingles allow him to combine his training in statistics with his creative side. The jingle that brings the most satisfaction is one for a dishwashing detergent that will leave American housewives feeling "both married and sexy,"[37] thereby dissolving the restrictive dialectical tension between marriage and sexuality.

Clearly, matters regarding sexuality and same-sex relations continue to engage Gloria Naylor's creative energies. For her, the issue is not so much society's refusal to carve out a niche for those practicing same-sex love as it is the effort on the part of gays/lesbians to redefine the terms of their sexuality. Much of that process of redefinition involves adopting multiple subject positions, even as gays/lesbians enlarge the sphere of their influence. Her fiction critiques the institutions of black America that internalize the hegemonic practice of the white world rather than embrace all individuals, regardless of difference. At the same time, however, her expanding canon reveals the myriad ways in which gays/lesbians have adapted creatively to their restrictive world. In this regard, her portrait of same-sex love encourages the reader not only to see the world from the vantage point of those on the margins, but to also rethink established ideological notions formulated within the social mainstream.

NOTES

1. Gloria Naylor, "Gloria Naylor," *Conversations with Gloria Naylor*, ed. Maxine Lavon Montgomery (Jackson: University Press of Mississippi, 2004), 71–72.
2. Offering a glowing, unequivocally positive perspective of the home as a poetic space, Gaston Bachelard posits the domestic arena as being a welcoming, maternal site in *The Poetics of Space* (New York: Orion Press, 1964). Sandra Gilbert and Susan Gubar utilize a feminist approach in their discussion of "architecture of patriarchy" and the myriad ways nineteenth-century women's writing reveals female anxiety over containment within the domestic arena in *The Madwoman in the Attic: The Woman Writer and the Nineteenth-Century Literary Imagination* (New Haven: Yale University Press, 1979).
3. Homi Bhabha, *The Location of Culture* (New York: Routledge, 1994).
4. Patricia Hill Collins, *Black Feminist Thought: Knowledge, Consciousness, and the Politics of Empowerment* (New York: Routledge, 1991), 95.
5. Gloria Naylor, *The Women of Brewster Place* (New York: Viking Press, 1982), 131.
6. Ibid., 129.
7. I base my assessment on Naylor's comments in which she refers to the community's view of Theresa and Lorraine as "an alien social solution." See Naylor, "A Talk with Gloria Naylor," by William Goldstein, in *Conversations*, 5.
8. Gloria Anzaldua, Preface to *Borderlands/La Frontera: The New Mestiza* (San Francisco: Aunt Lute Books, 1987).
9. Naylor, *The Women of Brewster Place*, 142.
10. Ibid., 138.
11. Marilyn Farwell, *Heterosexual Plots and Lesbian Narratives* (New York: New York University Press, 1996).
12. Naylor, *The Women of Brewster Place*, 141.
13. Anzaldua, Preface, 41.
14. Naylor, *The Women of Brewster Place*, 153.
15. Ibid., 142.
16. Naylor, "A Conversation with G.N.," by Angels Carabi, in *Conversations*, 119.

17. Naylor, "A Talk with Gloria Naylor," by William Goldstein, in *Conversations*, 5.

18. Ibid., 54.

19. See Barbara Smith, "The Truth Never Hurts: Black Lesbians in Fiction in the 1980's," *Wildwomen in the Whirlwind: Afro-American Culture and the Contemporary Literary Renaissance*, ed. Joanne Braxton and Andree Nicola McLaughlin (New Brunswick: Rutgers University Press, 1990). Smith finds Naylor's representation of gay/lesbian relations to be unrealistic and pessimistic. In my interview with Naylor, however, she responds to Smith's criticisms by asserting that her gay/lesbian characters are no more tragic than her other (straight) characters. See Naylor, "A Conversation with Gloria Naylor," interview by the author, tape recording, Brooklyn, New York (May 3, 2003).

20. Naylor, *The Men of Brewster Place* (New York: Hyperion, 1998), 166.

21. Ibid., 76.

22. Ibid., 78.

23. On the concept of the counterhegemonic, see bell hooks, "Choosing the Margin as a Space of Radical Openness," in *Yearning: Race, Gender, and Cultural Politics* (Boston: South End Press, 1990), 68–82.

24. Naylor, *The Men of Brewster Place*, 80.

25. Ibid., 80–81.

26. Henderson bases her theory in part on Mikhail Bakhtin's discussion in *The Dialogic Imagination: Four Essays*, ed. Michael Holquist, trans. Caryl Emerson and Michael Holquist (Austin: University of Texas Press, 1981). See Mae Henderson, "Speaking in Tongues: Dialogism and the Black Woman Writer's Literary Imagination," in *Changing Our Own Words: Essays on Criticism, Theory, and Writing by Black Women*, ed. Cheryl Wall (New Brunswick: Rutgers University Press, 1989).

27. Naylor, *Linden Hills* (New York: Tricknor and Fields, 1985), 75.

28. Naylor, "A Conversation," interviewed by the author.

29. Henry Louis Gates, Jr., sees a homoerotic attraction between Lester and Willie and between Lutheer and Willie. See Gates, "Significant Others," *Contemporary Literature* 29 (1988): 606–23.

30. Naylor, *Linden Hills*, 26, 54, and 73.

31. Ibid., 28.

32. Ibid., 273.

33. Ibid., 79–80.

34. Naylor, *Bailey's Café* (New York: Harcourt, Brace, and Jovanovich, 1992), 193.

35. Naylor, "A Conversation with G.N.," by Virginia Fowler, in *Conversations*, 130–31.

36. Naylor, *Bailey's Café*, 171.

37. Ibid., 215.

4

Postmodernism, Paul Auster's *The New York Trilogy*, and the Construction of the Black/Woman of Color as Primal Other

Lawrence W. Hogue

Much has been made of the conjecture that postmodern fiction—along with the poststructural/postmodern theories of Jacques Derrida, Michel Foucault, Jacques Lacan, Luce Irigaray, Jean Baudrillard, Hélène Cixous, and others—suggests a culture or social formation beyond instrumental reason and other Enlightenment ideas, existential humanism, the patriarchy, the nuclear family, the ego-centered subject, the Freudian psyche, and hierarchies of class, race, and gender—in short, beyond modernity and modernism. A close scrutiny of postmodern fiction in general and Paul Auster's *The New York Trilogy* in particular shows that they play with instrumental reason and other Enlightenment ideas, opening up and validating all kinds of excluded/unacknowledged psychological, social, and nonrational human dimensions and experiences. They expand human possibilities and create new languages and new ways of thinking about existence—outside Freud, the patriarchy, and the ego-centered subject.

But because postmodern fiction in general and Auster's *The New York Trilogy* in particular are written within the modern, Eurocentric horizon, they still become entrapped in some of its structures, definitions, values, conventions, and stereotypes. For example, as with modern American literature, they tend to redact modern, Eurocentric (male) subjectivity as privileged and fixed. They also tend to victimize/fetishize the Other, assuming that it exists outside of Western history and rationality. Here, when I speak of Other, I am referring to the global periphery, Woman, the dominated classes of the marginalized, the African American, the Native American, and, in Paul Auster's case, the black/woman of color. Here, also, I am not just concerned with the Other being constructed as a fixed and ontological subject, in the modern sense. I also want her to be defined as a subject of postmodernity. I want him to be defined in terms of what Jacques Lacan would call a network of contextual, partial, contradictory, and shifting identifications.[1]

I want to situate my discussion of Auster's *The New York Trilogy* within the context of postmodernity as a critique of modernity and as a Eurocentric paradigm. Also, I want to examine how Auster treats the Other, particularly the black/woman of color. In "Beyond Eurocentrism," Enrique Dussel identifies two basic paradigms of modernity—the Eurocentric and the planetary—and he argues that the type of critique one offers modernity, and subsequently one's choice of postmodernity, is determined by the paradigm of modernity he chooses. Dussel's Eurocentric paradigm conceptualizes the phenomenon of modernity (and later postmodernity) as exclusively European, with Europe and the West as the center and the rest of the world as Other, the periphery. Dussel's planetary paradigm—which he defines as "the coexistence of systems that include differences, with variable degrees of complexity"[2]—formulates the phenomenon of modernity (and later postmodernity) as the culture of the *center* of the first-world system, through the incorporation, the intermingling, of the periphery. These two paradigms of modernity construct the world and history differently.

Paul Auster's *The New York Trilogy* both presupposes and challenges Dussel's Eurocentric paradigm of modernity. As a part of the second generation of postmodern, Euro-American, male writers, Auster is concerned with assailing instrumental reason. He is rebelling against what he calls the "conventions of so-called realistic fiction" where "everything's been smoothed out . . . , robbed of its singularity, boxed into a predictable world of cause and effect."[3] Instead, Auster wants to normalize mystery, chance, doubling, the corporealized subject, and coincidence, which he defines as being a part of everyday life and a social reality. In an interview with Joseph Mallia, Auster states:

I believe the world is filled with strange events. Reality is a great deal more mysterious than we ever give it credit for . . . . We're surrounded by things we don't understand, by mysteries, and in the books [the three novellas of *The New York Trilogy*] these are people who suddenly come face to face with them.[4]

Thus, Auster wants to reconfigure the world into a place where the rational and the nonrational intermingle, where differences coexist and interact. This reconfiguration signifies planetary postmodernity.

But, despite Auster's signification of planetary postmodernity and the creation of a differ/defer chain of signifiers in the male narrator's Hegelian, enlightenment, transcendental, racially *unmarked* "I," which undermines the notion of a unified self, the "I" of his quest narrative in all three novellas of *The New York Trilogy*, with its underpinning of white male desire, is never deconstructed. It maintains a self/Other binary opposition, thereby erasing differences. In failing to engage the reason of the Other and in asking the Other to give up its histories, cultures, and distinct subjectivities in order to be accommodated by the Euro-American, male narrative, Auster still practices the violence of the myth of modernity. As a consequence, *The New York Trilogy* reads postmodernism as a narrative about the identity crisis of a few, relatively privileged, Western white males. Auster's postmodernism is still Eurocentric subject–centered.

In *The New York Trilogy*, the place that Auster wants to get to is a postmodern fiction where chance is a part of reality, where mystery and coincidence "operate as governing principles that are constantly clashing with causality and rationality."[5] It is a postmodern fiction where "chance and synchronicity move the plot forward," where there is intertextual play of names and identities, and where the author becomes a part of this intertextual play. "Like everyone else," Auster states in an interview, "I am a multiple being, and I embody a whole range of attitudes and responses to the world. Depending on my mood, the same event can make me laugh or make me cry; it can inspire anger or compassion or indifference."[6] In short, Auster's postmodern fiction, unlike straightforward realistic/modern fiction, has the "presence of the unpredictable, the utterly bewildering nature of human experience."[7]

To get at this "utterly bewildering nature of human experience," Auster in *The New York Trilogy* uses and abuses the Western detective story to write his postmodern fiction. In the interview with Mallia, he states:

I use certain elements of detective fiction . . . . But I felt I was using those elements for such different ends, for things that had so little to do with detective stories . . . . I tried to use certain genre conventions to get to another place, another place altogether.[8]

Auster begins *The New York Trilogy* with the detective and the search for the missing person. Then he highjacks his detective search and pursues an investigation of linguistic, metaphysical, and philosophical absences.

> So the detective really is a very compelling figure, a figure we all understand. He's the seeker after truth, the problem-solver, the one who tries to figure things out. But what if, in the course of trying to figure it out, you just unveil more mysteries? I suppose maybe that's what happens in the books [*The New York Trilogy*].[9]

Auster subverts the conventions and expectations of the detective story, which is end-dominated, by resisting closure and resolution and by unveiling "more mysteries."

In each of the three novellas in *The New York Trilogy*, the central character is a writer/detective. Daniel Quinn of *City of Glass*, Blue of *Ghosts*, and the narrator of *The Locked Room* are each given separate, but similar, case assignments that require them to observe, investigate, and report on the lives of Peter Stillman, Sr., Black, and Fanshawe, respectively. As Hegelian, Enlightenment subjects, they are governed by the rules of reason. They appropriate the search for the missing person into the search for absolute knowledge, the logocentric Father, and/or the self. For the detectives, it is a journey of reason alone, unhindered by the senses. They have a singleness of purpose.

Traditionally, plots of detective novels further themselves through various connections, revelations, and causalities. Madeleine Sorapure notes that in a conventional detective story, "the detective is successful only insofar as he is able to attain the position of the author, a metaphysical position, above or beyond the events of the text."[10] But, instead of giving his detectives authority over the narrative, elevating them to metaphysical positions, Auster unravels/undresses the singularly constructed modern identities of the protagonists, pushing them to the brink of disintegration and beyond, into madness and annihilation. Meaning eludes them. Obsessed with what he thinks is "his case," spying on a man named Stillman, Daniel Quinn in *City of Glass* trails Peter Stillman, Sr. through the streets of Manhattan, hoping initially to solve the crime/mystery and later to find Truth, Meaning, the logocentric Father, or the self. Quinn suspects "that Stillman's red notebook contains answers to the questions that he has been accumulating in his mind."[11] If he can ascertain and decipher the meaning of the red notebook, he would have the answer to the mystery, absolute knowledge. But he is never able to decode the notebook. This suspicion teases the reader and defers Meaning.

Similarly, in the second novella, *Ghosts*, Blue is a detective forced into becoming a writer. He, like Daniel Quinn, is unable to comprehend the facts of his case, to become the author of his subject. He, too, is looking for Origin, Meaning, Truth, the logocentric Father, and/or the self. In *Ghosts*, a man named Blue is commissioned by White to keep Black under constant watch from a room across the street. Blue is not told why he is watching Black, who is writing a book. As the days pass, Blue finds himself in the position of a man condemned to sit alone in a room reading a book about the man sitting alone and writing a book.

At the end of *Ghosts*, it seems that the novel Blue holds in his hand is the very book that Black, the writer in the story, was writing. It is possible, argues Anna T. Szabo, that while Blue watched Black, Black was watching Blue, and Black wrote exactly the story of this double-spying.[12] This supposition is grounded on Blue's thorough knowledge concerning the contents of Black's book: "He [Blue] reads the story right through, every word of it from beginning to end . . . . Black was right, he says to himself. I knew it all by heart."[13] Thus the story does not reflect anything but itself, it is the story of a story, a mirror reflecting another.[14] Again, Blue, like Daniel Quinn, is searching for Truth, Meaning, the logocentric Father, and/or the self.

While *City of Glass* and *Ghosts* end in failed attempts at authorship, at mastering logocentric Truth and Meaning, at finding the logocentric Father, with both Quinn and Blue experiencing a psychic death, regression, and eventual disappearance from the text, Auster is clearly saying that to seek for absolute knowledge and final resolution, to solve the mystery of the detective story, leads to a form of madness. But what is of significance in the third and final section of *The New York Trilogy*, *The Locked Room*, is not that it upholds the concept of authorship, but that it does so in a manner that synthesizes the three separate novellas into an indeterminate, authored text.

Whereas Daniel Quinn and Blue are able to confront Peter Stillman, Sr. and Black physically, the narrator of *The Locked Room* cannot find the material body of his childhood friend, Fanshawe, who has mysteriously disappeared. The narrator has only Fanshawe's unpublished novels, plays, and poems. When Fanshawe disappears and Sophie, Fanshawe's wife, calls him, the narrator believes initially that Fanshawe has not only disappeared but is dead.

As soon as he gains possession of Fanshawe's manuscripts, the narrator usurps the life of his friend. He marries Fanshawe's wife, adopts his son, and considers the idea of publishing Fanshawe's books as his own. The more the narrator immerses himself in the details of Fanshawe's life and work, the more he "becomes" him. Just when the narrator has published successfully Fanshawe's novel, he receives a letter from Fanshawe, thanking him.

Learning that Fanshawe is alive and, later, being asked by Stuart Green, their publisher, to write a biography of Fanshawe, the narrator of *The Locked Room* becomes a detective and sets out to find him. The narrator searches for him (and himself) at Fanshawe's mother's and childhood home. Later, he looks for Fanshawe in his letters, at Harvard, in telephone calls to his shipmates, and in Paris. In *The Locked Room*, finding Meaning, the logocentric Father, or the self is still being deferred. During the month that he is coming apart in Paris, the narrator claims authorship of *The New York Trilogy* and states his interpretation of the book.

But the narrator will have to change before he can own, write, or account for *The New York Trilogy*. He does. Early in *The Locked Room*, the narrator wonders "what it means when a writer puts his name on a book, why some writers choose to hide behind a pseudonym."[15] In attempting to write a biography of Fanshawe, the narrator realizes that

> [e]very life is inexplicable. . . . No matter how many facts are told . . . the essential thing resists telling . . . . We imagine the real story inside the words, and to do this we substitute ourselves for the person in the story, pretending that we can understand him because we understand ourselves. This is a deception. We exist for ourselves, perhaps, at times we even have a glimmer of who we are, but in the end we can never be sure, and as our lives go on, we become more and more opaque to ourselves, more and more aware of our own incoherence. No one can cross the boundary into another—for the simple reason that no one can gain access to himself.[16]

This is the problem of the writer and his subject. *The Locked Room* is a "locked room" for Auster himself: it contains the life of Auster, not only in the sense that it contains his words; it also contains elements of his biography.[17] But Auster cannot capture himself successfully in language.

In Paris, instead of finding a material body, the narrator finds a decorporeal body. The identification between narrator and double intensifies as he loses "track of [him]self" and comes "apart"[18] and as figures virtually blur and dissolve into each other. The narrator names a young woman in a bar Fayaway; he names himself Herman Melville. When he meets a vaguely familiar young man on the street, he decides that this person will be Fanshawe: "This man was Fanshawe because I said he was Fanshawe."[19] When the man objects and says his name is Peter Stillman, the two fight, reenacting the battle for identity between Blue and Black in *Ghosts*. The narrator becomes exhilarated by this freedom of language and his ability to name things at random.

> Stillman was not Fanshawe—I knew that. He was an arbitrary choice, totally innocent and blank. But that was the thing that thrilled me—the randomness of it, the vertigo of pure chance. It made no sense, and because of that, it made all the sense in the world.[20]

Unlike Daniel Quinn in *City of Glass* and Blue in *Ghosts*, the narrator of *The Locked Room*, at this moment, comes to accept chance as a part of his world. He accepts the Saussurean idea that the relationship between the signifier and the signified, the word and the object, is arbitrary.

In the final scene of *The Locked Room*, the dying Fanshawe gives the narrator the red notebook, which is suppose to have the answers/insights. Finally, the reader thinks she/he will get closure. The narrator describes the contents of the red notebook thus:

> All the words were familiar to me, and yet they seemed to have been put together strangely, as though their final purpose was to cancel each other out .... Each sentence erased the sentence before it, each paragraph made the next paragraph impossible . . . I lost my way after the first word, and from then on I could only grope ahead, faltering in the darkness, blinded by the book that had been written for me.[21]

But, instead of answers/insights, the narrator finds contradictory sentences, indeterminacy, open-ended-ness, and ambiguity. Again, in a postmodern manner, *The New York Trilogy* has refused to provide closure and resolution. This action of accepting chance signals a shift in paradigms. For those characters searching for Truth/Meaning, the red notebook has been used throughout. It is equivalent to a written representation of a life, the Truth. But it can never be accessed. In accepting the world as one of play, chance, and mystery, the narrator is no longer searching for Meaning. He now knows that you cannot achieve absolute knowledge.

Unlike Daniel Quinn and Blue, who disintegrate because they are unable to deal with or understand the nonrational things around them, the narrator of *The Locked Room* does not go mad or commit suicide. Rather, as I have stated earlier, he comes to accept the play of difference, chance, coincidence, reason, vulnerability, and the mysteries. In fact, he is thrilled by the randomness of arbitrary choice, the "vertigo of pure chance."[22] He comes to understand that life is messy, risky, and chance-laden, rather than some grandiose truth or fulfillment. Therefore, he, unlike Daniel Quinn and Blue, is able to write *The New York Trilogy*. Commenting on the change in the narrator of *The Locked Room*, Auster states:

> He finally comes to accept his own life, to understand that no matter how bewitched or haunted he is, he has to accept reality as it is, to tolerate the presence of ambiguities within himself. That's what happens to him with relation to Fanshawe. He hasn't slain the dragon, he's let the dragon move into the house with him. That's why he destroys the notebook in the last scene.[23]

The narrator points to the end of modern subjectivity and demonstrates a new capacity to think outside the framework of modern binaries and modern identities, to a thought of plurality and multiplicity.

Auster solves the problem of authorship and mastery of Meaning by privileging difference at the authorial and narrative levels. Auster achieves this effect of authorship through postmodern narrative strategies, including the introduction early in *City of Glass* of a fictional character named "Paul Auster." By introducing the name "Paul Auster" into the text, Auster creates a fictional self within the narrative. He magnifies variations in the agency of the "author function" within the discourse. When asked by Sinda Gregory in an interview why he introduced himself into the narrative, Auster replied,

> I think it stemmed from a desire to implicate myself in the machinery of the book. I don't mean my autobiographical self, I mean my author self, that mysterious other who lives inside me and puts my name on the covers of books. What I was hoping to do, in effect, was take my name off the cover and put it inside the story. I wanted to open up the process, to break down walls, to expose the plumbing . . . . The self that exists in the world—the self whose name appears on the covers of books—is finally not the same self who writes the book.[24]

The author/self has many selves.

Not only with the fictional Paul Auster, but throughout *The New York Trilogy*, Auster plays intertextually with doubles, names, and identities, making them fluid. He produces Euro-American, male subjects that are fractured, decorporealized, decentered, and multiple. In *City of Glass*, the distinction among author, narrator, and character—that is among Daniel Quinn, Paul Auster, Paul Auster, Max Work, and William Wilson—is increasingly blurred.

Similarly in *Ghosts*, we get intertextual play with doubles, identities, and names. Blue, who is aware that Black and White are the same person, asks who is writing the book, Black or White. Blue and Black are doubles. They all have fluid identities. Throughout *Ghosts*, we get this intertextual play with names and identities, creating a fluid/multiple male subject.

Finally, in *The Locked Room*, Auster continues constructing Euro-American, male subjectivity as fluid and multiple entities. From the beginning, the narrator admits that Fanshawe exists inside him as "a ghost [he] carried around inside [him], a prehistoric figment, a thing that was no longer real."[25] In creating multiple names and identities for author and characters, Auster in *The New York Trilogy* is undermining reason and communicating to the reader a different notion/concept of subjectivity. The modern subject has the temporal unification between the past and the future in the present. In *The New York Trilogy*, Auster decorporealizes the subject, allowing other aspects and dimensions besides its unified material body. For Auster, subjectivity moves relatively free through past, present, and future experiences. Auster's subject, argues Steven E. Alford, "is a textual construct and [is] subject to the difference and deferral inherent in language."[26] In the postmodern sense, in *The New York Trilogy* there is no longer a unified Euro-American male self. For Auster, the Euro-American male self is a nexus of meaning rather than an unchanging entity, except insofar as it is unitary and stable in being Euro-American and male.

The narrator's Hegelian, transcendental, racially *unmarked* "I" in *The New York Trilogy* comes to accept a chain of signifiers of the white masculine within the quest narrative and thereby deconstructs the notion of a unified self. But, in representing itself in language as the "center" and "end" of history, as a self-reflexive subject, and as not being dependent upon or attached to an other outside himself, this privileged, white, sovereign, masculine, Hegelian "I" remains unturned. It remains Eurocentric subject–centered. This chain of Euro-American male signifiers that comes to embody the subject is the Selfsame. It always comes back to a story of phallocentrism. It does not engage differences. It is never challenged. It appropriates constantly the world as the Same in order to be at home in it. It refuses to move beyond the Euro-American patriarchal Symbolic

Order. It refuses to live in a world of difference. Therefore, it murders the Other.

According to Jacques Lacan, the Real, which is excluded from representation, resists "symbolization absolutely."[27] Therefore, the subject we get in language is fractured and distorted. This distortion is manifested as a lack of being, and it is this lack that desire constantly attempts to fill. For Lacan, desire is born from a fundamentally lost object and is defined in a subjective, sexual arena. The subject's desire is always already the "desire for the Other."[28] It has an excluding/self-enclosing feature that produces the need for an Other against which it defines itself as whole. The formation of the self, argues Luce Irigaray, "results from the impact of other bodies, of matter that is foreign to [it]."[29] But in using other subjects as the objects of desire, modern, questing, racially *unmarked* middle-class Euro-American males in Auster's *The New York Trilogy* cannot recognize the exteriority/reason of the Other. Although the narrator's "I" is constituted in relation to the Other, it denies it. Also, these privileged, Hegelian, masculine subjects never intermingle and intermix with the repressed/marginalized, *marked* Other in the text. They simultaneously refuse to accept and identify with Others in their separateness and difference.

In *The Phenomenology of Mind*, Georg Hegel states that in the process of recognizing itself and constituting its own self-consciousness, the (masculine) subject must constantly overcome or "cancel" the Other.[30] The Otherness that he self-consciously seeks to overcome is actually and ultimately his own Otherness, which he displaces onto others. Because the narrator's "I" in *The New York Trilogy* is imperialistic and because it defines itself against an Other, it still maintains a binary opposition between self and Other, which connotes domination and subordination. Thus, as a consequence of this binary opposition, a problem arises in the text. Modern stereotypes about the Other are reinforced and differences within the Other are erased. Auster's narrator's "I" in *The New York Trilogy* never recognizes the Other as a subject. Women, the homeless, prostitutes, and the African American are parked without agency and subjectivity in the margin of his Western white male quest narrative.

The racially *unmarked*, Euro-American female characters—Mrs. Blue, Virginia, and Sophie (Mrs. Fanshawe)—in *The New York Trilogy* inhabit the margin of quest narratives, serving to articulate and reinforce the patriarchal, capitalist, compulsory heterosexual, masculine order. They are domesticated and kept in their familial place. Cixous writes in *The Newly Born Woman*: for women, the masculine order says, "[t]here is no place for your desire in our affairs of State."[31] And, as patriarchally constructed women, when the masculine order wants it, they nurture and support it in its dreams. But they do not play in the plots. In the economic structure of capitalist society, they are assigned the responsibility of unpaid domestic labor. Therefore, they stay home while their husbands work more creative, adventurous jobs in the public arena, where they "succeed," "climb the social ladder" and even enjoy the "temptation that encourages [them], drives [them], and feeds [their] ambitions."[32] Virginia Stillman is "Peter's wife."[33] She says, "with Peter there's a purpose to my life."[34] She will take care of him. In *Ghosts*, Blue uses the prostitute Violet, the "blowsy tart," as exotic Other, and gets "tipsy enough to get invited back to her place."[35] He goes to the movies, "for the stories they tell and the beautiful women he can see in them."[36] With Blue, we have "[t]he erotic potential of the gaze, [and] its potential to violate its object and to arouse the self."[37] "If traditionally," argues Irigaray, "woman represents *place* for man, such a limit means that she becomes *a thing*."[38] In parking women in the margin, Auster repatriates the potential threat of her sexual specificity, assuming its power for the masculine order.

Likewise, the future Mrs. Blue's only significance in *Ghosts* is to be a companion to Blue. Before White arrived at his office with the new case, Blue and the future Mrs. Blue "were planning to go out."[39] After the case arrives, she is abandoned. She is completely marginal and tangential to his life. While on his search for his identity and the Meaning of Black, "*unfortunately*, thoughts of the future Mrs. Blue occasionally disturb his growing peace of mind" (emphasis mine).[40] He thinks about calling her for a chat, but refuses: "He doesn't want to seem weak. If she knew how much he needed her, he would begin to lose his advantage, and that wouldn't be good. The man must always be the stronger one."[41]

Finally, Sophie is the wife of both Fanshawe and the narrator in *The Locked Room*. She plays the role of the dutiful wife. As Fanshawe's wife, she took care of him while he wrote. When the two began living together, Fanshawe did not work. Sophie took "a job teaching music in a private school, and her salary could support them both."[42] There were times when Sophie wanted to smuggle one of Fanshawe's manuscripts out to a publisher, but refrained. "Here were rules in a [patriarchal] marriage that couldn't be broken, and no matter how wrong-headed his attitude was, she had little choice but to go along with him."[43] In the situations of Virginia, Mrs. Blue, and Sophie, they are what Luce Irigaray calls "use-value for men . . . in other words, a commodity."[44]

These women, according to Luce Irigaray, are a "more or less obliging prop for the enactment of man's fantasies."[45] Their objectification and subordination are central to the Masculinist order. They never become the subject of their desire, which is expressed through passivity and subordination. Rather, as Other, they are reduced to "being the other of the same, its inferior, reflection, 'excess,' hence still defined by and an extension of it."[46] They gain more value in being wives than in being women, or in belonging to what Irigaray calls the female "gender" or female "sexual culture."[47] (They are not called or obligated to participate in the big social *fete* of Auster's *The New York Trilogy*.)

Unlike Daniel Quinn, Peter Stillman, Sr., Blue, and all the other Euro-American, male characters in *The New York Trilogy*, these women lack difference and fluidity. Although Paul Auster argues that chance, strange events, coincidence, mystery, and the play of difference are a part of the (postmodern) human condition and, therefore, are a part of reality in *The New York Trilogy*, his women are totally untouched by this postmodern reality. The absence of *female* specificity in Auster's quest narratives particularizes these narratives as masculine.

Likewise, in Auster's *The New York Trilogy*, the differing/deferring Euro-American, male narrative "I" constructs the African American as Other. He/she functions as a metaphor for the Western notion of the un-self-conscious primal state. But in constructing the African American as Other, as the primal state, the text also uses the African American as a vehicle to achieve Truth, Meaning, the logocentric Father, Origin, or the self. There is "the old black man . . . for example, who tap-dances while juggling cigarettes—still dignified, clearly once a vaudevillian, dressed in a purple suit with a green shirt and a yellow tie, his mouth fixed in a half-remembered stage smile."[48] This black man is the image of a "passive spectator" who is not touched by the narrator's world.[49] He exists completely outside of the malaise and the alienation and fragmentation and doubling that pervade the lives of Euro-American, male characters such as Daniel Quinn, Blue, the narrator of *The Locked Room*, and Peter Stillman in *The New York Trilogy*.

Also, Jackie Robinson is constructed in *City of Glass* as being Other, outside Auster's postmodern world. He becomes stable Meaning, the space of energy, affirmation, clarity, and positive vibes. When Quinn arrives at Ebbetts Field, he is struck by the sharp clarity of the colors around him: the green grass, the brown dirt, the white ball, the blue sky.

> Each thing is distinct from every other thing, wholly separate and
> defined. . . . Watching the [baseball] game, [Blue cannot] take his eyes
> off Robinson, lured constantly by the blackness of the man's face and
> he thinks it must take courage to do what he is doing, to be alone like
> that in front of so many strangers, with half of them no doubt wishing
> him to be dead. As the game moves along, Blue finds himself cheering
> whatever Robinson does, and when the black man steals a base in the
> third inning he rises to his feet, and later, in the seventh, when
> Robinson doubles off the wall in left, he actually pounds the back of the
> man next to him for joy.[50]

In moving into Jackie Robinson's Otherized space, Blue finds clarity;
he has joy, and "Black did not cross his mind even once."[51] Yet, in
order to clarify the self, Blue has to annihilate Robinson, the Other.
Blue never allows Robinson to reveal himself as an individual with
subjectivity and agency. Auster/Blue also assumes that Robinson is a
passive spectator, that he is "wholly separate and defined," and that he
is outside Western history and rationality.

Furthermore, Auster in *The New York Trilogy* says very little about
the historical experiences of Jackie Robinson. In constructing
Robinson as Other, as the color black, Auster extrapolates him from
other important racial, social, and cultural factors in contemporary
United States. Auster gives us no sense of the insults and racial slurs
Robinson endures from the American public, the fans, and/or his
teammates. He excludes any discussions about the threats on his life.
He does not tell us that when Robinson's team, the Brooklyn
Dodgers, made its first road trip with him on the roster, the team was
denied accommodation at a hotel in Philadelphia because Robinson
was black. By not giving us this background information, Auster
occludes the historically specific experiences of the first professional
black baseball player in the Major League in a racist America in 1947,
transforming him into a prop for discussions about the crisis in
Western modernity/postmodernity.

The desire for power/knowledge, the Lacanian lost object, is
associated with sexuality, and the sexuality of the racially *marked*
black/woman of color is considered exotic Other/taboo/primal by
Western patriarchies. To be racially marked is to have a label or
category, which is loaded with stereotype, replace one's individuality/
subjectivity. As with Robinson and the black tap dancer, the black/
woman of color in *The New York Trilogy* is constructed as existing outside of (Western) history and rationality, outside of the social. She,
according to Cornel West in *Race Matters*, is defined by normative
America as "exotic 'other'—closer to nature (removed from intelligence

and control) and more prone to be guided by base pleasures and biological impulses."[52] She has been constructed by the West to represent the idea of "sexual insatiability, the illicit thrill of unbridled desire, and the fantasy of an orgiastic sexuality."[53] The black/woman of color represents the desire to reclaim "origins and pure states."[54]

In *The New York Trilogy*, the racially *marked* black/woman of color becomes the exotic feminine Other, in sharp contrast with the Euro-American female characters, including Violet the prostitute, who are never constructed as sexually free. As male fantasy, the black/woman of color appears in the text at those crucial moments when Euro-American males are searching intensely for themselves. As a consequence, Euro-American, male characters inscribe her body with all of their dark illicit secrets, desires, fears, inhibitions, weaknesses, and fantasies. The black/woman of color becomes more than desirable human flesh. She becomes the projection of their own denied Otherness, and they are seduced by their own projections. She becomes what Lacan would call enlightenment men's *jouissance* (sexual enjoyment). The economy of the imaginary re-creation of *jouissance* does not find its solution in a "real" *jouissance* but in "the *jouissance* of the other."[55]

In *The Locked Room*, the narrator and Fanshawe, at fifteen years of age, lose their virginity in a brothel to a young and beautiful racially *marked*, black woman, who, according to the conventions for representing the primitive, "was so *casual and friendly about her nakedness*" (emphasis mine).[56] For the narrator, the "nakedness" creates cultural difference, distance, and hence, eroticism. As Fanshawe has sex with the young, beautiful black prostitute, the narrator sits at the kitchen table with the "fat madam" who calls him "sugar, reminding [him] every so often that she [is] still available."[57] She is the "black" woman driven by a raging libido. But her size makes her a desexualized mammy or arch-mother. Therefore, she is ignored. Auster constructs black/women of color as inhabiting an unselfconscious primal state. Unlike the Euro-American female characters discussed earlier, these black/women of color are racially and sexually marked as free and obscenely desiring.

Later, in Paris after he comes apart and wanders in the streets seeking answers/the self, the narrator of *The Locked Room* picks up prostitutes to sleep with, singling out the racially *marked*, black/woman of color. "[M]y head burning with the thought of bodies, an endless jumble of naked breasts, naked thighs, naked buttocks . . . . I see an enormous black woman spreading her legs on a bidet and washing her cunt."[58] Auster's prostitutes are sexualized body-parts, and the racially *marked* black woman is a *dirty*, exotic, primitive, unselfconscious Other.[59] These are pornographic images of the black/woman of color, the embodiment and manifestation of Euro-American, male fetishistic desire. Lastly, still searching for the self, the narrator of *The Locked Room* encounters another black/woman of color in a bar: "The girl was Tahitian . . . and she was beautiful: no more than nineteen or twenty, very small, and wearing a dress of white netting with nothing underneath, a crisscross of cables over her smooth brown skin. The effect was *superbly erotic*" (emphasis mine).[60]

Fanshawe defines his/their pursuit of these black/women of color as " 'tasting life,'" as "*searching for the unknown*"[61] (emphasis mine). Julia Kristeva argues that the feminine is the "uncanny strangeness,"[62] the *unknown*, which is feared and desired by Enlightenment Eurocentric men. Kristeva would define searching for the unknown as a way for the Enlightenment man to get in touch with his unconscious, his repressed Otherness. He "projects out of [him]self what [he] experiences as dangerous or unpleasant in [him]self" onto the Other.[63] Here, the narrator's phallic *ego* shows "domination concomitant with economic domination."[64]

For Auster in *The New York Trilogy*, the black feminine is not only the uncanny strangeness, the unknown, it is also taboo and the animate—the unselfconscious primal. It is the gateway to the Other, an ultimate referent or foundation outside the play of language. The black feminine functions as a counternarrative to the undesired sexuality and the repressed hysteria of the white feminine signified in Sophie. Discussing the construction of white female sexuality (particularly in the South) in *White Racism*, Joel Kovel argues that Southern American culture (like America in general) forces the "white woman into being the most worshipped, the purest, the least vital, and certainly the least sexual of females."[65]

Because she/it represents the unknown, the black feminine invokes the unactualized, white masculine, and possessing/fucking/controlling the black feminine becomes intensely exotic and more pleasurable. The desire to dominate begins with a sexual urge. It becomes his repository of joy and revivification. The idea is that if you can "fuck" successfully the black feminine without shame, possessing her without fear or deference, you have the potential to fill the Lacanian lack, to achieve "true" liberation, to return to the primal state, or to achieve selfhood. Fanshawe does "fuck" and possess the Other, the black feminine. Yet he does not achieve freedom, unity of the self, or transformation. His encounter "did not change the monotopically conceived [Eurocentric] hermeneutic, for the understanding subject [the narrator's I] and his . . . locus of enunciation maintained a European [American] position."[66] Fanshawe's primal desire for the absolute and the infinite that the black feminine represents is too deep to be fulfilled. Like Daniel Quinn and Peter Stillman, Sr., who also attempt to return to the unselfconscious primal state, he ends up committing suicide.

The uninhibited, extroverted sexuality, which Fanshawe and the narrator of *The Locked Room* attribute to the black/woman of color's primal state, also serves as a reason for rejecting her, for her primitive existence is a stage that is past, condemned, and even feared. She is written to represent a rejected/demonized part of the modern Eurocentric self. Therefore, she represents attraction and repulsion. She exists as the repository for those qualities that the Enlightenment man has denied himself and now wishes to reclaim.

Blue, Fanshawe, and the narrator of *The Locked Room* have no desire/intention to fulfill the desire of the Other, of black/women of color. At no point does Auster consider the black feminine as individuated or as subjects. These black women cannot choose, as Sophie does. They are not provided for, as Sophie is. They are singularly mythic, defined *only* as sexual, reflective objects. For Auster, the desire for the Other, the black feminine, is *not* about love interest, for she does not measure up to white beauty standards, which play a "weightier role in sexual desirability for women in racist patriarchal America."[67] In fact, the concern is not about relationships with other people/the black woman/the feminine.

Rather, at issue is the Western, Euro-American male fantasy of colonizing the black/woman of color in order to get in touch with his unknown, his denied otherness, and to achieve masculine freedom. This is about the Euro-American male's struggle between his intellect and his libido. More importantly, it is about the Euro-American male's refusal to deconstruct his privileged, transcendental, racially *unmarked* "I." Although Blue, Fanshawe, and the narrator of *The Locked Room* desire both transformation and confirmation of selfhood, they resist identification with the Other and affirm the privileged, sovereign, Euro-American, compulsory heterosexual, masculine self. But in using the black feminine (and prostitution) to taste life, to come to grips with the strangeness/unknown/Otherness within themselves, Fanshawe, the narrator of *The Locked Room*, and Blue in *Ghosts* inflict violence on the black feminine and the prostitute. "Love of [the modern European male] self," writes Irigaray, "would seemingly take the form of a long *return* to and through the other. A unique female Other."[68]

In their search for the self, they objectify and push the black/ woman of color into cramped spaces where her subjectivity, complex human existence, sexual presence, desire, and agency are denied. She is denied herself, her daughter(s), her mother, and/or her female history. She is also denied self-assertion and competitive relations with other women, black and white, and denied her complex racial history. Finally, the representation of the black woman as primitive Other who is sexually free from cultural constraints and morality justifies the continuing sexual abuse of her in social reality. Auster is not attuned to those aspects of his fetishistic interest in these women that link him to what bell hooks calls "collective white racist domination"[69] and to racist myths of black sexuality.

More important, though, in his desire to construct black/women of color as primitive Other, Auster in *The New York Trilogy* ignores signs of the modern/postmodern in their historical existence. He denies the actual lives of these black/women of color and masks the connection between them and Euro-American males. black/women of color do not exist in some unselfconscious primal state but are radically implicated in patterns of modernization. The fact that these black/women of color are in Paris and the United States means that they are the product of European colonialism, capitalism, and modernity. Their agency is sharply circumscribed by a world system in which power is unequally distributed and the economic interests of some sharply constrain the destinies of others. They are hybrids, for they belong to more than one tradition. They are either a part of the international migration of labor or they are descendants of those Africans who were purchased in the sixteenth and seventeenth centuries in exchange for European products such as arms and iron tools. They were later bartered in Bahia, Hispanic Cartegena, Havana, Port-au-Prince, and in the ports of the colonies south of New England for gold, silver, and tropical products. They arrived in the West as capitalist commodities. Their slave labor made them an integral force in producing modern society. And more specifically, the fact that the black/women of color are selling their bodies in exchange for money means they have internalized the capitalist value system. They are working women. How can they possibly be the un-self-conscious Other? Or exist outside Western history and rationality? How could they not be touched by modernity/postmodernity?

The crucial question is why does Auster at the sunset of the twentieth century have the need to continue to define the complex, modern African American as the primitive Other, as the unknown? Why does Auster have the need to reproduce in postmodern fiction the nineteenth-century image of the black/woman of color as a sexualized prostitute? Why does Auster have the need to reproduce the same primitive representation of the African American as Hume, Kant, and Hegel? Maybe it has more to do with him than with them? In Otherizing/essentializing the African American, *The New York Trilogy* assumes that the African American is "without history" and therefore never changes. This notion, argues Marianna Torgovnick in *Primitive Passions,* "has perpetuated ideas of European superiority to Others."[70] It dramatizes the advancement, the distance the West has traveled. It reinforces the self/Other binary opposition. It erases the world of difference, where subjectivities are different but equal.

Also, despite the fact that Auster's world in *The New York Trilogy* embraces chance, mystery, the decorporeal subject, and the textual play of names and identities, gender and sexual roles/categories remain "boxed into a predictable world."[71] The man/woman, heterosexual/homosexual binaries remain in place, thereby ignoring/ repressing the fact that sex and gender are textual constructs and therefore are also subject to the difference and deferral inherent in language. This Daniel Quinn/Paul Auster/William Wilson/Peter Stillman/Blue/Black/Fanshawe business can be defined as an example of the masculine self-arousal that Irigaray sees in "philosophical discourse, which gives privileged status to self-representing."[72] Although it represents itself as a site of freedom, adventure, wholeness, and liberation, this Western, Euro-American, male discourse is actually a site of repressed differences. Here, in *The New York Trilogy,* differences are reduced to a confirmation of the superiority of the (masculine) self-same. Auster seems unaware of how deep gender, sex, class, and race have been concealed in hegemonic linguistic, social, historical, and psychological structures, or how gender, sex, class, and race affect his thinking.

The narratorial I's perception of the quest narrative and of himself as narrator is not deconstructed. This "I" defines itself as the only truly existing reality, refusing to accept an "alternative politics of location with equal rights to claim and truth."[73] It does not know how to use the foreignness within itself to connect ethically with others. Despite the desire for both transformation and a confirmation of self, Quinn, Blue, and the narrator of *The Locked Room* never change. There is no transformation, as this would require recognition of their relationship with the Other. Auster's failure to challenge this hegemonic, Euro-American, male position in culture suggests that Auster's postmodernism is still (modern) Eurocentric subject–centered. Unlike the feminine that desires a relationship between two subjects, *The New York Trilogy*'s narrator's I, to use Irigaray's words in *to be two*, "prefers a relationship between the one and the many, between the I-masculine subject and others: people, society, understood us *them* and not as *you*."[74]

Auster demonstrates how Eurocentric postmoderns may criticize modern reason as a reason of terror but still practice the sacrificial violence of the myth of Eurocentric modernity by failing to engage *the reason of the Other*. In leaving the white male/Other binary opposition in place and erasing difference, Auster in *The New York Trilogy* reproduces gender, racial, and class systems that generate relations of domination. He defines white males as normative and superior and represents the African American, Woman, the poor of the center, and homosexuals as devalued Other—all victims of Eurocentric post-modernity's "irrational action in contradiction to its own rational ideal."[75] In *The New York Trilogy*, Auster produces a narrow/limited conception of postmodernism, one whose truth-claim is circumscribed by a racially *unmarked*, Euro-American male desire/reality, one that generates Euro-American male supremacy. His deconstructionist process stops short of deconstructing white male subjectivity.

NOTES

1. Jacques Lacan. *Ecrits: A Selection*, trans. Alan Sheridan, *Seminar* I (New York: W. W. Norton, 1977), 287.
2. Fernando Gomez, "Ethics is the Original Philosophy; or, The Barbarian Words Coming from the Third World: An Interview with Enrique Dussel," *Boundary 2* 28.1 (Spring 2001): 19–73; 26.
3. Paul Auster, Interview, *The Art of Hunger: Essays, Prefaces, Interviews* (Los Angeles: Sun & Moon Press, 1991), 270.
4. Ibid., 260, 262.
5. Ibid., 270.
6. Ibid., 289.
7. Ibid., 271.
8. Ibid., 261.
9. Ibid., 262.
10. Madeline Sorapure. *The Detective and the Author: City of Glass. Beyond the Red Notebook: Essays, on* Paul Auster, ed. Dennis Barone (Philadelphia: University of Pennsylvania Press, 1995), 72.
11. Ibid., 73.
12. Anna T. Szabo, "*The Self-Consuming Narrative:* Paul Auster's *The New York Trilogy*," *The Anachronist 19–21* (1996): 266–79.
13. Szabo, *The Self-Consuming Narrative*, 232.
14. Ibid., 269.
15. Ibid., 279.

16. Paul Auster, *The Locked Room. The New York Trilogy* (New York: Penguin Books, 1996), 291–92.

17. Alison Russell. "Deconstructing *The New York Trilogy:* Paul Auster's *Anti-detective Fiction*," *Critique* 31 (1990): 80.

18. Auster, *The Locked Room*, 345.

19. Ibid., 348.

20. Ibid., 351.

21. Ibid., 370.

22. Ibid., 351.

23. Auster, Interview, *The Art of Hunger*, 264.

24. Ibid., 293.

25. Auster, *The Locked Room*, 236.

26. Steven E. Alford. "*Mirrors of Madness*: Paul Auster's *The New York Trilogy*." *Critique* 37 (1995): 17.

27. Lacan. *Ecrits*, 66.

28. Ibid., 312.

29. Luce Irigaray, *An Ethics of Sexual Difference*, trans. Carolyn Burke and Gillian C. Gill (Ithaca, NY: Cornell University Press, 1993), 3.

30. G.W.F. Hegel, *The Phenomenology of Mind*, trans. J.B. Baillie (New York: The MacMillan Company, 1931), 225.

31. Hélène Cixous and Catherine Clement, *The Newly Born Woman*, trans. Betsy Wing (Minneapolis and London: University of Minnesota Press, 1986), 67.

32. Cixous and Clement, *The Newly Born Woman*, 67.

33. Ibid., 16.

34. Ibid., 33.

35. Paul Auster, *The Ghosts, The New York Trilogy* (New York: Penguin Books, 1996), 190.

36. Auster, *The Ghosts*, 190.

37. Marianna Torgovnick, *Gone Primitive: Savage Intellects, Modern Lives. Passion* (Chicago and London: University of Chicago Press, 1990), 111.

38. Irigaray, *An Ethics of Sexual Difference*, 10.

39. Auster, *The Ghosts*, 165.

40. Ibid., 173.

41. Ibid., 165.

42. Auster, *The Locked Room*, 241.

43. Ibid., 242.

44. Irigaray, *An Ethics of Sexual Difference*, 31.

45. Ibid., 25.

46. Jane Flax, *Thinking Fragments: Psychoanalysis, Feminism, and Postmodernism in the Contemporary West* (Berkeley and London: University of California Press, 1990), 172.

47. Irigaray, *Je, Tu, Nous: Toward a Culture of Difference*, trans. Alison Martin (New York: Routledge, 1993), 12, 53.

48. Auster, *The New York Trilogy*, 129.

49. Enrique Dussel, "Beyond Eurocentrism: The World-System and the Limits of Modernity," in *The Cultures of Globalization*, ed. Fredric Jameson and Masao Miyoshi (Durham: Duke University Press, 1999), 17.

50. Auster, *The City of Glass*, 189–90.

51. Ibid., 190.

52. Cornel West, *Race Matters* (Boston: Beacon Press, 1993), 88.

53. Jonathan Rutherford. "Who's That Man?" *Male Order: Unwrapping Masculinity*, ed. Rowena Chapman and Jonathan Rutherford (London: Lawrence & Wishart, 1988), 64.

54. Torgovnick, *Gone Primitive*, 5.

55. Lacan, *Ecrits*, 42.

56. Auster, *The Locked Room*, 255.

57. Ibid., 254–55.

58. Ibid., 346.

59. This idea that being black also means being dirty goes way back in European/American history. It was present from the very beginning as an element of the European's reaction to the black. Joel Kovel in *White Racism: A Psychohistory* (New York: Vintage books, 1970) goes to the Oxford English Dictionary and examines the meaning/symbol of blackness before classical European colonialism. "Deeply stained with dirt; soiled, dirty, foul. . . . Having dark or deadly purposes." What ever objects the European/American could conceptualize as bad, the abstract idea of badness itself, became coordinated with blackness (62). Anthropologist Mary Ellen Goodman in *Race Awareness in Young Children* (Cambridge: Addison-Wesley, 1952) concludes that the uniform fantasy of the black being dirty implies a sense of basic inferiority (Kovel 86).

60. Auster, *The Locked Room*, 347.

61. Ibid., 254.

62. Julia Kristeva, *Strangers to Ourselves*, trans. Leon S. Rourdiez (New York: Columbia University Press, 1991), 185.

63. Kristeva, *Strangers to Ourselves*, 183.

64. Enrique Dussel, "Beyond Eurocentrism: The World-System and the Limits of Modernity," in *The Cultures of Globalization. Philosophy*, ed. Fredric Jameson and Masao Miyoshi (Durham: Duke University Press, 1999), 83.

65. Kovel, *White Racism*, 69.

66. Walter D. Mignolo, *The Darker Side of The Renaissance: Literacy, Territoriality, and Colonization*. 2nd Edition (Ann Arbor: University of Michigan Press, 1995, 2003), 18.

67. West, *Race Matters*, 90.

68. Irigaray, *An Ethics of Sexual Difference*, 61.

69. bell hooks, *Black Looks: Race and Representation* (Boston: South End Press, 1992), 24.

70. Marianna Torgovnick, *Primitive Passions: Men, Women, and the Quest for Ecstasy* (New York: Alfred A. Knopf, 1997), 153.
71. Auster, Interview, *The Art of Hunger*, 270.
72. Irigaray, *Speculum of the Other Woman*, trans. Gillian C. Gill (Ithaca, NY: Cornell University Press, 1985), 232.
73. Mignolo, *The Darker Side of The Renaissance*, 15.
74. Irigaray, *An Ethics of Sexual Difference*, 17.
75. Enrique Dussel, "Beyond Eurocentrism," 137.

Part II

Histories

5

THE MEMSAHIB MYTH:
ENGLISHWOMEN IN
COLONIAL INDIA

Indira Ghose

In his travel journal J. R. Ackerley, a close friend of E. M. Forster, reports an anecdote related to him by an Englishwoman living in India. The memsahib had been returning to her bungalow in the evening, accompanied by a servant.[1] Suddenly a krait—one of the most venomous snakes in India—slithered onto the middle of the path. Ackerley quotes the memsahib as saying, "Then the servant did a thing absolutely without precedent in India—he touched me!—he put his hand on my shoulder and pulled me back . . . Of course if he hadn't done that I should undoubtedly have been killed; but I didn't like it all the same, and got rid of him soon after."[2]

One might read this anecdote as a miniature allegory of empire. It has the staple ingredients of a hostile environment and inscrutable natives; centre stage is the Englishwoman in India, woefully or wilfully—depending on one's viewpoint—blind to the loyalty of the native. Unspoken in the background lurks the fear of native men lusting after white women. But above all, the story serves to reinforce the stereotype of the memsahib. It was the women who were blamed for exacerbating distrust and hostility between the races. Memsahibs were portrayed as intolerant, viciously racist, and abusive to servants. Their only interests were gossip and extramarital affairs. Interestingly, the image of the memsahib remains remarkably consistent, whether presented by opponents of imperialism such as E. M. Forster in his caricature of the memsahib Mrs. Turton in *A Passage to India*, or by supporters of the empire such as Rudyard Kipling. In 1909 the liberal-minded traveller Wilfrid Blunt announced, "it is a fact that the

Englishwoman in India . . . has been the cause of half the bitter feelings there between race and race. . . . it is her constantly increasing influence now that widens the gulf of ill-feeling and makes amalgamation daily more impossible."[3] And contemporary imperial historians such as Ronald Hyam conclude, "the idea that memsahibs were at least in part centrally involved in the deterioration of race relations from the 1860s still will not quite go away."[4]

Feminist historiography has attempted to rewrite the history of the memsahib by presenting her as a much maligned monster, arguing that "colonialism is men's business; women do the best they can within it."[5] For critics such as Helen Callaway, white women were merely "pawns in imperial politics."[6] Indeed, these critics held that women had set about trying to undermine the empire from within. Callaway claimed that by means of what she terms feminine qualities—sympathy, diplomacy, understanding—women had tried to bridge the gap between colonizer and colonized. Other critics set out to explain the role of the memsahib in terms of imperial policy. Ann Stoler has pointed to the fact that social distance was a cornerstone of British colonial rule. The role delegated to the Englishwoman in the colonial scenario was precisely that of patrolling racial boundaries. Stoler goes on to argue that British women in the colonies "confronted profoundly rigid restrictions on their domestic, economic and political options, more limiting than those of metropolitan Europe at the time." Imperial policies determined the way in which "women's needs were defined not *by*, but *for* them."[7]

Since the 1980s, however, a spate of criticism has uncovered the deep investment women had in imperialism.[8] Antoinette Burton, for instance, has discussed the way Victorian feminism used the image of the downtrodden Indian woman to negotiate an arena for Englishwomen in imperial politics.[9] Running an empire required the superior moral sensibilities of women, Victorian feminists argued. Thus the suffragette movement used the idea of the imperial mission of Britain to carve out a space for women in the public sphere. In a recent study of memsahibs, Mary Procida has looked at the way women forged a place for themselves within the British empire.[10] By focusing solely on the role women were assigned within colonial policy, their agency is elided—and concomitantly, their complicity.

Instead of attempting to isolate the accounts of women's lives, historians such as Joan Wallach Scott and Elisabeth Fox-Genovese have called for enmeshing the narratives of women in the larger context of history. Furthermore, they warn against the fallacious notion that the chronicle of women's lives is continuous. As Joan Scott argues,

"Identity as a continuous, coherent, historical phenomenon is revealed to be a fantasy, a fantasy that erases the divisions and discontinuities, the absences and differences that separate subjects in time."[11] There is no universal experience of womanhood. Indeed, the same women might experience specific historical constellations in contradictory ways. The truth is that Englishwomen were both victims and agents of empire. And as Fox-Genovese points out,

> the undervaluation of women has not only led to the slighting of women's participation in slave revolts, but also of their formidable contribution to the building of slave societies . . . The prevailing myth of woman-as-Other would encourage us to lump the wide range of women's experiences under the oppression of womanhood. But if we have learned anything, it must be that we must uncover the history of women in all its tragic complexity.[12]

In other words, we need to explore women's contribution to history in all its facets and examine the contradictions and complexity of women's relation to power.

In this chapter, I wish to look at the intersection of race and gender in the context of the British empire. Memsahibs offer a case study of how gender is constructed through racial privilege. My focus will be particularly on the way power affects gender, drawing on Max Weber's definition of power as "the possibility of imposing one's will upon the behaviour of other persons."[13] While Weber sees power as embedded in the structure of social relationships, he clearly attributes agency to those who exert power. I will be drawing mainly on autobiographical writings written by Englishwomen who had settled in India for a number of years. These memoirs are, of course, not transparent reflections of the lives of memsahibs in India. They are documents of social and cultural history that reveal less about the reality of the Raj than about how the memsahibs defined themselves, the stories they told themselves to make sense of the colonial experience.[14] A look at their own writings reveals a more complex view of the memsahib than the stereotype that dominates colonial fiction.

With the advent of the steamship in the 1830s, women regularly travelled to India, increasingly taking the overland route through Egypt to avoid the arduous voyage around the Cape. The opening of the Suez Canal in 1869 reduced the trip to India by sea from four to six months to a matter of weeks. The role of the memsahib reflected the changes in colonial policy in the course of the century. During the seventeenth and eighteenth centuries, the East India Company consisted of a band of merchants whose main aim was to amass as much

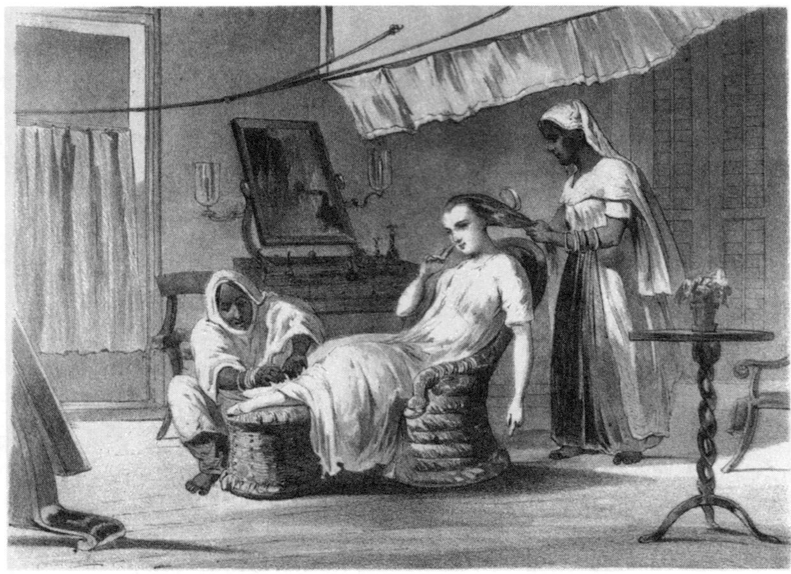

Figure 5.1   A view of Memsahib Culture.

fortune in the East in as little time as possible. It was Edmund Burke who, in his passionate attack on the rapacious exploitation of Indian provinces, laid the foundation of the notion that the British had a responsibility toward the people they governed. By the 1790s, the shift toward serious administration of an empire had been cemented. The main concern of the British now centred on upholding the prestige of the rulers as incorruptible and an exemplar of moral rectitude. To this end Indian wives or mistresses (*bibis*) were looked down upon and Eurasians categorically denied access to the higher echelons of the British administration. The rising tide of evangelical disapprobation at home added pressure on British society in India to maintain a social distance from Indians, in particular women. The early nineteenth century still witnessed significant cultural exchange between British administrators and the new middle class, particularly in Bengal, where English colleges were first founded. However, the 1840s were marked by the "birth of the nigger" (as native Indians were called) and by the increasing contempt for the natives and the segregation between the races.[15] As imperial historian Kenneth Ballhatchet points out, "English class attitudes are transformed into racial attitudes in an imperial setting."[16] Englishwomen fulfilled the role of both guardians of home values and policing agents in charge of upholding racial exclusiveness.

One of the turning points to change the position of women in the Raj was the Mutiny of 1957. The rebellion of a number of Indian soldiers in the British army began on May 10, 1857 and spread throughout northwestern India, propelled by discontent about British rule. A coalition of disgruntled rulers disempowered by the British, mutinous soldiers, and peasants with tax grievances produced the greatest threat to the edifice of British rule in the nineteenth century. One of the atrocities committed during the uprising was the slaughter of several hundred Englishwomen and their children at Cawnpore by Indian insurgents. This event remained seared on the colonial collective memory, fuelled by sensationalist accounts of the rape and mutilation of Englishwomen by rebels. One of the first to cast doubt on these rumours was the reporter Sir William Howard Russell, who gained fame in the Crimean War as the first war correspondent, exposing the shocking conditions under which the British army fought.[17] Even though historians such as George Trevelyan and a committee set up by the British after the rebellion could uncover no evidence of rape, the myth of lascivious natives posing a sexual threat to white women remained firmly etched on the public imagination. Throughout the nineteenth and the early twentieth century, an idealized view of the white woman as the embodiment of innocence and Englishness remained in circulation—side by side with the denigration of the memsahib.

THE LIFE OF A MEMSAHIB

Despite the diversity among memsahibs—some travelled extensively, some wrote colonial romances, and some were active in social causes—a number of characteristic motifs thread their memoirs. Probably the most important literary strategy was the construction of India as "a land of exile."[18] Irrespective of the number of years that the women spent in India, the idea of Britain as home was continually cultivated in these texts. It is important to remember that the British in India were at all times a tiny minority—145,000 were counted in the first census in 1881, out of a total population of a quarter billion.[19] Furthermore, colonial wives in India were constantly on the move. The writer Flora Annie Steel casually mentions the fact that in the fifteen years she lived in India she moved house sixteen times.[20] Far from the network of family and relatives that they could draw upon in Britain, women faced a further obstacle in forming close friendships among themselves. As Mrs. Sherwood points out, "There is no solitude like the solitude of a civilian's lady in a retired situation in India."[21]

The cult of home was the keystone of colonial ideology. For this was the function that the memsahib was expected to fulfil—to represent forever England in the Raj. What they did was stage one continual performance of Englishness. This is visible precisely in the trivial details of their lives—the food they ate, the clothes they wore, and the sweet peas they grew in their gardens. Englishwomen proved their mettle precisely by not adapting to the Indian climate in any way. As Mrs King reveals, their clothing weighed about four pounds (without shoes) in the summer heat.[22] It was a matter of pride to obtain all one's clothes and household articles from Britain. Travellers to India such as Emily Eden were amazed to learn that English ladies in Calcutta scorned luxury items such as silks and upheld the honour of English fabrics instead.[23] What this implied was that they were expected to be continually on their guard against the dangers inherent in life in India.

In the earlier part of the Raj, the lives of the British were indeed shadowed by illness and sudden death. In the course of the nineteenth century, the focus shifted to the ceaseless war waged against the heat and dust. Maud Diver, who wrote an ardent defense of the memsahib, speaks of "daily battles against heat, dust, cholera, and that insidious inertia of soul and body that is the moral microbe of the East."[24] Significantly, she collapses the distinction between physical phenomena and moral corruption. India was felt to pose a threat on all fronts and seemed to call for constant vigilantism and the policing of borders. Diver explains, "It is a known fact that the Indian climate . . . tends to promote an astonishingly rapid waste of nerve tissue." This is what lies at the root of "that curious slackness—mental and moral—of which the Anglo-Indian woman stands accused."[25] Unsympathetic visitors to India such as Christine Bremner remark, "if this is true, and many are to be found who assert it, it points to some errors in diet that could be avoided," drawing attention to the mounds of meat consumed by the British twice a day in the heat.[26]

Social relations with Indians were kept to a minimum. The mutual interdining that took place during the eighteenth century ceased abruptly with the large influx of Englishwomen from the 1840s onward. As Lady Wilson remarks ironically, the policy of social distance was not conducive to social interaction: "some Europeans of the old school would not allow a lady to accept an Indian gentleman's proffered hospitality. They would not permit her to drive through an

Indian town, be a spectator of tent-pegging, or receive an Indian as visitor, far less dine with him. They would, in short, prefer her to be as wholly absent from every kind of Indian society as are the inmates of zenanas."[27] The reasons put forward by the British were that they disdained to invite anyone into their homes who refused to introduce them to their own wives. Indeed, a traditionalization of Indian society did take place in the course of the nineteenth century.[28] One reaction to colonialism was the insistence of conservative Indian groups on the sanctity of the domestic sphere by setting it outside the control of the colonial state. The image of the Indian woman as the repository of traditional values was deployed by traditional groups to help mark themselves off from the British. What Lady Wilson hints at is the fact that English ladies were no less secluded than were the Indian women. In fact, Englishwomen were relegated precisely to the same role for the self-constitution of the British in India as Indian women—that of upholding the boundaries between the British and Indians. Interestingly, even reformist Indians who advocated the education of Indian women warned against the example of the memsahib. Memsahibs were seen as a test case of the education of women gone badly wrong. They were accused of being assertive, self-indulgent, indolent, immodest, and neglectful of domestic duties. An article in a Bengali women's magazine in 1870 admonishes its readers: "give no place in your heart to *memsahib*-like behaviour. This is not becoming in a Bengali housewife."[29]

To a culture that advocated a rigid control of sexuality, Indian culture seemed scandalously sensual. To quote Ackerley's memsahib once again: she gives the newcomer one last word of advice: " 'You'll never understand the dark and tortuous minds of the natives,' she said; 'and if you do I shan't like you—you won't be healthy.' "[30] But it was above all Indian women against whom the memsahibs defined themselves. Relations to Indian women were marked by ambivalence.[31] Invariably they took the form of visits to the zenana or purdah parties (all-women's parties organized by English wives). Indian women were either described in the purple prose of Orientalist fantasies or in the compassionate style favoured by philanthropists. They were seen either as obsessed with sensuality, or as degraded specimens that inspired pity and contempt. Either way they served to reinforce the self-image of the Englishwomen as more enlightened, deflecting any critique of the gender relations in their own societies. Even in the case of women who were engaged in social reform, for instance in the field of female education, their self-definition was constructed against the foil of Indian women as less emancipated than they were.[32]

The most intensive contact with Indians that memsahibs had was with their servants. Many English memsahibs developed surprisingly close relations to their servants. Servants were an important issue for Englishwomen in Britain, too, and many a memsahib lamented the "absolute heathenism" among the working classes in London and the airs that domestic servants gave themselves.[33] In India, however, the numbers of servants were vastly superior to those an average middle-class family could afford at home. In 1831, Fanny Parkes lists a total of fifty-seven servants as the minimum that she and her husband "as quiet people" required.[34] A further difference was that most domestic servants in India were male.

The memsahib Julia Maitland pokes fun at the plethora of servants every household maintains:

> I have an ayah (or lady's maid), and a tailor (for the ayahs cannot work); and A—[her husband] has a boy: also two muddles—one to sweep my room, and another to bring water. There is one man to lay the cloth, another to bring in dinner, another to light the candles, and others to wait at table. Every horse has a man and a maid to himself—and every dog has a boy. I inquired whether the cat had any servants, but found that she was allowed to wait upon herself; and, as she seemed the only person in the establishment capable of so doing, I respected her accordingly.[35]

She goes on to describe the indolent life of a typical memsahib:

> The real Indian ladies lie on a sofa, and, if they drop their handkerchief, they just lower their voices and say, "Boy!" in a very gentle tone, and then creeps in, perhaps, some old wizen, skinny brownie . . . who twiddles after them for a little while, and then creeps out again as softly as a black cat, and sits down cross-legged in the verandah till "Mistress please to call again."[36]

Servants were consistently compared to children. "The Indian servant is a child in everything save age, and should be treated as a child," declares Flora Annie Steel authoritatively.[37] At the same time, a lingering fear of the devious native recurs. They were suspected to be in possession of mysterious powers and capable of poisoning their masters at will. One memsahib hints darkly: "Servants . . . have been known to wash the cups and plates from which their master's child take their food, in so subtle a juice or distillation that everything they took disagreed with them, until the parents . . . have hastened back to where the natives would be."[38]

The site of greatest vulnerability was, of course, the memsahib's child. During most of the nineteenth century, colonial doctors forbade breast-feeding as too debilitating for the middle-class mother, and for this purpose native wet-nurses were employed.[39] As numerous memsahibs lament, these servants gleefully exploited their potential to blackmail their mistresses:

> The amah [wet-nurse] is a Caste woman, and her whims are the plague of my life: I am obliged to keep a cook on purpose for her, because her food must all be dressed by a person of her own caste; and even then she will sometimes starve all day rather than eat it, if she fancies anybody else has been near it: she has a house built of cocoa-nut leaves in the compound, on purpose to cook her food in.[40]

On occasion the wet-nurse would use even more brutal means of extortion:

> An "amah" also, or native wet-nurse, offended by some word or action of her mistress, will revenge herself by causing her milk to dry up, or "backen," as it is technically termed, in a few hours, and what is more extraordinary, will, when perhaps in possession of the dismissal she coveted, bring the draught back again almost as quickly. . . . one can scarcely blame the maternal instinct of the animal which prompts her to retain all her milk for the little one for whose use it was given her: but it is not so easy to feel amiable towards a reasoning creature who undertakes to perform the part of mother towards a helpless infant, and will then deprive it of its nourishment without the least regard to its health, in order to gratify her own caprice.[41]

The passage attempts to set up a contrast between natural maternal instincts in animals and the lack of these instincts in the perverse and callous wet-nurse. It is another memsahib, the evangelical Mrs. Sherwood (known for her pious tales set in India) who lays bare the true state of affairs. She describes a conversation with an English nanny:

> "But the wet-nurse's baby," I remarked; "what can be done for the little black infant?" "Oh!" replied the amiable white woman, "something handsome is always paid for their being reared; but they commonly die." "My lady," she added, "has had six nurses for different children, and the babies have one and all died." "Died!" I remember I exclaimed, "but this is murder." She answered coolly, "But this can't be helped; the mothers never fret after them. Whenever they nurse a white baby they cease to care for their own; they say, 'White child is good; black child his slave.'"[42]

What Mrs. Sherwood reveals is passed over in silence in later texts. Instead, occasionally the native servant was accused of deliberately sacrificing her child: "they are so careless about their own children when they are nursing other people's, that she and her husband would let the poor little creature die from neglect, and then curse us as the cause of it."[43]

This brings us to the hidden cost exacted from the memsahib. Colonial ideology decreed that all children be sent back to Britain between the age of five and seven. The choice memsahibs were left with was either to leave their husbands and accompany their children back home, or to part with their children. The reasons given were invariably the corruption of the tender mind through contact with natives—colonial lore passed on from one memsahib to the next. Helen MacKenzie declares, "I could not repeat the dreadful stories I have heard of the early depravity and knowledge of wickedness acquired by children from their Ayahs [nannies], *even* under vigilant superintendence."[44] And Florence Marryat notes, "I have been told that the conversation of the natives, as a rule, is too filthy to be imagined, which always gave me a great horror of permitting my children to pick up the Tamil language from their ayahs."[45]

There might have been an element of rivalry at work here— dispassionate commentators such as Emma Roberts (a journalist and a spinster) remark on the fact that the Anglo-Indian children were far closer to their Indian nannies than their mothers and often spoke Indian languages fluently, with only a halting command of English.[46]

In characteristically maudlin style, Maud Diver expatiates at length about the tragic shadow haunting the memsahib's lives—"that tragic shadow of separation, which is the keynote of Anglo-India— unavoidable always, and always a tragedy":

> But early or late the cruel wrench must come—the crueller, the longer deferred. One after one the babies grow into companiable children; one after one England claims them, till the mother's heart and house are left unto her desolate. Empty nurseries, empty verandahs; only the haunting music of small footsteps and clear voices still troubles and glorifies her dreams. Yet in all likelihood she will continue to dance and ride and entertain with undiminished zest. Heartlessness? Frivolity? In a few cases, possibly, but in most the sheer pluck of the race that has a prejudice in favour of making the best of things as they are, and never whimpering over the inevitable . . . [47]

Personal loss is transmuted into a trademark virtue of the imperial race. The lonely mother is celebrated as an imperial heroine who has sacrificed her domestic happiness at the altar of a higher cause. Anne Wilson finds less pretentious (and more eloquent) words to describe the pain of parting from her child:

> A dreadful thing happened to me the last night I was in England. I was sitting in a small inner room in the big London hotel, only one other woman there, and I meant to be so brave, when into the room there rushed a boy, just like my own boy, the same age, the same height, with the same radiant joyous face, the same dear loving eyes. He came with arms outstretched, and calling 'Mother,' threw himself into the arms of the other woman, and covered her happy face with kisses.[48]

Deprived of their children, the memsahibs spent their days either as "a complete victim to languour and ennui,"[49] or in larger stations in a stultifying ritual of calling, taking the obligatory evening drive, and attending dinner parties. These activities were regulated according to rigid rules of precedence, enshrined in a Warrant of Precedence issued by the government as a guide for official social occasions. Hostesses consulted it as a bible, enforcing a strict adherence to its norms.[50] An important mainstay of colonial social life was the season spent in hill-stations such as Simla in northern India, where society indulged in a frenzied round of calling, driving to the Mall, amateur theatricals, paper chases, fancy dress parties, balls and dinner parties. As Christine Bremner, a visitor to India, explains, "The great thing is to get up a good visiting list, to know nice people, nice being almost synonymous with those who give pleasant parties, have good tennis courts, can introduce you to a set you want to know, or advance some relative of yours. And ladies are said to be extremely powerful in India in advancing men in whom they have an interest."[51] It was life at Simla that gained memsahibs a reputation for intrigue and frivolity. However, Bremner insists, social life in the Raj was marked by true heroism. In a brilliantly satirical set-piece that bears quoting at length, she mocks the social etiquette of calling, always reserved for the hours between noon and two in the afternoon:

> So in this hottest part of the Indian day, courageous woman, ever in the van of social self-sacrifice, emerges . . . Exhausted with cawing, the crows are gaping open-mouthed on the trees of the compound, the lizards have crept into shady corners, the terrier has moved off the spot in the verandah where the sun's rays had found him out. His nose lying on extended paws, his blinking eyes and unwagging tail say . . . : "I am determined to keep cool from twelve to two.". . . but poor mem-saheb, in her tight dress and kid-encased extremities, sallies out with more of

a smile on her face than the crows, which are perhaps gaping at her courage as much as at the heat. I never heard of any lady being struck by heat apoplexy, and would have you note that English courage and daring are not confined to one sex among Anglo-Indians.[52]

THE PLEASURES OF IMPERIALISM[53]

Why, one wonders, would generations of women accept the strictures of an ideology that claimed such a high price from them, both in terms of personal loss and the inanity of the lives they led? I wish to suggest that life in the Raj offered the memsahibs compensations in the form of both prestige and gender power. Colonial society in India was made up of middle-class officials aspiring to the life of the aristocracy—and pursuing a lifestyle they would never be able to maintain at home.[54] For middle-class Englishwomen, colonial life brought a rise in status and privileges such as they could hardly hope for in the home society. Furthermore, the relation between domesticity and empire changed significantly in the course of the nineteenth century. As critics such as Nancy Armstrong have argued, within the agenda set by the evangelical movement, women gained power in the home by forgoing public power.[55] In late eighteenth and early nineteenth century, English domesticity was defined in opposition to the empire.[56] Indeed, colonial wealth amassed in India was seen as a corrupting influence in English society, as was slavery in the West Indies. Englishwomen in the empire were widely regarded as decadent. In the wake of the shift in policy that sought to establish imperial rule on a firm moral base, an attempt was made to import ideas of Englishness into the empire—linked to the large-scale influx of memsahibs. In the nineteenth century, domesticity became women's contribution to the empire. Called upon to fulfil an important function in the empire, women gained a meaningful public position.

The most striking feature about the memsahibs was that they lived public lives—the British in India were constantly aware of performing on a public stage. As the sister of Emily Eden, Fanny, reflected, "it seems to me that we are acting a long opera."[57] In fact, it was in the empire that Englishwomen foiled the two spheres ideology that relegated them to the home—by redefining the private as the political. The memsahibs undermined the ideology of domesticity by explicitly foregrounding the symbolic dimensions of the home as a microcosm of empire.[58] This enabled the memsahib to stake a claim to a share in the imperial mission. The colonies offered late Victorian and early twentieth-century Englishwomen the opportunity to destabilize and challenge the boundaries between the private and the public—the domestic sphere itself was transformed into a political space indispensable to the smooth functioning of the empire. The authors of the authoritative *The Complete Indian Housekeeper and Cook: Giving the Duties of Mistress and Servants, the General Management of the House, and Practical Recipes for Cooking in all its Branches* (1889), Flora Annie Steel and Grace Gardiner, summed up the situation in these terms: "an Indian household can no more be governed peacefully, without dignity and prestige, than an Indian Empire."[59]

In the British empire, women's home management was upgraded to a political act—Englishwomen's contribution to the task of running the empire. Significantly, Steel and Gardiner couch their recommendations for the daily routine in militaristic rhetoric: "Inspection parade should begin, then, immediately after breakfast . . . The cook should be waiting—in clean raiment—with a pile of plates, and his viands for the day spread out on a table. . . . Luncheon and dinner ordered, the mistress should proceed to the storeroom, when both the bearer [valet] and the khitmatghar [table servant] should be in attendance." Half an hour (after breakfast) was sufficient for the arrangements for the day, they advise. And in words that chime with contemporary feminist sentiments, they insist, "it is not necessary, or in the least degree desirable, that an educated woman should waste the best years of her life in scolding and petty supervision. Life holds higher duties"[60]

The critic Rosemary George has argued that the empire "established one of the primary arenas in which Englishwomen first achieved the kind of authoritative self associated with the modern female subject."[61] In other words: the first emancipated Englishwoman was a memsahib. However, the stifling constraints that shaped Englishwomen's situation in the empire need to be taken into account. There were very few avenues open to women in the empire, careers in politics or administration being firmly closed to them. The women were subjected to enormous social pressure. Newcomers in particular were bullied into adapting to a social mindset that disapproved of all signs of individualism and that instilled into them above all the importance of not letting the side down. As we have seen, Englishwomen paid a personal price for the position they acquired as representatives of imperial power, be it in the form of homesickness or the loss of their children.

Nonetheless, a closer look reveals that life in the Raj also offered women certain pleasures. For memsahibs, the empire presented an opportunity to transgress the norms of the private and the public and thus acquire a significant political role in upholding imperial rule. In addition, memsahibs exerted pressure on the image of women in imperialist ideology to create new selves. Isabel Savory, who travelled to India to indulge a passion for big-game hunting at the end of the nineteenth century, noted that "time has changed the Mem-sahib" and explained, "The *mem-sahib* of the nineteenth century is an energetic, tennis, Badminton, calling and riding—sometimes sporting—creation."[62] Books such as Mrs. R. H. Tyacke's *How I Shot My Bears* appeared (1893). A significant shift took place in the image of the Englishwoman in the empire—by the early twentieth century, the idea of the weak and vulnerable woman that circulated in Mutiny lore no longer held center stage.

As regards their relationship to power, what one might term the Thatcher-syndrome seems to be in operation here.[63] Women have historically used a raft of strategies to open up new conceptual spaces in their engagement with power. They have deployed the insignia of femininity only to undermine its signification, traditionally associated with powerlessness. In addition, they have drawn on male sources of authority and prestige by identifying themselves with men. Alternatively, they have tapped into traditional cultural stereotypes of female modes of authority. These strategies that served to create representations of women as powerful nonetheless remained overtly conservative and thus defused the threat they posed to gender norms.

While memsahibs negotiated a form of power both on a national and on a personal level through their rise in status, it is notable that in their writings scorn is invariably poured on other women who are seen to fulfil the memsahib stereotypes. Julia Maitland described meeting a memsahib settled in India for many years. She asked her what she had seen of the country and its inhabitants since she had been in India. "'Oh, nothing!' the lady answered, 'Thank goodness, I know nothing at all about them, nor I don't wish to: really I think the less one sees and knows of them the better!'"[64] For Englishwomen in India the memsahib stereotype served as a foil against which they sought to differentiate themselves. Memsahibs were *other* Englishwomen.

For some memsahibs, the pleasures bound up with imperialism were more palpable than it was for others. Flora Annie Steel describes how she chastises a servant who earns her ire by mistreating a mule:

> Then my temper gave way; I sent for the mule man. I seized him by the scruff of the neck—I was still in my habit with my whip—and I belaboured him with it till I nearly dropped, he shrieking with terror, thinking a female demon had got him . . . it was done, and if anyone

blames me for having horse-whipped a man, I don't blame myself. I confess that I never do get angry without an intense desire to hit, but I know it is unladylike, and I condemn myself, *as a rule*, to inaction.[65]

Lady Isabel Burton, a passionate campaigner for animal rights, describes how she patrolled the streets on the lookout for natives abusing animals, boasting that "if my husband did not keep me in order in this matter, I should always be in the 'lock-up' for assault, for these sights make me forget that I am a lady."[66]

It is Steel, too, who gives the following advice to other memsahibs who might have difficulties with recalcitrant servants—she recommends the forced administration of castor oil.

> This is considered a great joke, and exposes the offender to much ridicule from his fellow-servants; so much so that the words, "*Mem Sahib tum ko zuroor kaster ile pila dena hoga*" (*The Mem Sahib will have to give you castor oil*), is often heard in the mouths of the upper servants when new-comers give trouble. In short, without kindly and reasonable devices of this kind, the usual complaint of a want of hold over servants *must* remain true until they are educated into some sense of duty.[67]

In her autobiography Steel muses on "the absolute necessity for high-handed dignity in dealing with those who for thousands of years have been accustomed to it—they love it."[68] Steel's authoritative style flaunts a command of the language and an insight into the mentality of the native that can hold its own against the professional expertise of any colonial administrator.

This might bring us closer to the reasons behind the hostility universally directed at the memsahib. In their exercise of power, they demolished the idea of frail and defenceless womanhood so cherished by Victorian society. In reality, the main threat they embodied was not directed at race relations with Indians—it was aimed at the gender privileges of British men. What made their appropriation of power difficult to rebut was the fact that they claimed to act in the name of empire. This power was exercised in relation to the colonized as well as in the form of social influence within the Anglo-Indian community. The lives of leisure they led, unburdened by domestic and motherhood chores, created resentment on the part of other social classes at home, who clearly perceived that what was at stake was a community of middle-class origins aspiring to the lifestyle of the aristocracy in England. Indian men felt threatened in their plans for carefully controlled social reform of their wives—memsahibs seemed to represent precisely the dangers of educated women against which conservative critics had warned them. Finally, Englishwomen themselves had an interest in distancing themselves from other, more decadent, memsahibs. The myth of the memsahib served as a convenient means to defuse male anxieties about women's access to authority in empire.

To be sure, a number of women in colonial India refused to conform to the stereotypical image of the memsahib.[69] Flamboyant examples at the turn of the century include Margaret Noble and Annie Besant, both of whom became actively involved in nationalist politics, the former converting to Hinduism and becoming a Hindu nun.[70] There were women who were engaged in the field of women's education, such as Annette Beveridge and the redoubtable Flora Annie Steel, who was an inspectress of girls' schools in the Punjab.[71] There were intrepid adventurers, such as Fanny Parkes, who travelled around India on a breathless quest for the picturesque. Other women, such as Anne Wilson, immersed themselves in learning Indian music or studying the tenets of Indian religions. Some memsahibs were professional writers who produced a prolific oevre of colonial romances. Works by authors such as Maud Diver, Flora Annie Steel, or Alice Perrin were highly popular at the time, though their reputation has not survived the demise of the empire.

Even more remarkable than the range of different types of Englishwomen in colonial India is the fact that their autobiographical writings are riven with ambiguities. The same writers who pour scorn on the devious native display a warm affection toward their own servants. Memsahibs who lament the constrictions of life in India can on occasion demonstrate a deep interest in Indian culture. However, a consistent feature in their texts is the remarkable evasion of the fact that their position as women in British India was based on racial privilege. Two points are significant in this connection: their denial of power and their denial of pleasure.

The truth of their narratives and the veracity of the stories that circulated about them is not at issue here. Instead, what is of interest is the function their texts serve. Their self-stylization as leading a life where pleasure was sacrificed to duty was closely bound up with the ethos of the British in India. The British viewed their rule in terms of a thankless duty to uplift the downtrodden and inculcate order into Oriental minds. The mission to civilize the "silent, sullen peoples" of the East was a burden imposed upon them by destiny.[72] According to the Victorian cult of good conduct that shaped this ethos, frivolity and the pursuit of pleasure was destructive of character-building. Consequently, as historian Francis Hutchins argues, "India came to be valued not for its pleasures, or promise, but precisely because it was possible to be desperately unhappy there."[73] Memsahibs shared this view of life in India as one long exile. To be sure, many memsahibs endured a lonely life in colonial outstations with admirable fortitude. Nevertheless, what is specific about the women's experience was the fact that the empire gave them access to sources of power that were unthinkable in the context of Britain. There is an inherent incongruity between their self-image as victim and the role they staked out for themselves as an indispensable pillar of the empire. Above all, their writings denied the pleasures of power grounded on racial privilege. This ranged from the ability to shape new gender roles for themselves to at times exerting real political clout. Perhaps there was too much at stake; laying bare the influence they wielded might have provoked measures to curtail their power. Furthermore, the form of power they exercised was highly precarious since it lacked legitimation within the colonial state.[74] A case in point is the Ilbert Bill controversy of 1883. The bill, introduced by the Viceroy Lord Ripon, advocated a minor legal amendment that would enable Indian magistrates to try Europeans in provincial courts. At the time, only two native members of the Indian Civil Service were qualified to do so. Nevertheless, a wave of outrage swept the British community in India, much of which centred on the idea of Englishwomen being tried by Indian judges. "Would you like to live in a country," the *Friend of India* thundered, "where at any moment your wife would be liable to be sentenced on a false charge, the magistrate being a copper-coloured Pagan?"[75] The campaign against the Ilbert Bill was spearheaded by memsahibs, who orchestrated petitions and protests with such skill that the bill was revoked. However, in the course of the twentieth century, memsahibs were increasingly sidelined while imperial politics were negotiated between British administrators and Western-educated nationalist leaders such as Gandhi, Nehru, and Jinnah.

Memsahibs were ready to deploy the myth of the native violating white womanhood when it served their own ends. The self-construction of the memsahibs in their texts is that of long-suffering martyrs to the imperial mission, not as active agents of the empire. In fact, disclaiming authority served to authenticate and sustain women's empowerment in the empire. A denial of imperial privilege was a crucial strategy of power for women in the Raj.

NOTES

1. The term memsahib refers to married English ladies in colonial India, mainly the wives of officials or army officers.

2. J. R. Ackerley, *Hindoo Holiday: An Indian Journal* (1932; London: Penguin Books, 1960), 22.

3. Winfrid Scawen Blunt, *India Under Ripon: A Private Diary* (London: T. Fisher Unwin, 1909), 261.

4. Ronald Hyam, *Empire and Sexuality: The British Experience* (Manchester: Manchester University Press, 1990), 208.

5. Jane Haggis, "Gendering Colonialism or Colonising Gender? Recent Women's Studies Approaches to White Women and the History of British Colonialism," *Women's Studies International Forum* 13 (1990): 105–15; 110.

6. Helen Callaway, *Gender, Culture and Empire: European Women in Colonial Nigeria* (Urbana: University of Illinois Press, 1987), 5.

7. Ann Laura Stoler, "Carnal Knowledge and Imperial Power: Gender, Race, and Morality in Colonial Asia," in *Gender at the Crossroads of Knowledge: Feminist Anthropology in the Postmodern Era*, ed. Micaela di Leonardo (Berkeley: University of California Press, 1991), 51–101; 52. Emphasis in the original.

8. See *Western Women and Imperialism: Complicity and Resistance*, ed. Nupur Chaudhuri and Margaret Strobel (Bloomington: Indiana University Press, 1992), Vron Ware, *Beyond the Pale: White Women, Racism and History* (London: Verso, 1992), and *Gender and Imperialism*, ed. Clare Midgley (Manchester: Manchester University Press, 1998).

9. Antoinette Burton, *Burdens of History: British Feminists, Indian Women, and Imperial Culture, 1865–1915* (Chapel Hill: University of North Carolina Press, 1994).

10. See Mary A. Procida's insightful study *Married to the Empire: Gender, Politics and Imperialism in India, 1883–1947* (Manchester: Manchester University Press, 2002). Many of her theses are corroborated by my own research.

11. Joan W. Scott, "Fantasy Echo: History and the Construction of Identity," *Critical Inquiry* 27 (2001): 284–304; 292.

12. Elisabeth Fox-Genovese, "Placing Women's History in History," *New Left Review* 133 (1982): 5–29; 29.

13. Max Weber, *Max Weber on Law in Economy and Society*, ed. Max Rheinstein, trans. Edward Shils and Max Rheinstein (Cambridge, MA: Harvard University Press, 1954), 323.

14. The Raj denotes British rule in India.

15. For an overview of this development, see Peter Mudford, *Birds of a Different Plumage: A Study of British-Indian Relations from Akbar to Curzon* (London: Collins, 1974).

16. Kenneth Ballhatchet, *Race, Sex and Class under the Raj: Imperial Attitudes and their Policies and their Critics, 1793–1905* (London: Weidenfeld and Nicolson, 1980), 121.

17. See William Howard Russell, *My Diary in India, in the Year 1858–9*, 2 vols. (London: Routledge, Warne & Routledge, 1860).

18. Maud Diver, *The Englishwoman in India* (Edinburgh: William Blackwood & Sons, 1909), 33.

19. Margaret Macmillan, *Women of the Raj* (London: Thames and Hudson, 1988), 42. Only a tiny percentage were high-ranking colonial officials and army officers and their wives, the majority comprising British soldiers. Unfortunately, no accounts left by soldiers' wives, maids or governesses have come to my notice.

20. Flora Annie Steel, *The Garden of Fidelity* (London: Macmillan, 1929), 184.

21. Mary Martha Sherwood, *The Life and Times of Mrs Sherwood (1775–1851) from the Diaries of Captain and Mrs Sherwood*, ed. F. J. Harvey Darton (London: Wells Gardener & Co., 1910), 405.

22. E. Augusta King, *The Diary of a Civilian's Wife in India 1877–1882*, 2 vols. (London: Richard Bentley, 1884), 2:141.

23. Emily Eden, *Letters from India*, ed. by her Niece, the Hon. Eleanor Eden, 2 vols. (London: Richard Bentley, 1872), 1:225–26.

24. Diver, *Englishwoman in India*, 129.

25. Ibid., 8–9.

26. Christina Sinclair Bremner, *A Month in a Dandi: A Woman's Wanderings in Northern India* (London: Simpkin, Marshall & Co., 1891), 45.

27. Lady Anne Campbell Wilson, *Letters from India* (1911; London: Century, 1984), 33–34. Zenanas were the secluded women's quarters in upper-class Indian homes, both Muslim and Hindu.

28. See C. A. Bayly, *Indian Society and the Making of the British Empire*, The New Cambridge History of India 2.1 (Cambridge: Cambridge University Press, 1988), 136–68.

29. Quoted in Dipesh Chakrabarty, "The Difference-Deferral of (A) Colonial Modernity: Public Debates on Domesticity in British Bengal," *History Workshop* 36 (1993): 1–34; 9.

30. Ackerley, *Hindoo Holiday*, 23–24.

31. I discuss this issue in further detail in *Women Travellers to Colonial India: The Power of the Female Gaze* (New Delhi: Oxford University Press, 1998), particularly in connection with Englishwomen's forays into the zenana.

32. Barbara Ramusack has used the term "maternal imperialism" for this relationship. See her "Cultural Missionaries, Maternal Imperialists, Feminist Allies: British Women Activists in India, 1865–1945," in Chaudhuri and Strobel, 119–36.

33. Steel, *Garden of Fidelity*, 264.

34. Fanny Parkes, *Wanderings of a Pilgrim in Search of the Picturesque*, ed. Indira Ghose and Sara Mills (1850; Manchester: Manchester University Press, 2001), 158.

35. Julia Charlotte Maitland, *Letters from Madras, during the Years 1836–39, by a Lady* (London: John Murray, 1843), 37–38.

36. Maitland, *Letters from Madras*, 38. The British used the term "Indian" or "Anglo-Indian" for the British in India. Indians were referred to as "natives."

37. Flora Annie Steel and Grace Gardiner, "The Duties of the Mistress, The Complete Indian Housekeeper and Cook: Giving the Duties of Mistress and Servants, the General Management of the House, and Practical Recipes for Cooking in all its Branches" (1889), in *Empire Writing: An Anthology of Colonial Literature 1870–1918*, ed. Elleke Boehmer (Oxford: Oxford University Press, 1998), 126–32; 127.

38. Florence Marryat, *"Gup": Sketches of Anglo-Indian Life and Character* (London: Richard Bentley, 1868), 165.

39. See Nupur Chaudhuri, "Memsahibs and Motherhood in Nineteenth-Century Colonial India," *Victorian Studies* 31.4 (1988): 517–35; 28. In Britain, wet-nurses were often Irish.

40. Maitland, *Letters from Madras*, 106–7.

41. Marryat, *"Gup,"* 165–66.

42. Sherwood, *Mrs Sherwood (1775–1851)*, 402.

43. Maitland, *Letters from Madras*, 107. Similar accusations were leveled against Irish wet-nurses in England.

44. Helen MacKenzie, *Six Years in India* (London: Richard Bentley, 1857), 70–71.

45. Marryat, *"Gup,"* 55.

46. Emma Roberts, *Scenes and Characteristics of Hindostan, with Sketches of Anglo-Indian Society*, 3 vols. (London: W. H. Allen, 1835), 2:114–25.

47. Diver, *Englishwoman in India*, 45–46.

48. Wilson, *Letters from India*, 203.

49. Sherwood, *Mrs Sherwood (1775–1851)*, 405.

50. Macmillan, *Women of the Raj*, 48.

51. Bremner, *Month in a Dandi*, 54.

52. Ibid., 17–18.

53. In a well-known essay on Kipling's *Kim*, Edward Said discusses the pleasures of imperialism evoked by the novel in terms of surveillance and the fantasy of crossing cultural boundaries at will. See Edward W. Said, "The Pleasures of Imperialism," *Culture and Imperialism* (London: Chatto & Windus, 1993), 159–96. I wish to point to alternative pleasures that the empire offered British women, pleasures that are bound up with transgressing gender norms of the time.

54. See Bernard S. Cohn, "The British in Benares: A Nineteenth-Century Colonial Society," *Comparative Studies in Society and History* 4 (1961–1962): 169–99.

55. See Nancy Armstrong, *Desire and Domestic Fiction: A Political History of the Novel* (New York: Oxford University Press, 1987).

56. See Jon Mee, "Austen's treacherous ivory: Female patriotism, domestic ideology, and Empire" in *The Post-Colonial Jane Austen*, ed. You-me Park and RAJESWARI Sunder Rajan (London: Routledge, 2000), 74–92.

57. Eden, *Letters from India*, 1:91.

58. See Procida, *Married to the Empire*, 56–80.

59. Steel and Gardiner, "Duties of the Mistress," 132.

60. Ibid., 131–32; 126.

61. Rosemary Marangoly George, "The Authoritative Englishwoman: Setting Up Home and Self in the Colonies," *The Politics of Home: Postcolonial Relocations and Twentieth-Century Fiction* (Cambridge: Cambridge University Press, 1996), 35–64; 36. I am indebted to George's findings.

62. Isabel Savory, *A Sportswoman in India: Personal Adventures and Experiences in Known and Unknown India* (London: Hutchinson, 1900), 201; 338.

63. See Maureen McNeil, "Making and not Making the Difference: The Gender Politics of Thatcherism," in *Off-Centre: Feminism and Cultural Studies*, ed. Sarah Franklin, Celia Lury, and Jackie Stacy (London: Harper Collins, 1991), 221–40. I discuss this idea in connection with women travelers in *Women Travellers in Colonial India*, 140.

64. Maitland, *Letters from Madras*, 53.

65. Steel, *Garden of Fidelity*, 154. Emphasis in the original.

66. Isabel Burton, *A. E. I. Arabia Egypt India: A Narrative of Travel* (London: William Mullan, 1879), 235.

67. Steel and Gardiner, "Duties of the Mistress," 128. Emphasis in the original.

68. Steel, *Garden of Fidelity*, 133.

69. For a defense of the other memsahibs, see Kumari Jayawardena, *The White Woman's Other Burden: Western Women and South Asia during British Rule* (New York: Routledge, 1995).

70. On Annie Besant see Nancy Paxton, "Resistance and Complicity in the Writings of Annie Besant and Flora Annie Steel," in Chaudhuri and Strobel, 158–76.

71. On Steel see Paxton, "Resistance and Complicity," in Chaudhuri and Strobel, as well as Rebecca Saunders, "Gender Colonialism, and Exile: Flora Annie Steel and Sara Jeannette Duncan in India," in *Women's Writing in Exile*, ed. Mary Lynn Broe and Angela Ingram (Chapel Hill: University of North Carolina Press, 1989), 304–24.

72. See Kipling's "The White Man's Burden" (1899), in *A Choice of Kipling's Verse*, ed. T. S. Eliot (London: Faber and Faber, 1948), 137, 1:47.

73. Francis G. Hutchins, *The Illusion of Permanence: British Imperialism in India* (Princeton, NJ: Princeton University Press, 1967), 29.

74. See Max Weber's distinction between the power exercised through influence and the power legitimized through various types of authority.

75. Quoted in Dennis Judd, *The Lion and the Tiger: The Rise and Fall of the British Raj, 1600–1947* (Oxford: Oxford University Press, 2004), 106. On the Ilbert Bill controversy also see Mrinalini Sinha, *Colonial Masculinity: The "Manly Englishman" and the "Effeminate Bengali" in the Late Nineteenth Century* (Manchester: Manchester University Press, 1995), 33–68.

6

RACE, GENDER, AND LEADERSHIP: (EN)COUNTERING DISCOURSES THAT DEVALUE AFRICAN AMERICAN WOMEN AS LEADERS

Patricia S. Parker

This essay explores "othering" processes revealed in discourses about women, work, and leadership. Fifteen years ago, when I began to study women in management, I encountered a broad literature on gender and leadership that, among other things, advanced a "distinctly feminine" approach to leadership.[1] The feminine model was intended as a counternarrative to the dominant masculine approaches that stifle women's values. However, models of feminine and masculine leadership were based on the socially constructed identities and cultural values of Western, white, middle-class women and men, but presented as race-neutral, universal depictions of how the leadership process is accomplished. Broadly defined, leadership is a process of influence between leaders and followers in the pursuit of goals. Theories of leadership attempt to explain how that process unfolds to yield the most effective outcomes. But the meanings of "organizational leader" also take on high symbolic importance in Western culture.[2] Organizational members come to expect leaders to look, act, and think in ways that are consistent with certain iconic images.

In mainstream academic journals and popular press there are two distinct images of leaders, "The Great White Masculine Man" and The Ideal Feminine Woman."[3] An understanding of the leadership process flows from these symbolic representations. "Feminine" leadership is characterized as a noncontrolling, nurturing, emotional, and relationship-oriented process, which is in stark contrast to "masculine" leadership viewed as a controlling, aggressive, rational, and distant process. There is a debate in the literature that centers on which model is better, with one popular book announcing that there is a distinct "female advantage."[4] Excluded from these dominant Western visions of leadership are the experiences of other groups and cultural traditions that view the very notions of "feminine" and "masculine" differently and that should be influencing the production of leadership knowledge. In the dominant popular discourses on gender and leadership of the 1980s and early 1990s, there was not a great deal of interest in the question "What can be learned about leadership from Black women, Asian women, Latina women, poor women, and other marginalized groups?" At the same time, critiques by black feminist writers in women's studies, communication, management, sociology, and psychology boldly called for a revisioning of the white-washed theories about women in society.[5] So I set out to study organizational leadership from black women's standpoints.

I wondered how we might redefine the notions of feminine and masculine leadership if we took into account black women's cultural history of resistance and empowerment. What would processes of control and noncontrol look like if we dislodged them from the context of white privilege and reexamined them from the standpoints of resistance to oppression? I explored these questions through research on the history of black women's work and community activism. I also conducted interviews and observations of African American women senior executives who came of age during the civil rights movement. And I recently began a project with African American teen girls in low-income urban neighborhoods. In my research, I found evidence of a tradition of African American women's leadership that disrupts traditional notions of "feminine" and "masculine" leadership. It is a tradition that I argue can be traced to creative resistance and community building during the era of slavery and is visible in contemporary culture. In this chapter, I share some of what I have learned about leadership from African American women's standpoints.

I recognize that tradition is a complicated and often politically charged concept with multiple meanings. It is sometimes used as shorthand in our institutions to maintain or reclaim race, gender, or sexual oppression and domination. It also can be highly oppressive as members of a community rigidly adhere to rules out of fear of cult leaders. However, I am using the concept of tradition to emphasize positive cultural continuity in black women's history as one way to counter historical and contemporary discourses that devalue black women. The rites of passage that ensure some middle- and upper-class white men privileged positions of leadership at the top of America's corporations and institutions are socially constructed as the "standard" for success in the traditional leadership literature.[6] However, the experiences and knowledge that have, as historians Darlene Clark Hine and Margaret Thompson note, "enabled Black women to shape the raw materials of their lives into an extraordinary succession of victories" have been ignored and unexamined.[7]

A TRADITION OF BLACK WOMEN'S LEADERSHIP

I begin by briefly tracing the development of this leadership tradition, and then describing what I believe is its embodiment in the leadership approach of the civil rights activist Ella Baker. I will end with a discussion of how this approach finds expression among black women and girls in contemporary culture. The seeds of the tradition were planted as black women struggled to find ways to resist the oppression of centuries of slavery. Space does not allow a comprehensive retelling of that history; however, I do want to give a brief sketch of some of the ways enslaved black women were able to empower themselves and remain self-defined in racist and patriarchal systems that relied upon their devaluation as a primary means for reproducing power and domination. Indeed, the hegemonic "othering" of black women is well-documented in critical studies of enslaved black women who were constructed as "fallen womanhood" and as "natural laborers." This was accomplished through derogatory stereotypes in literature, theater, the press, and everyday life.[8] Controlling popular images of black women as mammy, Sapphire, and the black matriarch shaped a composite picture of what Morton refers to as a "defeminized female failure." At the same time these discourses reinforced a "White feminine ideal" that privileged particular expressions of "femaleness" and "femininity" that are echoed in contemporary notions of "feminine leadership." Yet the racial ideology of "Black-women-as-failed-women" allowed for their exploitation, humiliation, and brutalization as laborers alongside men in the slavery-based economy.

It is within this context that black women's strategies for resistance and empowerment are revealed as the seeds of a tradition of leadership. Their resistance and empowerment took shape in both enslaved communities and among their freed sisters of the north. In the context of the southern plantation, direct resistance was often met with brutal punishment from white slaveholders and overseers. Therefore, the more usual course was to find a covert way of resisting the conditions of slavery, and this often took on the character of negotiation.

Recent critical histories of this period document hundreds of instances where black women found ways to remain self-defined and self-determined. They supported and drew strength from their communities and used creativity and resourcefulness to assert their voices as black women and to maintain some control over their own lives. In one remarkable example of initiative, negotiation, and market savvy, enslaved black women of mid-1600 Charles Town (later Charleston, South Carolina) seized control of the town market through selling, buying, and reselling goods. Drawing on their skills as former west African traders, the women negotiated with their slaveholders to take a portion of the money from selling plantation goods to buy other goods and resell them, making a larger profit, paying the slaveholder a stable wage, and keeping the rest of the profits for themselves. Through this practice, frequently challenged (to no avail) by laws and procedures to stop it, some of the women amassed considerable wealth.[9]

In the larger community of enslaved people, black women created important leadership roles as they worked to help preserve the community through education, healthcare, spiritual leadership, and support for the slavery resistance movement. Elderly women were especially revered for their knowledge of the healing arts, and their service as midwives, healers, and spiritual leaders. Some black women supported their communities by covertly challenging the slaveholder's authority. For example, as the persons in charge of food preparation for both whites and their own families, women sometimes clandestinely fed runaways to keep them out of harm's way for as long as possible.[10]

Formerly enslaved women or those born into freed families in the north were able to influence their communities more directly through resourcefulness, entrepreneurship, and oratory. During the nineteenth century, women such as Anna Julia Cooper, Maria Stewart, Mary Ann Shadd Cary, and Sojourner Truth actively promoted black self-determination, especially for black women. Maria Stewart is noted for lecturing publicly to audiences of both black and white women and men. She emphasized self-determination and economic independence for African Americans and "demanded that black women take an active part in business, politics, and education," and that they work to "refute the myths of the [W]hite South that said [B]lack women were ignorant, lazy, and degenerate."[11]

My primary premise is that there are specific themes that are borne out of black women's resistance to the oppression of slavery, themes that are the seeds of a tradition of leadership. The first theme is *self-determination* and *self-definition*. Black women resisted discourses that would define them as "failed women" according to a racially biased ideal, and reconstructed a culture of black womanhood that is grounded in strength, independence, creativity, and resourcefulness. A second theme born of this resistance is *staying connected to and building community*. The women used community work to strengthen family and kinship ties, combat racism, and empower communities to survive, grow, and advance. A final theme relates to finding ways to *develop one's voice* and then *exercising agency*, and *working for social justice*.

These themes are visible throughout African American women's history of labor and community activism, not only during slavery, but also through reconstruction and beyond. One important example is the black women's club movement in which black women across the country, under the motto "Lifting as we climb," formed *thousands* of organizations to promote the welfare of their communities and to fight the widespread poverty, illiteracy, and discrimination.[12] The themes are evident also in the experiences of black women who were the first to enter into the professions, in the practices of black women activists who resisted the oppression of women in the African American church, and in the experiences of black women in the worker resistance movements of the early twentieth century.

The above is part of the reclaimed history of black women in America that, until recently, was not deemed important enough to be recorded. The voices of African American women are excluded from the production of leadership knowledge, because the idea of valuing black women's potential contributions is counterintuitive in a society in which our devaluation is so deeply ingrained in literature, the media, and political discourse. However, within this reclaimed history is a leadership tradition that emerges from black women's unique location in sociohistorical racial politics of the Americas. Moreover, it is quite difficult to envision this tradition as a "feminine" model of leadership, given that the symbolism associated with "feminine" and "masculine" ideals were created through the enactment of racist and sexist ideologies that relied on the exploitation of black women and men. Rather, this is a culturally distinct leadership tradition that took root during the era of slavery, flourished, and is still accessible today.

CIVIL RIGHTS ACTIVIST ELLA BAKER: THE TRADITION EMBODIED

One example of how this tradition was passed down and put into practice is found in the collective leadership approach of civil rights activist Ella Baker. Indeed, countless black women exemplified this kind of collective leadership as they worked mostly behind the scenes in their churches, community centers, and homes, especially during the early years of the civil rights movement. However, I emphasize Ella Baker as a vivid example of African American women's leadership traditions as exemplified in historical accounts of her life and work.[13] A graduate of Shaw University in Raleigh, North Carolina, Baker moved to New York in 1927 and quickly became involved as an activist and organizer. In 1941, she became the National Association for the Advancement of Colored People (NAACP) field secretary and two years later was named director of branches. She was a major force in the development of the Southern Christian Leadership Council (SCLC) and was instrumental in organizing the Student Nonviolent Coordinating Committee (SNCC), from the corps of young people who were staging sit-ins to protest the segregated lunch counters and public facilities across the country. Like other early organizers of the civil rights movement, Baker's understanding of leadership was deeply entrenched in communal and family traditions that she herself traced back to a tradition of resistance during the era of slavery. Over a period of about thirty years, she honed her own understanding of those traditions into an approach to leadership that emphasized the long-term development of leadership in ordinary women and men. It is an approach that I believe crystallizes a tradition of black women's leadership.

Baker enacted a leadership approach that allowed people "to formulate their own questions, to define their own problems, and to find their own solutions."[14] Her style was characterized by direct communication that would not fit easily into traditional notions of "feminine" leadership; neither would her directness fit the characteristic detachment and aggressiveness of masculine models. Rather, Baker's style was one that seemed to flow from her experience of encountering oppression and seeing opportunities for resistance. It is in that space—between encountering problems and finding solutions— that the possibility for leadership happens. This is where developing leaders learn to draw upon resources available to them from culture, experience, and formal training. It is the space in which Ella Baker found her leadership voice in a modern context as she drew upon the traditions that had been passed down to her from her forebears' experiences resisting race and gender oppression.

Her central strategy was that of collective leadership reinforcing the theme of *connecting and building community*. Just as enslaved black women combined an African heritage with American exigencies to create new opportunities, and as nineteenth-century clubwomen sought to unite African American women in the rural and urban communities, Ella Baker enacted a tradition that enabled people across class statuses, races, ages, religions, and ethnicities to identify with each other. She used specific strategies for enacting her collective leadership approach that reinforced traditions of resistance and transformation.

Like her foremothers, Baker emphasized *self-definition* and *self-determination*, but in this new context, they informed specific tactics and processes for leadership development and social change. She not only used mechanisms and created structures that challenged people to speak from their own experiences but also gave them support to implement their ideas. She was relentless in her attack on the rigid centralized decision-making at the national headquarters of the NAACP, recognizing that the challenge of organizing the huge mass base of the national organization—four hundred thousand members by 1944—was in helping local branches identify and act on their local concerns. She advocated creating regional offices of the NAACP so that local leaders would have a source of assistance nearer than New York, and made it possible for small groups of people to maintain effective working relationships among themselves.

Another leadership strategy Baker used was *developing and using voice*—her own and others'. She developed ways to first, invite participation in a collective effort, and second, to work against the intrusions of hierarchy. As Baker put it, "Everyone has a contribution to make. Just as one has to be able to look at a sharecropper and see a potential teacher, one must be able to look at a conservative lawyer and see a potential crusader for justice."[15] Always trying to find ways to surface potential contributions, especially among the youth and the disenfranchised, she held marathon rap sessions, leadership training seminars (some were called, "Give the People the Light, and They Will Come"), and grassroots-oriented conferences as common forums. Baker was responsible for institutionalizing listening at the highly formal annual conferences that brought together members of the organizing effort. She designed a structure so that instead of staff members making speeches, several delegates from local branches were designated to talk out of their branch experiences.

AFRICAN AMERICAN WOMEN'S TRADITIONS OF RESISTANCE AND CHANGE IN CONTEMPORARY CULTURE

I turn now to address several questions that are raised by the notion of a tradition of African American women's leadership, the most fundamental question being, does the tradition continue in more recent times? And if so, in what ways does that tradition contradict, redefine, or expand models of feminine and masculine leadership? Also, how does the tradition find expression in an increasingly fragmented postmodern culture?

In 1997, I completed a leadership study with fifteen African American women senior executives who at the time were in the top ranks of major corporations and government agencies across the United States.[16] Following the established protocol in leadership studies, I conducted life histories with the women, interviewed their coworkers, and observed many of them in interaction as they went about their leadership duties. My study with the executives was intended as a direct response to the kinds of studies that had been done up to that point that focused mostly on white women executives. It was an opportunity to center the experiences of African American women in the current production of knowledge about leadership.

I found that the leadership traditions revealed in the history of black women in America are exemplified in the experiences of the women executives. The women shared personal histories that reinforced an organic view of black culture, providing threads that tied the women's experiences together. In recounting their life histories, the executives emphasized the inner strength and knowledge they gained through the stories, messages, and interpersonal influence from their parents, grand-parents, "othermothers," and members of their extended families and communities. The traditions passed down to them strengthened their identity as black women and influenced their approaches to leadership.

The recurring theme across the women's narratives—whether they were born into working-class or middle- and upper-class families— was "Remember who you are," referring to the history of struggle, survival, and triumph in African American experience. Mirroring the themes of the black clubwomen from the well-to-do families of nineteenth-century Boston, here is how one executive in her early Fifties described the traditions of her family:

> I knew that we were special. I knew that we were different. I knew that we had advantage, but with awareness of whatever this "special-ness" was, came the obligation to do for and to give to and support others,

especially in education. [My family had] strong roots to the church and public activism. My grandfather was a physician. My grandmother on that side, my maternal grandmother, had the distinction of helping to build public support for the first public library for Negroes, as we were then called. . . . I have recollection of [my maternal] grandmother whose back porch was always filled with clothing, clean, folded clothing in sizes that she routinely gave to others. . . . And she was always identifying people, some of whom . . . worked in her restaurant, who needed help. She brought thirteen of her relatives out of that almost plantation-like environment in southwest Virginia, to see them educated as well. So, the family tradition was of leadership and also a great sense of responsibility for the broader community.[17]

Several other executives emphasized their more recent histories of their family's involvement in the civil rights struggle. One executive told the story of how her father courageously confronted the Klan on a dark and deserted road, as she waited for him in their truck with instructions to use if necessary the gun he had left on the seat next to her. She was seven years old at the time.

Another executive shared how her parents instilled in her the courage to confront systems of oppression, even if it meant standing alone:

My parents were always involved and they were always committed to making a difference. I can remember at a very young age my mother and father were involved in the Civil Rights Movement. I always knew my parents were not afraid. They were never afraid of leadership. They were never afraid of taking a difficult stand . . . I think that is what definitely probably developed most of my personality. When I was in the second grade they sent me to a school that at the time was pre-dominantly White and by that I mean there was [*sic*] two Blacks, my next door neighbor and me. It was *way* before [schools were legally integrated] . . . and so they always stepped out ahead and made me do the difficult thing for whatever reason. They had to write letters and had to, you know, they had to go through a bunch of mess, but I mean of course they couldn't keep us out. . . . And I remember . . . telling my mother I don't want to be going to a White school. My mother said, "Don't worry; it's not White it's red brick." And so that kind of helped shape my ideas. You know, in terms of it's okay to stand alone. It's okay to do the difficult thing because, you know, this is life. So that's the leadership thing for me.[18]

Even with the diversity in geographic location and socioeconomic background, there are striking similarities in the ways the executives said they learned leadership. Collectively, these accounts reveal how the women, from very early stages of their life, were encouraged and taught to develop self-confidence, to be independent and resilient, and to remain true to themselves, no matter what the circumstance. These messages and sources of influence served as a powerful force that helped them deal with the racism and sexism they encountered as they advanced in their careers. They also strengthened their capacities to enact leadership with dominant corporate cultures in ways that continue the traditions in black women's history.

Reminiscent of Ella Baker's collective leadership approach in the early civil rights movement, the women enacted a philosophy that brought together diverse interests and viewpoints. However, this philosophy is expressed quite differently within the context of dominant corporate culture. As workforce diversity has increased, organizations are seeing the need for structures and processes that help all of its members—from the boardroom to the shop floor to the service centers—work through politics, contradictions, and preconceived notions as they encounter difference in the workplace. Decades of paying lip service to diversity initiatives has done little to address the underlying conflicts related to racism, sexism, homophobia, classism, and ageism that lie just below the surface of workplace interactions. The purpose of leadership in such a context is to facilitate dialogue and allow members of the organization to see themselves as valued. My research shows that African American women's traditions of leadership and organizing provide a way of envisioning this process.

The women's overall leadership approach can be described as *simultaneously* collaborative *and* control-oriented, defying categorization in both the feminine and the masculine models. Rather than viewing collaboration as an *alternative* to control, where control is defined in terms of traditionally "masculine" values such as distance, detachment, and competition, the women enacted a leadership philosophy where directness and control *are a means for collaboration*. In this sense, control is redefined as personal and interactive. The focus is on the other as a way of assessing points of view and levels of readiness to perform.

This paradoxical co-mingling of control and collaboration was most evident in the way the women's coworkers described their leadership. All of the women were described as being direct communicators, but not in the pejorative sense that is often associated with African American women.[19] Their staff members and peers used words and phrases such as "direct," "straightforward," "shoots it straight," "demanding," "all business" "precise," "focused," and "dynamic" to describe the women's leadership. Also, each of the executives described herself in similar terms such as "to the point," "opinionated," or "focused." However, when asked to elaborate on these words or phrases, the interpretation of directness that emerged was a kind of openness in communication not meant to intimidate, but to negotiate. To the executives and their coworkers, directness is a positive style useful for (a) bringing important issues into the open, (b) making sure voices (including their own) that need to be heard on a certain issue get that opportunity, and (c) having no hidden agendas. In this way, the women's leadership was a kind of conduit through which a diversity of viewpoints can be brought together, negotiated, and enacted.

This view of leadership counters the hegemonic discourses that have suppressed black women's ideas, and it expands traditional views of organizational leadership. By placing black women at the center of analysis, we can begin to see the contours of black women's voices. Behavior deemed as controlling or conflictual in a larger cultural text that devalues African American women is understood here as the capacity for African American women to see the infinite possibilities of individual characteristics through a lens of constructing a solution. The result is a process of leadership that produces what Patricia Hill Collins terms "contextualized truth." Based on Mae Henderson's metaphor of "speaking in tongues," contextualized truth emerges through the interaction of "logic, creativity, and accessibility."[20] Implicit in the process of producing contextualized truth is the willingness and ability to construe knowledge and values from multiple perspectives without loss of commitment to one's own values.

The women emphasized that their positions afforded them opportunities that are specific to them as black women in majority-culture organizations. In keeping with black women's leadership traditions, this included being able to connect in positive ways with members of the black community, both those who work for the organization and those who do not. The women spoke of how important it was to other African Americans, especially other black women, to see them in positions of power in their organizations. One executive told me about a moving experience she had when she was reassigned to the Los Angeles headquarters where there is a large population of African American employees, mostly in their twenties and thirties, who have not had the opportunity to have anyone of color, especially a black woman, in senior management. She spoke at an employee forum consisting of all members of the region, white and black, and made it clear that she was accessible and willing to listen to their needs. In her talk, the executive emphasized that she understood their frustration over trying to tackle problems and never even touching the levels that could really make a difference. Her address was very energetic and involved some call and response engagement with the audience and a question and answer period at the end.

Weeks later, during one of her visits to the regional office, a young African American woman approached the executive in the cafeteria and said that a lot of the African American employees had been talking about the forum and wanted her to know that "we see your light shining. We want you to know that we will be praying for you, because you have taken LA by storm, and we just want you to be successful and we've got your back."[21]

Outside the organization, and in the traditions of their foremothers, many of the women stayed connected to the black community by being active in their churches, sororities, and other community organizations that address black women's issues. Also, several of the women served on boards that allowed them to impact on issues facing the African American community, in sectors such as health, education, and labor.

CONTINUING THE TRADITION?

In this chapter, I have argued that reclaiming and celebrating a tradition of leadership grounded in black women's culture and values is a powerful way to counter discourses that devalue black women as leaders. However, the notion of a tradition based on collective history also raises new questions about women and othering in contemporary culture. In a postmodern world marked by fragmentation and indeterminacy, is it possible to imagine a black women's tradition of leadership that is based on collective group identity and to at the same time resist "othering" processes within the group? In my study of African American women executives, there are at least two reasons to justify why I found such strong evidence of cultural continuity among the women I interviewed. First, there may have been a degree of self-selection among my participants, as they responded to the request of a black woman doing research on black women's leadership. Second, these were all women who came of age during the civil rights era and seemed to be deeply immersed in the black cultural values that I have emphasized throughout this chapter. However, that cultural continuity is not readily apparent in the broader, more complex context of African American women's group identity. Divisions related to economic class, gender, age, geographic region, sexuality, nationality, and other community politics make it difficult to imagine a monolithic expression of African American women's leadership traditions. The challenge is to reclaim the core values of the tradition, as I have attempted to do in my work, and then examine black women's agency in accessing this cultural knowledge to construct individual expressions of self.[22]

The core values of African American women's traditions of leadership borne out of collective struggle and resistance—self-definition, self-determination, remaining connected to and building community, and developing voice and agency through the fight for social justice—provide a touchstone for evaluating contemporary expressions of leadership. The U.S. secretary of state Condoleezza Rice provides one salient example. On the one hand, Rice's image as a black woman serving in one of the most powerful positions in the world creates a counterimage to the spate of derogatory images of black women currently being exported around the world in gangsta rap videos and reality television shows. On the other hand, her image has been reconstructed in the language of stereotypical, Western, white femininity (The French praised her "perfect size six" elegance). At the same time, Rice's support and enactment of the current administration's domestic and foreign policies that disproportionately place economically poor people, African Americans, and other marginalized groups at a disadvantage run counter to the values that form the foundation of African American women's traditions of leadership.

The point is that not all black women have access to or choose to seek expression for black women's leadership traditions. However, as I have argued elsewhere, the values that form the foundation of African American women's traditions of leadership can be and should be accessible not just to black women, but across groups.[23] These values inform a fresh approach to leadership that would accommodate the multiple, often contradictory, viewpoints and paradoxical situational challenges of twenty-first-century society. As exemplified in the life and work of Ella Baker and other contemporary African American women, and counter to the either-or focus of traditional models, it is a process-based model that focuses on *simultaneously* negotiating self-identity and social justice in context.

Perhaps the greatest opportunity for witnessing new expressions of black women's leadership is among young African American women and girls. Current shifts in the economic and social structuring of society present new challenges and opportunities for continuing the traditions in African American women's history. Patterns of deindustrialization, declining labor markets, and continued residential segregation by race fragment the social world of contemporary African

American girls and young women, as well as of other groups.[24] In the current economy, African American girls and young women in working class and poor socioeconomic contexts are among the most vulnerable populations. Those living in impoverished neighborhoods with high crime rates are at risk of low academic achievement, teen pregnancy, drug abuse, and becoming victims of violence.[25]

Even across socioeconomic statuses, the potential of African American girls for success occurs within a complex social, cultural, and political environment that is becoming increasingly difficult for them to navigate.[26] They are contending with racial images created by the press and popular media of African American women as welfare queens, and video divas, juxtaposed with inaccessible images of the "overachieving black lady" and the "ideal White woman."[27] So the question remains open as to how, and in what form, black women's leadership traditions will continue into future generations.

I have recently begun a new project to study leadership development among African American teen girls living in urban and rural neighborhoods in North Carolina.[28] In my preliminary discussions with the young women, I see signs that, in the tradition of their foremothers, young African American women and teen girls are seeking to remain self-defined and express a range of identities as black women. Some of the young women's lives have been touched by drugs and violence, and they are very much aware of the social and economic changes that have ravaged their neighborhoods. They recognize the need for activism to bring about change. For example, Brianna (a pseudonym), a nineteen-year-old high school student I interviewed. During our conversation, Brianna talked with great emotion about her community, Riverton (also a pseudonym). Riverton is a black-majority, low-income, urban neighborhood that has a reputation for crime, drugs, and gang violence. Brianna described what it has been like growing up in Riverton:

> I remember in Riverton we use to have softball and track teams. We used to have everything . . . [W]e don't have that anymore. When I was like 10 or 11 we used to have everything. . . . Every so often we'll have a block party in Riverton; as a matter of fact about a month ago we had a block party in Riverton. But we don't have sports teams anymore. Those boys from Riverton could play some ball, so we were beating everybody. And so now they have gotten older now. They are selling drugs, and they don't care. They got the attitude that "I don't care about nothing." . . . Nobody does nothing until somebody get killed. . . . [A]bout a couple of months ago this boy named Thomas [not his real name] got killed in Riverton. We all knew him or whatever.

The first day they drove by and shot him, he got hit in the arm. He went home. He came out the very next day, standing in the same spot. [Then] he got killed. So, after he got killed they found his body down the street in this lady's yard a couple of houses down from me. The church paid for his funeral because his mama was on drugs and she couldn't really do it. For like a month after that they had prayer marches around the neighborhood, and then they just stopped. It was supposed to be every Saturday, but they just stopped. Me, my brother and my grandma did it too, but they just stopped. But it's like they don't want to act until somebody gets killed, then everybody wants to put their two cents in; not knowing what really happened, they just want to say something about it.[29]

Brianna's story illustrates that there is much to do in reclaiming the values that strengthened our communities in the past, and once again, black women are answering the call to "lift as we climb." There is renewed energy among black women in the professions who are starting community development organizations (CDOs) with holistic programs that create social capital through leadership, community participation, and networking with other organizations, such as churches, cultural institutions, other CDOs, and state legislators.

Also, many working, poor, African American mothers are speaking up as an empowerment strategy that emerges within the intensely raced context of negotiating the borders between home, welfare, the street, and low-wage, often temporary jobs.[30] The women are breaking the silence about race-based discrimination in low-wage jobs and employers' insensitivity to the needs of their children. In the tradition of black women's history of resistance and transformation, young working poor women are creating networks that must cross multiple boundaries, becoming in a sense *border guards*, managing the boundaries between work and family and between home and street, as they try to protect their children from gangs and gang violence rooted in the illicit drug economy. In their roles as border guards, these women employed collective forms of empowerment that included shared resources among families trying to keep their children and homes safe in neighborhoods riddled with violence and drug use.

So, I believe that hope for Brianna and other young girls and women like her lies in a tradition of black women's leadership. After almost quitting school in the ninth grade, Brianna is now a senior in high school, struggling to graduate. When I asked her to describe how she sees her life in the future, she talked in vivid detail about getting married to her boyfriend and having a large house with two huge cars. She also talked about giving back to her community and working to make it better for everyone. However, there is a gap between Brianna's aspirations to enjoy social mobility and her present situation in which the odds are stacked against her on many fronts. For me, this gap is the place where a tradition of African American women's leadership can take hold and flourish. I intend to continue exploring the ways in which the values of resistance and social change through self-definition and self-determination, voice, agency, and community support can find new forms of expression in lives of young black girls and women.

NOTES

1. Sally Helgesen, *The Female Advantage: Women's Ways of Leadership* (New York: Doubleday, 1990); M. Loden, *Feminine Leadership or: How to Succeed in Business Without Being One of the Boys* (New York: Times Books, 1985); J. B. Rosener, "Ways Women Lead," *Harvard Business Review* 68 (1990): 11–12.
2. J. C. Rost, *Leadership for the Twenty-First Century* (Westport, CT: Praeger, 1991).
3. Patricia S. Parker, *Race, Gender, and Leadership: Re-envisioning 21st Century Leadership From the Perspectives of African American Women Executives* (Mahwah, NJ: Erlbaum, 2005), 4–10.
4. I refer to the title of Helgesen's *The Female Advantage*.
5. bell hooks, *Ain't I a Woman: Black Women and Feminism* (Boston: South End Press, 1981); D. K. King, "Multiple Jeopardy, Multiple Consciousness: The Context of a Black Feminist Ideology," *Signs* 14 (1988): 42–72; S. M. Nkomo, "The Emperor Has No Clothes: Rewriting 'Race' in Organizations," *Academy of Management Review* 17 (1992): 487–513; B. Smith, *Home Girls: A Black Feminist Anthology* (New York: Kitchen Table Press, 1988).
6. Henry Mintzberg, *The Nature of Managerial Work* (New York: Harper and Row, 1973); J. Kotter, *The General Managers* (New York: Free Press, 1982).
7. Darlene Hine and Katherine Thompson, *A Shining Thread of Hope: The History of Black Women in America* (New York: Broadway Books, 1998), 5.
8. Barbara Christian, *Black Women Novelists: The Development of a Tradition, 1892–1976* (Westport, CT: Greenwood Press, 1976); Catherine Clinton, *The Plantation Mistress: Woman's World in the Old South* (New York: Pantheon Books, 1982); Patricia Morton, *Disfigured Images: The Historical Assault on Afro-American Women* (New York: Greenwood Press, 1991).
9. Hine and Thompson, *A Shining Thread of Hope*, 93.

10. Jacqueline Jones, *Labor of Love, Labor of Sorrow: Black Women, Work, and the Family From Slavery to the Present* (New York: Basic Books, 1985).

11. Hine and Thompson, *A Shining Thread of Hope*, 107.

12. Jones, *Labor of Love, Labor of Sorrow*, 43.

13. Joanne Grant, *Ella Baker: Freedom Bound* (New York: John Wiley & Sons, 1988); Charles M. Payne, *I've Got The Light of Freedom: The Organizing Tradition and the Mississippi Freedom Struggle* (Berkeley, CA: University of California Press, 1995).

14. Grant, *Ella Baker*, 5.

15. Payne, *I've Got the Light*, 89.

16. Patricia S. Parker, *African American Women Executives within Dominant Culture Organizations: An Examination of Leadership Socialization, Communication Strategies, and Leadership Behavior* (Unpublished doctoral dissertation, Austin: University of Texas, 1997).

17. Ibid., 107.

18. Ibid., 101–102.

19. R. Weitz and L. Gordon, "Images of Black Women among Anglo College Students," *Sex Roles* 28 (1993): 19–34.

20. Patricia Hill Collins, *Fighting Words: Black Women and the Search for Justice* (Minneapolis: University of Minnesota Press, 1998), 30.

21. Parker, *African American Women Executives*, 145–47.

22. My thinking here closely follows that of Collins, in her book *Fighting Words*. Collins calls for more research that investigates how Black women's collective, lived experiences in negotiating the category "Black woman" can serve a purpose in resisting current politics of containment for Black women (1998): 227.

23. Parker, *Race, Gender, and Leadership*, xiv.

24. *Latinas and African American Women at Work: Race, Gender, and Economic Inequality*, ed. I. Browne (New York: Russell Sage Foundation, 1999).

25. R. Arnold, "Black Women in Prison: The Price of Resistance," in M. Baca Zinn and B. Dill (eds.), *Women of Color in U.S. Society* (Philadelphia: Temple University Press, 1994), 171–84.

26. C. C. Holcomb-McCoy, and C. Moore-Thomas, "Empowering African-American Adolescent Females," *Professional School Counseling* 5 (October 2001), 19–27.

27. S. Fordham, "'Those Loud Black Girls': Black Women, Silence, and Gender, 'Passing' in the Academy." *Anthropology and Education Quarterly* 24 (1993): 3–32; Sheila Radford-Hill, "Keepin' It Real: A Generational Commentary on Kimberly Springer's 'Third Wave Black Feminism?'" *Signs: A Journal of Women in Culture and Society* 27 (2002): 1083–90.

28. Patricia S. Parker, "Learning to Lead: The Contemporary Context of Leadership Development and Career Socialization for African American

Female Adolescents in Low-Income Neighborhoods in North Carolina"
(Unpublished essay), Chapel Hill: University of North Carolina, 2005.
29. Parker, "Learning to Lead," 6.
30. Michelle Fine and Lois Weis, *The Unknown City: The Lives of Poor and
Working-Class Young Adults* (Boston: Beacon, 1998).

7

Gender, Race, and Sexuality in the American Christian Right

Andrea Smith

There's no question that white evangelical Protestants, especially in the South, were not only on the sidelines but were on the wrong side of the most central struggle for civil justice of the twentieth century, namely the struggle for civil rights . . . [U]ntil the pro-family, religious conservative movement becomes a truly biracial or multi-racial movement, it will not have moral resonance with the American people, because we were so wrong at that time. I want the Christian Coalition to be a truly rainbow coalition. I want it to be black, brown, yellow, white. I want it to bring Christians of all faith traditions, all denominations, and all races and colors together. I don't think that's going to happen over night. It's going to take years, but we're committed to it.[1]

This quotation by Ralph Reed, then director of the Christian Coalition, marked a growing concern among the Christian Right: race reconciliation.[2] The purpose of race reconciliation, as prominent evangelical Tony Evans puts it, is to "establish a church where everyone of any race or status who walks through the door is loved and respected as part of God's creation and family."[3]

Race reconciliation rose to prominence in the early 1990s with the growth of the Promise Keepers (PK) movement, an evangelical men's organization designed to encourage the participation of men in evangelical churches. When Bill McCartney organized the first PK rally in 1991, he was troubled by the fact that the attendees were all white. Since then, McCartney has made race reconciliation one of the *top* priorities of the PK, and his efforts have met with some success. While in general about 84 percent of the attendees at PK rallies are white, at

the 1996 rally in New York City, one-third to one-half of the attendees were men of color.[4] Typically, about one-third to one-half of
speakers at PK rallies are men of color, and racial themes sound
throughout most, if not all, speeches. The journal *New Man*, which
originally began as a PK publication, also focuses on race reconciliation and prominently features articles by and about men of color—
more so than left-leaning journals such as the *Nation* and the
Progressive. Over a dozen books on race reconciliation were published
in 1996 by evangelical publishers, and Bill Anderson, president of the
Christian Booksellers Association (CBA), directly attributes the
increased visibility of African American authors in CBA stores to the
PK.[5] Men of color are actually part of the group's organizational
structure as well; R. Leslie Jr. looked into the PK's Colorado headquarters and found that its board president is African American and
that 38 percent of its executive staff were men of color. The PK later
intensified its efforts by forming a "reconciliation division" with
national strategic managers for each major racial group.[6]

Evangelical Christian organizations everywhere followed suit and
began jumping onto the race reconciliation bandwagon in the early
1990s. In 1995, the Southern Baptist Convention (SBC) issued an
apology for slavery and racism. The mostly white Pentecostal
Fellowship of North America dissolved and reformed into the
Pentecostal/Charismatic Churches of North America with a 50–50
black-white board.[7] Billy Graham began intensive recruitment of
people of color for his Washington Crusade in 1986, his Atlanta
crusade in 1994, and his Minneapolis crusade in 1996.[8] The NAE in
its 1994 reorganization announced that it would prioritize combating
racism in the church and that it would initiate discussions with the
National Black Evangelical Association to cultivate closer relationships.[9] *Christianity Today* even went so far as to run a cover story
supportive of evangelical black nationalism.[10]

After the initial fervor behind the race reconciliation movement,
the reality of the difficulty in effecting true reconciliation has begun to
set in. Emerson and Smith's study on race relations, *Divided By Race*,
concluded that race reconciliation was largely unsuccessful, a conclusion that proved to be very disturbing to those involved in these
programs. Evangelical magazines began to document the stumbling
blocks faced by Christians interested in evangelicals. For instance, an
op-ed in *Charisma* noted that as of 2003, only 8 percent of employees in large evangelical organizations are not white, and white
evangelicals still do not believe people of color are victims of prejudice.[11]
The SBC became embroiled in controversy when it published a

Vacation Bible School curriculum called "Far Out Far East Rickshaw: Racing to the Son" (2004). Korean American minister Soong-Chan Rah condemned it as perpetuating Asian stereotypes and published a Web site to oppose it: <www.geocities.com/reconsidering-rickshawrally> He gathered 1,100 signatures in support of his cause within a month of publishing the Web site. The response of Lifeway (the Southern Baptist agency that published the curriculum) was to be "offended" by the charges because Lifeway is not racist. Southern Baptist ethicist Ben Mitchell at Trinity International University said that while he did not think it was realistic for Lifeway to withdraw the curriculum, it should apologize. "For many people, it will either confirm their view of Southern Baptists as parochial and culturally naive at best, it will make them suspicious of our commitment to racial justice and ethnic sensitivity."[12] Race reconciliation has proven to be the least popular program within the PK, and the issue of race reconciliation was much less prominent in the rallies of 2004 than in those of 1990s.[13] Nevertheless, race reconciliation efforts continue within evangelical venues.

Gender

Running parallel to the race reconciliation movement, but generally not intersecting with it, has been the evangelical feminist movement. The most prominent evangelical feminist group is Christians for Biblical Equality (CBE), which formed in 1986 as a splinter group from the Evangelical Women's Caucus when EWCI passed a resolution supporting gay/lesbian civil rights. This movement has grown in a context within conservative evangelicalism where there has been an increased effort to tie evangelical orthodoxy to gender hierarchicalism. The SBC amended its Baptist Faith and Message in 1998 to include a statement on male headship:

> A wife is to submit herself graciously to the servant leadership of her husband even as the church willingly submits to the headship of Christ. She, being in the image of God as is her husband thus equal to him, has the God-given responsibility to respect their [sic] husband and to serve as his helper in managing the household and nurturing the next generation.[14]

The Council of Biblical Manhood and Womanhood formed in 1987 to organize against the CBE. It, along with *World Magazine* and James Dobson's Focus on the Family, organized to stop efforts to translate the New International Version (NIV) of the Bible (the version commonly used by evangelical Christians) into gender neutral language. These groups derailed the translation temporarily, but later the translation efforts resumed. CBMW has also conducted campaigns against evangelical churches that support gender equality, such as the famous Willow Creek Church in Barrington, Illinois, which is one of the largest evangelical churches in the country.[15]

However, it is possible that this backlash may not in fact signal the triumph of gender hierarchicalists, but it may testify to the success of the evangelical feminist movement changing gender roles within evangelicalism. Pierre Bourdieu's description of "doxa" may be helpful in this analysis. Bourdieu separates fields of knowledge between doxa and opinion. Doxa is defined as undisputed, unquestioned understandings of the world—that which seems natural. The dominating class secures domination by making the processes of domination seem natural—within the field of doxa. Through crisis, however, Bourdieu argues, the field of doxa can enter the field of opinion—fields of knowledge that are understood as contestable. Once this process of change occurs, agents of reaction can attempt to institute an "orthodoxy" that intends to turn the field of opinion back to the state of doxa. However, it is never entirely able to do so.[16] Thus, we can interpret this backlash as a reassertion of orthodoxy based on gender hierarchy, but the extent to which orthodoxy needs to be reasserted is indicative of how much it has in fact eroded. Thus, what we may be seeing among conservative evangelicals is an increasing mandate to verbally assent to the demands of gender hierarchy while de facto living lives based on the at least partially economically determined need for gender equality. As a result, evangelicalism is marked by contestations between gender complementarians (those who support gender hierarchy in the church and/or the home) and egalitarians (those who support gender equality in the church, home, and society). Even in groups that seem to support complementarianism, important shifts in gender politics are apparent.

For instance, as mentioned previously, the CBMW makes its mission to root out egalitarianism. While its organizing efforts have certainly done much to undermine the work of egalitarians in evangelical communities, the fact that gender hierarchicalists found CBE sufficiently threatening to form a countergroup is significant. In addition, even within its literature we find unacknowledged shifts in terms of gender hierarchy. First, the fact that gender hierarchicalists now feel the need to call themselves "complementarians" instead of "hierarchicalists" indicates that they feel the need to distance themselves from male supremacy. In fact, in one flyer, the CBMW positioned its stance between "the effeminate left" and the "male dominant right." This signals an interesting shift as well, that the CBMW seems to want to distance itself from not only male dominance, but from the right as well. In addition, the Campus Crusade for Christ, which has affiliated itself with the CBMW and supported SBC's statement on male headship, announced a revision of its "Four Spiritual Laws," which now features inclusive language for humanity. Meanwhile, Concerned Women for America, although organized for the express purpose of countering "feminism," increasingly adopts (and co-opts) the history, principles, and issues of feminism, sometimes arguing that its members, and not contemporary feminists, are the women carrying on the true legacy of Susan B. Anthony. Clearly these developments did not occur in a vacuum but are the results of feminist struggles within evangelicalism that have shifted the terms of debate about gender roles.

Contestations in evangelical politics have become particularly pronounced in the rise of the PK movement. PK has perhaps been most severely criticized for its gender politics, particularly by liberal feminist organizations such as the National Organization for Women (NOW) and Fund for a Feminist Majority. Former NOW president and current president of Fund for a Feminist Majority, Eleanor Smeal declared:

> Don't be fooled by their [Promise Keepers'] outward appearances; the Promise Keepers are preaching that men are ordained to lead—women to submit or follow. We have been there, done that. These out-moded attitudes have led time and time again to low pay, low status, and the abuse of women.[17]

Yet the PK's gender politics are much more complex than articulated by its critics because PK is a coalition of "complementarians" and "egalitarians." Contrary to popular opinion, PK has not taken a stand on the issue of complementarianism versus egalitarianism.[18] Probably most of the leaders, such as McCartney, are complementarians.[19] However, a significant number in leadership positions are egalitarians. A prominent egalitarian among PK ranks is Bill Hybels (former board member and spiritual adviser to President Clinton) who heads the very influential Willow Creek church. In my research, I found that not all members of the PK (including PK staff) are in agreement about (1) What PK's position is on gender issues; (2) Where they stand on egalitarianism versus complementarianism; or (3) What defines complementarianism or egalitarianism. However, I have noticed that even while complementarians may vociferously defend their positions, what is considered complementarian sounds increasingly more egalitarian than it did a decade ago. Here was one exchange I had with a PK staff member:

Me: Is PK complementarian or egalitarian?

PK: Definitely complementarian.

Me: What exactly is complementarianism?

PK: That means men must exercise servant leadership in the home.

Me: So that means men have the final say in a marriage if there is an impasse in the decision-making process?

PK: No, they must work things out together. He can't just decide for them both.

Me: Does it mean that women and men have different roles? Perhaps women should be concerned more with the family and the husband with work?

PK: No, they both have the same roles. Women should have the same job opportunities as men.

Me: But men are to be servant leaders? What about women?

PK: They're supposed to be servant leaders too.

Me: So what exactly is the problem with egalitarianism?

PK: Hmmm. Well, I'm not exactly sure what egalitarianism is. Maybe I should find out.

As James Scott puts it: "Only when contradictions are publicly declared do they have to be publicly accounted for."[20] Husbands can let wives be in charge as long "as there is no public challenge to their authority" and so long as they are still given "credit for running things."[21] Evangelicals publicly subscribe to gender hierarchy while increasingly living their lives based on egalitarian principles.

RACE/GENDER

Gender analysis of the Christian Right has tended to exclude analysis of race; similarly, race analysis of the Christian Right has excluded analysis of gender.[22] For instance, Marie Griffith describes evangelical women's organizing as completely distinct from racial dynamics: "Cutting across distinctions of social class, race, ethnicity, and region, this is a culture representing thousands of American women who call themselves 'born again' or spirit-filled Christians."[23] Meanwhile, Michael Emerson and Christian Smith's book on race reconciliation in evangelical communities notes that men are much more likely than women to be familiar with or involved in race reconciliation efforts, but the book fails to theorize the importance of gender in shaping race relations within evangelicalism.[24] By contrast, this chapter suggests that race and gender are inextricably linked in Christian Right discourse in that both race reconciliation efforts and women's organizing habitually target women of color as scapegoats for social, religious, and political problems. Throughout this chapter, I will explore how the Bible interfaces with gender politics in the Christian Right.

Methodology

I base my research on Christian Right literature as well as on my attendance at national Christian Right events in order to ascertain how these ideas are being articulated, debated, and contested on a national basis. My methodology includes an exhaustive survey of conservative articles drawn from the Christian Periodical Index that are pertinent to understanding race reconciliation. I have surveyed all issues of *Christianity Today, World Magazine,* and *Charisma* (evangelical magazines that provide national surveys of issues particular to neoevangelicals, the conservative Christian Right, and charismatics, respectively) since 1991 (around the time race reconciliation appeared on the evangelical landscape). This survey was supplemented with a survey of periodicals published through the Christian Coalition, Concerned Women of America (CWA), and the PK, and with a survey of recent books by conservative Christians on race reconciliation and related issues.[25] In addition, I attend numerous national and local conferences organized by PK, the Christian Coalition, CBE, Concerned Women for America, Wiconi International, and the National Association of Evangelicals (NAE). This material is supplemented by data from thirty informal interviews conducted among those involved in the PK (while I staffed the PK project for the National Council of Churches in 1997).

The Gendering of Racial Politics

Race reconciliation efforts that mark the PK in particular are also fraught with gender politics. It is thus important to analyze how it is that race reconciliation efforts often reinscribe racism through sexism. Many black conservative evangelicals blame the "welfare queen" for the demise of the black family[26] and hold black female-led households, not a racist criminal injustice system, responsible for the large numbers of black men in prison.[27] Rodney Cooper argues that feminism, not racism or capitalism, is "the greatest enemy of black progress in America" because it encourages black women to rob black men of their jobs and their manhood.[28] *World Magazine* contends that the Moynihan report, which blamed female-dominated households for social decay in African American communities, was visionary: "A community that allows a large number of men to grow up in broken families, dominated by women, never acquiring any stable relationship to male authority, that community asks for and gets chaos."[29] The problem of poverty, according to *World Magazine*, has nothing to do with economic structures. Rather, poverty and family problems "all stem from a lack of marriage."[30] Similarly, according to the Urban Family Council's Chester Fatherhood Initiative: "When you get good, committed fathers in their homes, their daughters aren't going to be going out getting abortions, and their sons aren't going to be doing drugs and getting arrested."[31] In an opinion piece in *Christianity Today*, Stephen Carter critiques both the Democratic and Republican parties for inadequately addressing institutional racism post 9/11. However, his solution is an individual one that again targets women of color as the problem. "The sparkling world *Brown* hoped to build is yet in our grasp. But we will have to build it as individuals, with the small decisions of everyday life, rather than through bigger and better government programs. The nation is full of fatherless children to mentor, collapsed families to support, crumbling schools to visit-and human hearts to touch."[32]

Similarly, prominent African American Christian Right activist Star Parker positions herself as a former welfare recipient who is thus entitled to denounce current welfare recipients. At the 1996 Christian Coalition conference, Parker, who seemed not to know that whites have been the major recipients of welfare payments since the program's inception, claimed that if welfare is allowed to continue, whites will soon find themselves in the same degraded state as black people. Star Parker is one of the cheery proponents of the view that black people are on welfare because they live "raunchy lifestyles" and are "lazy." She goes so far as to claim that racism and economic discrimination bear no causal relationship *at all* to the perpetuation of black poverty. "Take a job, any job," she advises, "no matter how low-paying or demeaning," and considers it a character defect to refuse even the most exploitative work. (Parker also advocates exempting small businesses from the minimum-wage requirement,[33] although she never explains how subminimum-wage jobs can lift a person out of poverty.) Parker offers herself as the exemplar of up-by-your-bootstraps success: "I've been working for real welfare reform for years, and I know what

I'm talking about. After all, as a single mother I was once on welfare . . . My success came as a result of self-determination and support from my church and community. And that's the message I want to get out."[34]

Conservative articles on poverty, "illicit sex and drugs," and urban unrest always locate these "vices" in, and identify them with, African American or people of color communities.[35] CWA's *Family Voice* article "Is the Church Ready for Welfare Reform?" offers a portrait of black dependence and white patronage. In the pictures that accompany the article, welfare recipients are all black and their benefactors are all white. One fairly typical story describes a church minister who requires of the people who come to him for aid that they perform some manual labor and be a member of a home church. The minister is surprised that many "ungrateful" people balk at these requirements; nobody takes up the other side of the story—that the minister is taking advantage of the poor by paying them subminimum wages and compelling religious affiliation by threatening to withhold meager assistance.[36] Christian Right ideologies trace the roots of poverty among people of color to their "welfare mentality" and ignore the effects of corporate downsizing and the relocation of jobs to the Third World. So, the reasoning goes, if there are no structural reasons for poverty—and you would not see any if you keep your eyes really tightly shut—then poverty must be the fault of the poor. As Gary North states, there is a "right relationship between wickedness and poverty"[37]—which de facto means, between wickedness and skin color. The face of this "wickedness," in turn, is gendered in the figure of the welfare queen who refuses to live under the auspices of male headship.

The woman-blaming narrative in evangelical racial discourse is evident in Bishop T.D. Jakes's men's movement, Manpower, which appeals primarily to African Americans. He held a three-day conference for prison inmates in 1999 (inmates could participate by satellite and cable television). This conference featured a play called "Woman, Thou Art Loosed!" Once again, a woman contributes to the downfall of her children. The mother in the play refuses to have her live-in boyfriend arrested for abusing her daughter, and the daughter then grows up into a vicious cycle of hatred, violence, and promiscuity. The reason given for blaming the mother rather than the abusive live-in boyfriend for the daughter's problems is that "the one thing we didn't want to do in this play is male-bash."[38] The logical conclusion of this line of thinking is that only black men can be the victims of racism and not black women, who are, after all, part of the problem. Thus, a Christian Right favorite such as Clarence Thomas is allowed to be a victim of racism while Anita Hill is not.[39]

Conservative religious organizations also rely on gender hierarchies to win over men of color. They divide people of color against each other by offering men a chance to take control of a fragment of their lives at the expense of their wives, girlfriends, sisters, daughters, and other relatives. For instance, as I have argued in my previous work, many Native American men explain their conversion from radical American Indian Movement–like politics to Christianity in terms of rejecting male-dominated confrontations for a more feminine community based on love and relationship.[40] However, in doing so, they become associated with a religion that is often viewed as feminized, given that the majority of Christian parishioners are women. Hence it becomes necessary to assert a "muscular" Christianity that will enable men to bond with others in a community that stresses relationships without being deemed effeminate. Such a strategy has a long history in evangelicalism, such as the "muscular Christianity" and "Men and Religion Forward" movements at the beginning of the nineteenth century.[41] Such movements attempt to create a hypermasculine place that allows men to be Christian and manly. However, both in the nineteenth centuries and today, these movements have actually failed to change the demographics of church membership significantly. According to prominent evangelical pollster George Barna, despite the popularity of the PK movements in the 1990s, church membership of men actually *dropped*.[42] PK efforts to reach unsaved men by not charging for admissions failed to attract new constituents.[43] The organization downsized from a staff of 400 and a budget of $117 million to 96 workers and a $30 million budget.[44]

The PK tells its recruits that the black church has become "feminized," and that men of all colors need to assert their headship at home and in church.[45] The Nation of Islam, it avers, appeals to black male youth because it is more masculine than the "too female," too "male unfriendly" Christian church.[46] The PK hopes to provide a Christian alternative to the Nation of Islam; women are asked not to participate in PK events except as volunteer labor.[47] Latinos, too, apparently suffer from a "feminized" Church—the Catholic Church, which "worships Mary as a holy mother."[48] Latino men complain that Latinas, like black women, have much too much authority in the home. In Latin America, so-called female religious hegemony is thought to have "turned men into groveling worms who believe they are weak, incompetent, and loaded down with sin."[49]

Kimberle Crenshaw critiques the narrow definitions of racism that exclude the experiences of women of color: We must

> understand the need for—and summon—the courage to challenge groups that are after all, in one sense, "home" to us, in the name of the parts of us that are not made at home. . . . The most one could expect is that we will dare to speak against internal exclusions and marginalizations, that we might call attention to how the identity of "the group" has been centered on the intersectional identities of a few.[50]

Sexist and classist definitions of race not only exclude people of color who are poor or female, but ultimately serve to undermine the liberation of those who are male and middle-class as well. That is, femaleness and poverty are the boundaries of the liberation struggle for middle-class men of color; those who are regarded as too "extreme" risk being branded as "low-class" or "henpecked." In addition, the manner in which Christian Right discourse urges people of color to spout the most sexist or classist remarks promotes the idea that communities of color are in general politically unsophisticated. For example, as previously mentioned, the PK, despite its reputation as the promoter of women's subordination, actually has no official stance on male headship in the church or the family.[51] Speakers at PK rallies generally avoid making overtly sexist remarks; the exception seems to be black men. At the 1996 New York rally, Wellington Boone was the only speaker who explicitly espoused gender hierarchicalism (and he made it sound like a gift). When critics of PK want to highlight its sexism, they invariably quote African American Tony Evans,[52] who advises men to

> sit down with your wife and say something like this: "Honey, I've made a terrible mistake. I've given you my role. I gave up leading the family, and I forced you to take my place. Now I must reclaim that role." . . . I'm not suggesting that you *ask* for your role back, I'm urging you to *take it back* . . . there can be no compromise here. If you're going to lead, you must lead . . . Treat the lady gently and lovingly. But *lead!*[53]

In her speech at the American Academy of Religion, CBE'er Mary Stewart Van Leeuwen complained that men who make such statements should be disciplined by the PK. As these men are primarily black, the complaint suggests that black men are more of a problem than white men are, and that (white) women must be protected from them. In a society where media saturation of the Clarence Thomas, Mike Tyson, and O.J. Simpson stories has put a black face upon sexual harassment, battering, and rape, this promotion by the Christian Right of men of color as the vanguards of friendly patriarchy undermines community wholeness and preservation.

One almost never encounters literature on race reconciliation written by women, or even men, linking issues of race and gender. (One important exception was Don Argue's statement that the NAE needed to strive for race *and* gender inclusivity at its 1995 convention.[54]) As J. Lee Grady notes, the Pentecostal and Charismatic Churches of North America (PCCNA), which so vigorously "tackled the issue of racism in 1994, are more reluctant to deal with sexism."[55] Perhaps one reason for this reluctance is the understanding among evangelicals that "most commitments to Christ are made before the age of 18."[56] Since women play such a formative role in children's lives, it is important that they thoroughly internalize the hierarchy of gender roles in order to pass it down to their children. In addition, conservative Christian literatures stress the importance of ensuring that "non-Western" people do not fall under non-Christian (and hence non-Western) religions—particularly Islam.[57] The results, however, of Christianizing the world is that "whites comprise only about 40 percent of all Christians, and . . . the center of Christianity . . . has shifted to the Southern World, to Asia, Africa and Latin America . . . the third millennium will be shaped largely by the Southern Church."[58] As one ad for Christian Aid Mission suggests, we must now embark upon a neocolonial mission work in which indigenous missionaries can reach "hidden peoples" who can penetrate "the most difficult barriers of all—political, cultural, religious, language and locale" and travel "behind doors closed to North Americans."[59] Evangelical mission journals claim that one-fourth of cross-cultural mission work is done by people from non-Western countries.[60] This growth of non-European Christians threatens to fundamentally reshape the character of Christianity itself. Threatened by these possible shifts, evangelicals argue that it is imperative that Western missionaries train indigenous missionaries; otherwise, they leave open "the doors to syncretism, cults, and false teaching."[61] This perceived threat may explain the huge controversy over Chung Hyun-Kyung's presentation at the World Council of Churches (WCC) in 1991, where she was charged with exhibiting "a tendency toward syncretism with non-Christian churches."[62] It may also partially explain why 92 percent of all foreign missionaries work in heavily Christianized populations in predominately Christian lands.[63] Race reconciliation and indigenization of mission work are critical if the Christian Right is going to maintain its hegemony over the public meanings of Christianity. If it is not successful in its reconciliation efforts to unite with people of color in the United States and abroad, the majority of Christians in the world, who are not white, may redefine Christianity in a manner that is unacceptable to the Christian Right. It is thus particularly important that women of color accept their subordinate role if white Christian hegemony is to be maintained.

The Racialization of Gender Politics

At the same time that gender informs the race reconciliation movement, race also informs women's organizing in the Christian Right. Most analysts of right-wing women's organizations frame it as a reaction to the feminist movement. The primary question becomes, why do women seem to want to be complicit in their own oppression? In looking at groups such as Concerned Women for America, however, it is clear that a simple gender analysis does not explain the logic of this organizing. I would argue that, perhaps even more than antifeminism, this organizing is fundamentally based on white supremacy.

It is perhaps not a coincidence that evangelical women's groups do not stress race reconciliation because their targets of attack are racialized. As many scholars have noted, these groups focus on the maintenance of the good, Christian family that is the bulwark of society. However, what is the inverse image of this family? that is the kind of family these groups oppose, a kind that is seen as undermining society and the church? It is the welfare mother. It is the women of color who head day care programs. It is the single teenage mother. All of these figures are racialized within this discourse. One example is CWA's statement that describes single-mother families as the source of most social ills, from rape and murder to economic recession. Framing this discussion is the story of Clarence Thomas forced to raise his nephew who does not have a father in his home. The main social ills he has had to overcome are not racism or classism, but negligent black women. This narrative of Thomas's history is framed within a larger narrative of Thomas's supposed revictimization at the hands of another black woman—Anita Hill.[64]

As a variety of scholars have noted, one of the ways white women have been able to assert power and agency for themselves is through missionary work among indigenous peoples, people of color, prisoners, women in the third world, and in other such less-privileged locations.[65] Through these colonial relations in which white women assert their power over women from marginalized communities, white women strive for some power within a patriarchal society. Similarly, it is not a surprise that many CWA'ers find feminist analysis that they are victims or powerless uncompelling because these women exercise a tremendous amount of power and political clout. These women know the power brokers in the state legislatures, demonstrate tremendous political savvy, and have considerable influence in the political landscape of the country. The areas of political influence most open to them, however, revolve around opposing the political influence of other women, particularly women of color and poor women. In listening to women talk about their political and social commitments, it seems as though what concerns them most about feminism is that they are afraid that if they assert their political power, they will not be able to have relationships with men because men will be afraid of them. Thus, by subscribing to male headship, they attempt to carve out a space for themselves where they can have both things—marriage and political influence. As Linda Kintz argues:

> Describing women as inherently nurturing will, however, paradoxically legitimate their protective aggressiveness. That aggressiveness can then be seen not as abnormal for women, as in the manly aggressiveness of feminists, but as womanly, because it is now natural aggression or agency in defense of their children.[66]

In exchange for gender subordination to their husbands, they gain political power primarily over women of color. Thus, just as the Christian Right effects racial solidarity between men based on gender subordination, it simultaneously effects gender solidarity among whites based on colonialism and white supremacy.

One woman's explanation for why she supports male headship illustrates this relationship:

> In America, we get it really good as women. I can't believe that women sit around and cry about it. There are so many places that women are still considered about as good as a dog. . . . One time it really hit me was when I went on one ministry tour with my husband to Egypt. Women had to walk around with scarves over their faces. . . . They were like nonpeople. . . . Here, women can do anything they want.[67]

Dianne Knippers complains that antiviolence activism among liberal feminists and liberation theologians at the December 1998 WCC Assembly in Harare, Zimbabwe

> demeans and diminishes the plight of women who truly suffer the worst kinds of physical abuse. . . . It disgusted me to see women who enjoy

Western privileges and comforts claim a victim status along with women who suffer far more terrible abuses. Also there was no mention of the most serious abuses against women today—female genital mutilation in parts of Africa, bridal dowry burnings in Indian, or the enslavement of girls in Sudan. Of course, these are problems whose sources lie mainly outside the Christian faith. But, by ignoring these problems, the WCC festival created the impression that the Church is the major source of violence against women and that Christian teaching needs to be radically changed to address this problem. A more honest look at the world would produce a different conclusion–that biblical faith, in spite of its imperfect implementation, has been a force of protection and elevation of women in human history.[68]

Although locked in battles against feminism within the U.S. context, evangelicals often rely on feminist rhetoric to argue that Christianity can end the oppression of women in Arab and Muslim countries. This strategy was similar to that of the Bush administration who used feminist rhetoric to justify the invasions of Afghanistan and Iraq. As he stated in a *Charisma* interview: "We are dealing with extreme, radical people who have a deep desire to spread an ideology that is anti-women, anti-free thought, and anti-art and science."[69] Consequently, evangelical literature is replete with narratives of oppressed, veiled Muslim women who become "liberated" by converting to Christainity.[70] Elizabeth Farrell in her "exposé" on Christian women married to Muslim men, describes how women marrying Muslim men invariably seem to find themselves "trapped in a nightmare of oppression, abuse, and control."[71] In fact, an entire ministry, Zennah Ministries, was developed by W.L. Cati to reach out to women married to Muslims. Although she contends that she "is not bashing Muslims," Farrell argues that Muslim men are all wife batterers.[72] "You might be surprised by what some Muslims believe about wife-beating and male superiority," she states, ignoring the multitude of passages in the Christian Bible that also support male dominance, that command single women to marry their rapists, and that seem to condone the rape and sexual mutilation of women.[73] A highlight of the 2001 Global Celebration for Women, designed to be the evangelical counterpart of the Beijing Conference on Women, were tales from white Christian missionaries telling of their success in "liberating" Muslim women from the veil by teaching them how to apply makeup!

On the flip side of the Arab woman who needs saving is the Arab woman whose veil hides her terrorist activity. This ideology was also explicit within the 2003 Interfaith Alliance on Zionism held in Washington DC (May 17–18). There, Helen Freedman from Americans for a Safe Israel declared that there will be peace in Israel only when Arabs begin to love their children as much as they hate us. But she said Arabs are simply incapable of loving their children. Charles Jacob, who promotes Zionism on college campuses through the Davis Project, offered the following Power Point presentation to explain the difference between Israeli Jews and "Arabs/Palestinians."

Israel	Arab/Palestine
Teach kids songs of peace	Teach kids songs of hate (Sesame Street is about being a suicide bomber)
Every effort to prevent civilian death	Kill lots of civilizations
Anguish when civilians are hurt	Dancing when atrocities happen
Mothers do not want kids to fight	Mothers celebrate fighting

He thus summed up his presentation: I grieve for Palestinian people who have leaders who succumbed to evil and have fallen prey to evil because of their "perceived sense of oppression." They are filling their children with hate and death.

Another such example is a *World Magazine* article on a Palestinian woman who reportedly killed her daughter because she had been gang raped by two of her brothers and pregnancy ensued. According to *World Magazine*, this story shows we can dismiss complaints that U.S. evangelicals are supporting Western imperialist efforts by supporting Israel. Instead, Muslims "need the true light that alone brings peace," which is Christianity.[74] Thus, within conservative evangelical rhetoric, it is the woman of color who continues to inhabit the space of liminality in evangelical discourse about race and gender—she represents the threat of effeminacy for Christian men of color; she is the racialized bad mother who destroys her children, and against her white women must organize.

RACE AND SEXUALITY

Also important in the relationship between race and sexuality is the Christian Right attack on gay rights as "special rights." In this language, it is argued that people of color are a special group that needs special attention, unlike gays who are homosexual "by choice" and hence do not deserve special protection. The strategy is to divide gay rights struggles from racial justice struggles.[75] However, such groups often contradict themselves. For instance, the Traditional Values

Coalition argues that it is ludicrous to consider gays to be in the same category as people of color for receiving protection of hate crime legislation—but then goes on to oppose hate crime legislation wholesale.[76] Many African American evangelical leaders mobilized against same-sex marriage, particularly during the 2004 presidential elections. Pentecostal Paul Morton and Fred Price were among a group of African American ministers who denounced the Massachusetts move to legalize same-sex marriage. They criticized the push to liken gay rights to civil rights and called on the Congressional black Caucus to oppose civil unions.[77] In fact, not only has the rhetoric of the Christian Right rejected any comparison between the black civil rights and gay civil rights movements, but Matt Daniels of Alliance for Marriage, who crafted the Federal Marriage Amendment, likens the *anti*gay movement to the civil rights movement. "As with civil rights . . . traditional marriage will prevail."[78] Similarly, Alan Chambers cites Martin Luther King to support his antigay position in *Charisma*: "The church is neither the master of the state nor the servant of the state, but rather the conscience of the state."[79]

Thus, the discourse around sexuality is also racialized. For instance, *World Magazine* contended that black people are "almost uniformly opposed to homosexual marriage"[80] The AME voted unanimously in its national convention not to allow pastors to perform same-sex marriage. According to *World Magazine*, the reason is that the plight of African American communities is the result of deviant sexuality.

> One might say that black Americans are suffering the consequences of the sexual revolution. The whole culture has drifted away from sexual morality, and African-Americans have been paying the highest price, in the troubled children, the crime, and the poverty that accompany communities that do without marriage . . . The civil-rights movement of the 1960s was moral. The gay-rights movement is not. It's that simple.[81]

Similarly, the Alliance for Marriage positions itself as the defender of African American communities. Its motto: "more children raised at home with a mother and a father."[82] Taking this racialization of sexuality to the extreme, Charles Colson opined that same-sex marriage actually contributes to terrorism and is responsible for the prison scandals in Iraq. Apparently, same-sex marriage contributes to gender confusion, which, in turn, contributes to women abusing prisoners in Abu Ghraib. This abuse then contributes to more terrorist activity. Not passing the Federal Marriage Amendment "is like handing moral weapons of mass destruction to those who use America's decadence to recruit more snipers and hijackers and suicide bombers."[83] We must preserve traditional marriage in order to "protect the United States from those who would use our depravity to destroy us."[84]

WHAT IS TO BE DONE?

The gender and racial politics of the Christian Right do not always target women of color, however. One example of where Christian organizing supports women of color politics is its consistent critique of racist population-control policies sponsored by the U.S. government.[85] While supposedly "feminist" pro-choice activists and organizations have been known to promote contraceptives of dubious safety among women of color[86] and have often failed to criticize even the most blatant forms of contraceptive abuse, such as Quinacrine, CWA and other evangelical groups have denounced these practices for their racist nature. Thus, as I have argued elsewhere,[87] Christian Right groups cannot always be neatly lined up with the interests of white supremacy (and conversely, progressive groups are not always allies in struggles for racial justice).

Consequently, it is important to look at women of color organizations that critique organizing projects that lack an intersectional race/gender perspective on both the Right and the Left. The area of reproductive rights is an example where both the Right and the Left consistently marginalize women of color in their organizing practices and frameworks. From the point of view of progressive politics, there is the tendency of reproductive rights advocates to make simplistic analyses of who our political friends and enemies are in the area of reproductive rights. That is, all those who call themselves "pro-choice" are our political allies while all those who call themselves pro-life are our political enemies. As a result, we often lose opportunities to work with people with whom we may have sharp disagreements, but who may, with different political framings and organizing strategies, shift their positions.

To illustrate: Planned Parenthood is often championed as an organization that supports women's rights to choose with whom women of color should ally. Yet, as I have argued elsewhere, its roots are in the eugencist movement, and today it is heavily invested in the population establishment. It continues to support population control policies in the third world, it almost supported the development of Quinacrine in the United States, and it opposed strengthening sterilization regulations that would protect women of color.[88]

Meanwhile, the North Baton Rouge Women's Help Center in Louisiana is a crisis pregnancy center that articulates its pro-life position from an antiracist perspective. It argues that Planned Parenthood has advocated population control, particularly in communities of color. It critiques the black Church Initiative for the Religious Coalition for Reproductive Choice for contending that charges of racism against Sanger are "scare tactics."[89] It also attempts to provide its services from a holistic perspective—it provides educational and vocational training, GED (General Educational Development) classes, literacy programs, primary health care and pregnancy services, and child placement services. Their position: "We cannot encourage women to have babies and then continue their dependency on the system. We can't leave them without the resources to care for their children and then say, 'Praise the Lord, we saved a baby.'"[90]

Now, it would seem that while both groups support some positions that are beneficial to women of color, they both equally support positions that are detrimental to women of color. So, if we are truly committed to reproductive justice, why should one presume that we should necessarily work with Planned Parenthood and reject the Women's Help Center? Why would we not instead distance ourselves from both of these approaches and work independently to shift both of their positions to a stance that is truly liberatory for all women? Indeed, many women of color organizing projects such as Sista II Sista (New York), Communities Against Rape and Abuse (Seattle), Sisters in Action for Power (Portland), Incite! Women of Color Against Violence (national), and Sistersong (national) are organizing outside male-dominated discourses on race and white-dominated discourses on gender. Incite! and Communities Against Rape and Abuse in particular have articulated a women of color-centered reproductive justice platform that does not ally itself with either pro-choice or pro-life platforms. The work of such groups provides a critical role in counteracting groups that use sexism to promote racism and use racism to promote sexism.

NOTES

1. Quoted in William Martin, *With God on Our Side* (New York: Pantheon Books, 1996), 365–66.
2. There are many definitions of the Christian Right in circulation. For purposes of this paper, I define the Christian right as evangelical Christians who tend toward conservative politics (although they may disagree about the extent to which they think they should engage in politics). By "evangelical," I refer primarily to Protestants who generally subscribe to the five fundamentals of faith that have served as rallying points for evangelicalism: Biblical inerrancy; deity of Christ; substitutionary atonement;

bodily resurrection; and the second coming of Christ. This definition is inclusive of Pentecostals and those groups that do not trace their roots to the fundamentalist/modernist debates of the 1920s. I am not including the more explicitly racist Christian movements, such as Christian identity groups. See Ronald Nash, *Evangelicals in America* (Nashville: Abingdon, 1987); Edward Dobson, "Standing Together on Absolutes." *United Evangelical Action* 44 (September–October 1985): 4–10; William Trollinger "How Should Evangelicals Understand Fundamentalism?" *United Evangelical Action* 44 (September–October 1985): 7–9; Donald Dayton, *The Variety of American Evangelicalism* (Knoxville: University of Tennessee Press, 1991); Joel Carpenter, *Revive Us Again* (Oxford: Oxford University Press, 1997); Harold Ockenga, "From Fundamentalism: Through New Evangelicalism to Evangelicalism," in *Evangelical Roots*, ed. K. Kantzer (Nashville: Thomas Nelson Publishing Company, 1968). In addition, I use the term "Christian Right" loosely, understanding that many evangelicals support conservative politics while not necessarily identifying with the label "Christian Right." James Guth, "Southern Baptist Clergy: Vanguard of the Christian Right? " in *The New Christian Right*, ed. R. Liebman and R. Wuthnow (New York: Aldine, 1983); Christian Smith, *Christian America?* (Berkeley: University of California Press, 2000); Robert Zwier, *Born-Again Politics* (Downer's Grove: InterVarsity Press, 1982). The reason such a loose definition is appropriate for this study is that I am demarcating people who take part in a shared community of discourse about politics and religion even if they disagree about whether or not to term themselves members of the "Christian Right."

3. Tony Evans, *America's Only Hope* (Chicago: Moody Press, 1990).

4. Sheldon King, "We Must Come Together," *New Man* 4 (January–February 1997): 24.

5. Steve Rabey, "Where Is the Christian Men's Movement Headed?" *Christianity Today* 40 (April 29, 1996): 46–49, 60.

6. Ted Olsen, "Racial Reconciliation Emphasis Intensified," *Christianity Today* 41 (January 6, 1997): 67.

7. Stephen Strang, "Unity of Purpose," *Charisma* 20 (January 1995): 110.

8. Beth Spring, "Billy Graham's Washington Crusade Gains the Support of Black Church Leaders," *Christianity Today* 30 (June 13, 1986): 10–11; John W. Kennedy, "Deeper than a Handshake," *Christianity Today* 38 (December 12, 1994): 62–63; Ted Olsen, "Lutheran, Catholic, and Black Churches Join Graham Effort," *Christianity Today* 40 (July 15, 1996): 67.

9. Timothy Morgan, "NAE Reinvents Itself," *Christianity Today* 38 (April 4, 1994): 87.

10. Wendy Zoba, "Separate and Equal," *Christianity Today* 40 (February 6, 1996): 14–24.

11. David Aikman, "Racial Reconciliation," *Charisma* 29 (November 2003): 94.

12. Ken Walker, "Vacation Bible School Wars," *Christianity Today* 48 (March 2004): 26.

13. Michael Emerson and Christian Smith, *Divided by Faith* (Oxford: Oxford University Press, 2000).

14. Richard Land, "Questioning Biblical Submission," *Light* 6 (November–December 1999): 2–3.

15. Lauren Winner, "The Man behind the Megachurch," *Christianity Today* 44 (November 13, 2000): 56–60.

16. Pierre Bourdieu, *Outline of a Theory of Practice*, trans. Richard Nice (Cambridge: Cambridge University Press, 1998).

17. Eleanor Smeal, "Promise Keepers Hold No Promise for Women," (Washington, DC: Fund for Feminist Majority, 1997).

18. Mary Stewart Van Leeuwen, "Servanthood or Soft Patriarchy? A Christian Feminist Looks at the Promise Keepers Movement," *Priscilla Papers* 11 (Spring): 28–39.

19. Chuck Colson McCartney, Joseph Stowell, and Tony Evans (all prominent PK speakers) took out a page affirming the SBC's 1998 amendment to its faith and message that affirmed male headship. Land, "Questioning Biblical Submission," 2–3.

20. James Scott, *Domination and the Arts of Resistance* (New Haven: Yale University Press, 1990).

21. Scott, *Domination and the Arts of Resistance*. Similarly, Brenda Brasher contends that this gender flexibility is what allows gender insubordination to remain in place. "To the extent that male pastors are pressed by female congregants to address particular issues rather than redistribute authority in a nonsexist manner pastors are able to maintain an image of being responsive to women's concerns, thereby destabilizing women's impetus toward change and retaining congregational authority as a prerogative of males." Brenda Brasher, *Godly Women: Fundamentalism and Female Power* (New Brunswick: Rutgers University Press., 1998).

22. For an important exception, see Linda Kintz's *Between Jesus and the Market* (Durham: Duke University Press, 1997). She looks in depth at Christian Right female activists and how their doctrines of female submission promise security for white middle-class women from the destabilization caused by urbanization and multiculturalism. Linda Klintz, *Between Jesus and the Market* (Durham: Duke University Press, 1997).

23. C. Marie Griffith, *God's Daughters: Evangelical Women and the Power of Submission* (Berkeley: University of California Press, 1997).

24. Emerson and Smith, *Divided by Faith*.

25. As Sara Diamond points out, the frequent appearance of a topic in a community's periodical literature does not necessarily reflect that community's priorities. Periodical content depends on many other factors—for example, editors' and writers' particular preferences.

Nevertheless, this literature is very widely read by conservative Christians. So, while a prevalence of articles on a particular topic may not always reflect the interests of those at the grassroots, it certainly plays a role in determining the future shape of those interests. Sara Diamond, *Roads to Dominion* (New York: Guilford Press, 1995).

26. Jefferson Edwards, *Purging Racism from Christianity* (Grand Rapids: Zondervan, 1996).

27. Joe Maxwell, "Getting Out, Staying Out," *Christianity Today* 38 (July 22, 1991): 36.

28. Rodney Cooper, *We Stand Together* (Chicago: Moody Press, 1995).

29. "Black Family Betrayed," *Focus on the Family Citizen* 15 (February 2001): 24.

30. Ibid.

31. Rich Jefferson, "The War for Reparations," *Focus on the Family Citizen* 15 (February 2001): 25.

32. Stephen Carter, "Hope Deferred," *Christianity Today* 48 (July 2004): 64.

33. Christian Coalition Road to Victory Conference, 1996.

34. Star Parker, *Fundraising Letter for Coalition on Urban Affairs* (Los Angeles, CA: October 4, 1996).

35. See Ronald Nash, *Why the Left Is Not Right* (Grand Rapids: Zondervan, 1996); "Denominational Leaders Address Drug Crisis," *Christianity Today* 34 (November 19, 1990): 58–59; Maxwell, "Getting Out, Staying Out"; Brian Bird, "Christians Who Grow Coca," *Christianity Today* 33 (September 8, 1989): 40–43; Bob Lutpon, "How to Create a Ghetto," *World Vision* (October–November 1989), 11; Randy Frame, "Helping the Poor Help Themselves," *Christianity Today* 41 (February 3, 1997): 70–73; Amy Sherman, "STEP-ing Out on Faith—and Off Welfare," *Christianity Today* 40 (June 17, 1996): 35–36; Bill Wilson, "Why I Chose to Live in Hell," *Charisma* 22 (October 1996): 55–62; "Teen Sex: Black Youth Leaders for a Solution," *Christianity Today* 34 (September 10, 1990): 55; Dan Wooding, "God's Wake Up Call," *Charisma* 19 (July 1994): 29. Wooding implies that no whites are involved in gang activity in Los Angeles, for instance. Passantino wrote an article that was part of a larger collection of articles in *Moody* on several churches in different communities in the United States. Unlike all the other articles that focused on white communities, the names of the people mentioned in this article were changed "to preserve their dignity." Gretchen Passantino, "Surviving in the City," *Moody* 92 (September 1991): 36–38.

36. Trudy Hutchens, "Is the Church Ready for Welfare Reform?" *Family Voice* 17 (October 1995): 4–13.

37. Quoted in Michael Lienesch, *Redeeming America* (Chapel Hill: University of North Carolina, 1993).

38. Valerie Lowe, "Stand Up and Be Counted," *Charisma* 25 (December 1999): 70–76.

39. David Barton, "The Race Card," *Wallbuilders* (Fall 1995): 1–7.

40. Andrea Smith, "Bible, Gender and Nationalism in American Indian and Christian Right Activism" (Santa Cruz: University of California-Santa Cruz, 2002).

41. Margaret Bendroth, "The Search for 'Women's Role' in American Evangelicalism, 1930–1980," *Evangelicalism in Modern America*, ed. G. Marsden (Grand Rapids: Eerdmans Publishing Company, 1984); Gail Bederman, *Manliness and Civilization* (Chicago: University of Chicago Press, 1995).

42. Robert Andrescik, "Welcome to the New Men's Movement," *New Man* 7 (September–October 2000): 10; Patrick Morley, "The Next Christian Men's Movement," *Christianity Today* 44 (September 4, 1999): 84–86.

43. Mark Kellner, "Keeping Their Promises," *Christianity Today* 44 (May 22, 2000): 21.

44. Joe Maxwell, "MAB Men Are Back," *New Man* 7 (September–October 2000): 27–37.

45. B. Denise Hawkins, "Shoutin' from the Housetops," *Charisma* 20 (June 1995): 23–29.

46. Andres Tapia, "Churches Wary of Inner-City Islamic Inroads," *Christianity Today* 39 (January 19, 1994): 36–38.

47. Unlike men, evangelical women seem more reluctant to organize by themselves. For instance, women organized the Heritage Keepers as a counterpart to the Promise Keepers, but its events are not limited to women "so as to avoid the appearance of being feminist." "Women Becoming 'Promise Keepers,'" *Christianity Today* 40 (July 15, 1996): 63.

48. Steve Brouwer, Paul Gifford, and Susan Rose, *Exporting the American Gospel* (London: Routledge, 1996).

49. Ibid.

50. Kimberle Crenshaw, "The Intersection of Race and Gender," *Critical Race Theory*, ed. K. Crenshaw, N. Gotanda, G. Peller, and K. Thomas (New York: New Press, 1996), 377.

51. "Canadian Promise Keepers to be Established in Vancouver," *Faith Today* 12 (July–August 1994): 53.

52. After PK received so much criticism for this statement, PK's rhetoric around gender relations softened considerably. And as a very clever rhetorical strategy, PK placed Tony Evans as the speaker at the Stand in the Gap rally, where he reframed this quote so that it would not sound like it supported male supremacy. He explained that what "male leadership" actually entails is treating one's wife as an equal and recognizing that leadership is mutual, not oppressing or abusing one's wife.

53. Joe Conason, Alfred Ross, and Lee Cokorinos, "The Promise Keepers Are Coming," *The Nation* 263 (October 7, 1996): 11–19.

54. Helen Lee, "Racial Reconciliation Tops NAE's Agenda," *Christianity Today* 39 (April 3, 1995): 97.

55. J. Lee Grady, "Pentecostals Urged to End Bias against Women Ministers," *Charisma* 11 (December 1996): 15.

56. J. Alfred Smith and Ross Maracle, "Listening to America's Ethnic Churches," *Christianity Today* 33 (March 3, 1989): 25–41.

57. Sharon Mumper, "Resettlement Program Could Pave the Way for Outreach Among Indonesian Muslims," *Christianity Today* 29 (Marcy 15, 1985): 37, 39; Sharon Mumper, "New Strategies to Evangelize Muslims Gain Effectiveness," *Christianity Today* 29 (May 17, 1985): 75–76; Stan Guthrie, "Muslim Mission Breakthrough," *Christianity Today* 37 (December 13, 1993): 20–26; Adrian Jacobs, "New Songs and Ways of Worship," *Charisma* 18 (July–August 2000): 36; George Houssney, "Persistence Key in Muslim Evangelism," *United Evangelical Action* 49 (July–August 1990): 8–9; Stan Guthrie, "A Crescent for a Cross: Islam Prospers in America," *Christianity Today* 35 (October 27, 1991): 40; Terry Muck, "The Mosque Next Door" *Christianity Today* 32 (February 19, 1988): 15–20.

58. Roger Greenway, "A Shift in the Global Center of Christianity," *United Evangelical Action* 48 (November–December 1989): 4–7.

59. An advertisement, *Christianity Today* 29 (November 22, 1985): 15.

60. Gary Schipper, "Non-Western Missionaries: Our Newest Challenge." *Evangelical Missions Quarterly* 24 (July 1988): 198–202.

61. Glenn Kendall, "Missionaries Should Not Plant Churches," *Evangelical Missions Quarterly* 24 (July 1988): 218–21.

62. Rene Padilla, "Come Holy Spirit—Renew the Whole Creation," *Transformation* 8 (October 1991): 1–6.

63. Art Toalston, "AD 2000: Eleven Years to Reach the World," *Christianity Today* 37 (March 3, 1989): 48, 50.

64. Concerned Women for America. n.d. *Five Critical Trends for Fathers and Families in the New Millennium.* Washington, DC: Concerned Women for America. For other racializations of the "problem" of single-female households, see Janice Crouse, *Strengthening American Families: What Works and What Doesn't Work* (Washington, DC: Concerned Women for America, 1999).

65. Edwin Gausted, *A Religious History of America* (San Francisco: Harper Collins, 1990); Estelle Freedman, *Their Sisters' Keepers* (Ann Arbor: University of Michigan Press, 1981); Betty De Berg, *Ungodly Women* (Minneapolis: Fortress Press, 1990); Margaret Bendroth, *Fundamentalism and Gender, 1875–Present* (New Haven: Yale University Press, 1993); Valerie Sherer Mathes, "Nineteenth-Century Women and Reform: The Women's National Indian Association," *American Indian Quarterly* 14 (Winter 1990): 1–18; Wendy Wall, "Gender and the 'Citizen Indian,'"

Writing the Range, ed. E. Jameson and S. Armitage (Norman: University of Oklahoma Press, 1997).

66. Kintz, *Between Jesus and the Market.*

67. Brasher, *Godly Women,* 377.

68. Diane Knippers, "Violence, Ideology and Policy," *Faith and Freedom* 18 (Winter 1998–1999): 8.

69. Stephen Strang, "Faith Under Fire," *Charisma* 30 (August 2004): 50–58.

70. Tanya Green, "Mina's Story," *Family Voice* (Winter 2002): 14–17; 20–21.

71. Elisabeth Farrel, "Married to Muhammed," *Charisma* 25 (June 2000): 88–93.

72. Ibid., 89.

73. Ibid., 90.

74. Andree Seu, "Light Switch," *World Magazine* 19 (August 14, 2004): 47.

75. Andrea Sheldon. n.d. "The New Focus on 'Hate.'" *Traditional Values Report* 6 (1): 3.

76. "Federal Hate Crimes Legislation." n.d. *Traditional Values Report* 6 (1): 4.

77. News briefs, *Charisma* 29 (July 2004): 40.

78. John Kennedy, "Senate Showdown," *Christianity Today* 48 (September 2004): 23.

79. Alan Chambers, "Do We Want a Gay America?" *Charisma* 30 (October 2004): 40–44.

80. Gene Edward Veith, "Black & Right," *World Magazine* 19 (July 24, 2004): 25.

81. Ibid.

82. Sheryl Henderson Blunt, "The Man behind the Marriage Amendment," *Christianity Today* 48 (September 2004): 46–52.

83. Charles Colson and Anne Morse, "The Moral Home Front," *Christianity Today* 48 (October 2004): 152.

84. Colson and Morse, "The Moral Home Front," 152. This opinion piece was then criticized by Gary Roth of St. Andrew Lutheran Church in the letters section of *Christianity Today.* He stated that "blaming gays for broader social problems is like blaming a lesion for our illness when there is cancer throughout the entire body. 'Gay marriage' needs to be judged on its own merits (or demerits)—not on fear and suspicion, nor as a scapegoat for idolatries we would rather have go unchallenged." Readers Write. *Christianity Today* 48 (April 2004): 12–18.

85. Concerned Women for America. n.d. *Pro-Life Action Guide* (Washington, DC: Concerned Women for America).

86. Betsy Hartmann, *Reproductive Rights and Wrongs: The Global Politics of Population Control* (Boston: South End Press, 1995); Dorothy Roberts, *Killing the Black Body* (New York: Pantheon Books, 1997); Jael Silliman and Ynestra King, eds., *Dangerous Intersections: Feminist Perspectives*

on Population, Environment and Development (Boston: South End Press, 1999).

87. Smith, "Bible, Gender and Nationalism."

88. Andrea Smith, *Conquest: Sexual Violence and American Indian Genocide* (Boston: South End Press, 2005).

89. Sheryl Henderson Blunt, "Saving Black Babies," *Christianity Today* 47 (February 2003): 22.

90. Ibid.

8

The Future of Feminism: What Other Way to Speak?

Vron Ware

Throughout the Christian-majority world the subject of Islam often generates fear among audiences whose only knowledge of the subject is derived from hostile and stereotyped media representation. Factors such as the rise of Political Islam, and the changing geopolitical climate since 2001, have impacted on home-grown variants of racism to produce new levels of intolerance toward Muslim settler communities, and a readiness to see the entire Middle East as a hotbed of terrorism. This phenomenon is expressed in different but related ways in each country, but there is inevitably one unifying theme: the question of incompatible cultures fixed in "tradition" on one side, and "modernity" on the other. At the heart of this insidious "culture talk" there is a consistent emphasis on questions of sexuality and women's rights.[1] This chapter recognizes the urgency of exploring this explosive subject from a feminist perspective, and of applying pedagogical expertise to encourage wide-ranging, informed debate within the academic classroom. In doing so it will tackle some contemporary questions of the utmost importance: both to the study and practice of antiracism, and to the future of women's studies as a radical academic project.

The iconic figure of the veiled woman represents one of the most powerful symbols of multiculturalism as it excites deeply held views on culture, religion, subjectivity, identity, sexuality, agency, and the oppression of women. It is a volatile image used to evoke many different and often opposing agendas: from the openness of U.S. society to all-comers, for example, to the inimical presence of apparently incompatible cultures. One way to assess its significance as a symbol for both understanding and misunderstanding is to suggest that the question of women's rights is a priority in establishing an equitable and socially just society that can manage cultural difference without making exceptions. An alternative interpretation might argue that women's bodies have historically been used as a battleground for wider political conflict that has little to do with gender equality. It is the confusion, hostility, and ambivalence generated by this polyvocal symbol, rather than the study of the practice itself, that provides the rationale for this chapter.

Recent feminist scholarship has demonstrated that the struggle to improve women's lives has played a strategic role in the history of colonial missions to civilize peoples designated as heathen or beyond the realms of law. In part this can be traced to one of Euro-American feminism's founding arguments: that the quality or character of a civilization can be measured by the way it treats its women. Today the case for new forms of imperialist aggression can be made more readily if the evil posed by the enemy is linked to their oppression of women. The so-called clash of civilizations summons up a fundamental incompatibility between Christianity and Islam, secularism and religion. It pits Western modern freedoms against Oriental cultural traditions represented by veiled women and honour killings, relying on a notion of Islam as a timeless, homogenous religion impervious to change but in desperate need of modernization. At the same time, indigenous women's movements in many countries, regardless of the contexts and conditions in which they develop, are often tainted by association with a Western imperialist legacy and neocolonizing agenda.

The attack on the World Trade Center and the Pentagon in September 2001 and the subsequent declaration of the "war on terror" by the United States and European powers placed a particular burden upon international feminists to call attention to the centrality of gender discourse in the current geopolitical era.[2] I write as a member of a women's and gender studies program that, like many others, has been seeking both to "modernize" its curriculum and to assert its pedagogical relevance in a climate of hostility within the institution and among the student body. In the broadest terms, redesigning the feminist curriculum (or rather the required courses that engage with feminist theory) entails teaching a gender perspective that can open up new areas of contemporary life to academic scrutiny and make connections without expecting universally applicable solutions. This has entailed shifting to a more sustained transnational approach, using gender as an analytical framework that intersects with other categories of social division. A renewed emphasis on looking beyond national borders is tempered by an awareness of the politics of location that returns the critical gaze to the ground on which we stand.

Part of this pedagogical work involves introducing students to cross-cultural study: to the importance of listening and looking for disjuncture and conflict as well as common interests and solidarity along lines of gender identification. Most significantly, it means starting from home, recognizing that the country is at war, and coming to terms with the uncomfortable fact that aspects of Western feminism have been complicit with racism and imperialism since its inception in the nineteenth century.[3]

FEMINIST NETWORKS

Feminism has long been concerned with the ways in which some ideas about women—their rights, wrongs, entitlements, and essences—can be mobilized to inflame patriotism and nationalist fervor, to support and glorify war and to justify domination. In November 2003, *Glamour* magazine's Women of the Year award ceremony brought Iraq War veterans Jessica Lynch and Shoshana Johnson into the same space as Britney Spears, producing a photograph that circulated far and wide.[4] The forces that achieved this feminine trinity of celebrity, diversity, and belligerence are something to be reckoned with, even though at face value there is little mystery as to why the three are pictured together.

The vast body of feminist research and intellectual analysis accumulated in different countries over the past three decades and more serves as an invaluable resource that can be put to use to demonstrate how these ideas work—whence they are derived, where they draw their power from, how they worked in the past, what their consequences are in the present. This chapter draws on this unruly discourse as I think about the genealogies of feminism as a global movement, searching for noncolonizing, nonessentializing strands of connection that enable political solidarity at this time of war.

It is still too soon to tell what impact the activities and ideologies of the Bush administration have had on the way that differences between women are negotiated within U.S. feminism, but the so-called war on terror has certainly tested the resilience of home-grown feminist analysis, networks, political organization, and intellectual work. The dire necessity of reaction to geopolitical events within and outside the country, as well as a response to a major shift in domestic policies, has, ironically, given new impetus to a social movement that had been experiencing fragmentation and backlash throughout the 1990s. This has been equally true within those countries whose governments have signed up to the Coalition of the Willing to wage war.

One of the most valuable contributions to the global feminist debates that took place immediately after the 2001 attacks on the Twin Towers and the Pentagon and the ensuing invasion of Afghanistan came from Australian writers and activists Bronwyn Winter and Susan Hawthorne. Within a year of the attacks on the Towers, they had compiled *September 11th 2001, Feminist Perspectives*, a substantial collection of articles and essays from writers around the world, bringing voices from the global south into dialogue with women in the north.[5] The range of political analysis, personal testimonies, poetry, and stories suggested that transnational feminist politics rested on a firm foundation of collective outrage that had been building over several decades of struggle. There were other collaborations rushed into print with similar energy and focus—for instance, *Terror, Counter Terror: Women Speak Out*, edited by Ammu Joseph and Kalpana Sharma, first published by Kali for Women in 2003.[6] Feminism had equipped many women with networks and skills that could be used to coordinate responses from different geographical locations as well as provide a common language of solidarity with which to speak and listen to each other.

Despite the welcome appearance of these responses, which saw an exponential increase in academic journals and conferences throughout the United States, there are two aspects of this discourse on gender and war that remain relatively unexplored in that context. It is important to examine them because one of the greatest challenges of the current period is the urgency of intervening in what I referred to earlier as "culture talk." Since issues relating to women's rights, gender roles, sexuality, and family obligations are centrally implicated in the so-called clash of civilizations between Christianity, or secularism, and Islam, those in gender studies have a particular responsibility to help students navigate the various pitfalls of racism, ethnocentrism, cultural relativism, and plain ignorance that flow from using "culture" as an explanatory tool.[7]

The first problem that needs addressing is an old one: it is important to consider that one of feminism's most challenging tasks has been how to speak about women collectively and when to talk about gender. The difficulties inherent in qualifying women as a unitary category have provided feminists with endless creative insights that reveal and underscore deep ideological conflict. One added complication is the way that particular debates within countries—for example, the now historic conflicts among U.S. feminists over race, class, sexuality—are exported through publishing, development work, human rights, the UN, and NGOs. These inform popular culture, and even government policy. It is vital from the start to acknowledge that feminism in the north is in an inescapably hegemonic position. This makes it even more important to develop a politics of gender that comprehends the asymmetries inherent in any links that we make with feminists located in the global south.

There is currently a crisis facing feminists in the United States (and in Britain too) who have been struggling with the problem of how to deliver a women's studies curriculum that is relevant to younger students and is infused with political energies that gave rise to it in the first place. Collaborations such as *Women's Studies on Its Own*, edited by Robyn Wiegman, have provided a welcome reassessment of the institutionalization of feminist scholarship in the U.S. academy.[8] Contributors from universities all over the country write about teaching, curricula, pedagogy, and the politics of transforming the educational experiences not just of students but also of faculty hired to teach in this area. The urgency of this project is captured by Minoo Moallem in her essay " 'Women of Color in the U.S': Pedagogical Reflections on the Politics of 'the Name.' " She begins with the observation that "Turning the experience of teaching in a classroom in Women's Studies into a textual site of critical and analytical investigation is a crucial task."[9] Her contribution is useful here because it raises the question of how to approach feminist theories of difference from a historical perspective while also producing new forms of knowledge and insight.

The central theme of Moallem's piece is that the title of this course, which she has taught in several different places, raises among students expectations that are antithetical to the exploration of new ways of thinking that the course is designed to offer. Her critique of the phrase "women of color" echoes what is now a familiar complaint that the convergence of the terms "black women" and "Third World women" leaves important contradictions intact—not least of which is the fact that its vagueness—like the expression "global feminism"— has allowed it to be turned into one more U.S. export that carries the seeds of Western cultural imperialism. Moallem writes:

> Even as the term "women of color" has emerged institutionally to critique women within the United States, the stretching of the term to include a global oppositional category of women of color became problematic in the context of the 1990s and the elaboration of postcolonial theory and transnational feminist theories. A fissure appeared, quite predictably, between the U.S. category of "Women of Color" and the category "Third World" which constitutes in geopolitical terms subjects who are at the same time placed and displaced, resulting in serious contradictions and tensions.[10]

An earlier version of this critique was made just over ten years ago by Marnia Lazreg in her book *The Eloquence of Silence: Algerian Women in Question*.[11] In her introductory essay "Decolonizing Feminism," she explores some of the difficulties she has encountered writing about women not only from countries designated as Third World, but also "from a culture with a history of distortion."[12] Scornful of the mindset that groups Algerian women under headings such as Arab women, Muslim women, or Middle Eastern women, her critique centers on what she calls "the reductive tendency to present women as an instance of a religion, nation, ethnicity, or race." This form of ignorance, she argues, can be traced to the development of a crude form of racial thinking that emerged in the United States during the post–civil rights, post–cold war era. She writes:

> There is to a great extent continuity in American feminists' treatment of difference between women, whether it originates within American society or outside of it. There is, however, an added feature to feminists' mode of representation of women from the Third World: they reflect the dynamics of global politics. The political attitudes of the powerful states are mirrored in feminists' attitudes towards women from economically marginal states in a world rent asunder by the collapse of communism.[13]

Lazreg's anger at the destructive and patronizing legacy of identity politics, which, as she sees it, place too much emphasis on the "phenomenal manifestations of difference between women," is palpable. This undue emphasis, she argues, is sustained by the extension of standpoint theories that yield a *representation* of activity in the name of a situated truth. Racialized women claiming standpoint perspectives represent themselves in terms that already subsume and contain their representation. For women designated as Third World, this constitutes a sort of epistemological trap. Euro-American feminism invites individual women from this Third World to represent millions of women from their societies within the stereotype of the oppressed, in which case they find themselves classified as women of color at the end of the anthologies, or else they face the possibility of being dismissed for not keeping to the script.

One way out of this conundrum is for feminists in North America and in Europe to adopt a form of consciousness "that transcends their sense of specialness and embraces what is human at the heart of womanhood across cultures and races."[14] This entails a process of what she calls deracialization—implying, I think, that black and white feminists must shed their obsession with certain kinds of difference, seeing them as produced within a very particular (and powerful) sociohistorical space. Only under these conditions can "academic feminism" possibly become decentered so that other voices can be heard.

I have gone back to Lazreg's work as part of an attempt to listen more intently to feminist voices emerging from countries subsumed under the headings she so scorns: the Middle East, the Arab world, the Muslim world. Instead of relying on modes of seeing, of registering a concern with difference based on visual cues, I want to focus now on sound—in particular the sound of speech or its absence. I return to the final question asked by the convenors in their guiding questions for this symposium: What other way to speak? Now more than ever, we have to ask: What other way to *listen?*

INFO-WAR AND WOMEN'S RIGHTS

The changed nature of modern warfare is another feature of the current geopolitical climate that demands an informed feminist response. The colloquium that gave rise to this book coincided with the second anniversary of the invasion of Iraq by U.S. and British forces, a date commemorated by protest demonstrations all over the world. In the United States, the main focus was on the mobilization at Fayetteville, home of Fort Bragg, which was organized by a new and unprecedented coalition of organizations representing antiwar campaigners, veterans, and military families. Scores of regional protests targeted recruiting centers and other symbols of military power as they protested against the occupation and remembered all those who had died as a result of the war. The fact that these demonstrations received minimal coverage by the American press and TV news was a timely reminder that the "war on terror" is being carried out not just through the use of bombs, tanks, incarceration, torture, and "intelligence," but increasingly also through the manipulation of information. We face a situation in which the military, the government, and the corporate media are committed to a postmodern info-war waged through lies, news management, propaganda, spin, distortion, omission, and slant.[15]

It is worth recalling an extraordinary glimpse of this phenomenon in a celebrated article in the *New York Times* by Ron Suskind, former *Wall Street Journal* reporter and author of *The Price of Loyalty: George W. Bush, the White House, and the Education of Paul O'Neill.* In this piece, which was widely quoted after initial publication, Suskind described an encounter in 2002 with a senior adviser of the president that took place after Suskind wrote an article in *Esquire* criticizing Bush's former communications director Karen Hughes. The aide expressed the White House's displeasure at the article, and then "he told me something that at the time I didn't fully comprehend—but which I now believe gets to the very heart of the Bush presidency."

> The aide said that guys like me were "in what we call the reality-based community," which he defined as people who "believe that solutions emerge from your judicious study of discernible reality." I nodded and murmured something about enlightenment principles and empiricism. He cut me off. "That's not the way the world really works anymore," he continued. "We're an empire now, and when we act, we create our own reality. And while you're studying that reality—judiciously, as you will—we'll act again, creating other new realities, which you can study too, and that's how things will sort out. We're history's actors . . . and you, all of you, will be left to just study what we do."[16]

This quote has been used on countless occasions as an example of how the Neo-Conservatives pride themselves on their control of their own publicity machine. Writing more recently in the British newspaper the *Guardian*, diarist Julian Borger elaborated on this phenomenon with further examples: "When it comes to news and facts, however, the Bush Republicans are committed relativists. In their eyes, generally speaking, there is no single truth out there waiting to be discovered but rather competing points of view of the same reality. Your convictions or your faith will determine which view you choose."[17]

While this observation was hardly front-page news in itself, Borger's intention was to draw attention to a report that revealed the extent to which federal agencies, including the Pentagon, were producing carefully targeted propaganda items that were syndicated nationwide. These nuggets were routinely embellished with quotes from high-ranking officials and were rarely critical or controversial. Again, one might say that this is merely an example of routine political "spin" that has become integral to modern democracies. Naomi Klein, author of *No Logo: Taking Aim at the Brand Bullies* and, in recent months, a regular reporter from Baghdad, has added to this analysis by demonstrating how the Bush administration has consistently borrowed "cutting edge" tools from the corporate world. Arguing that the president's latest address on fighting terrorism in the Arab world bears resemblance to McDonald's advertising campaign urging Americans to fight obesity, she referred to U.S. foreign policy as "an orgy of redescription."

Central to her analysis is the question of women's rights in occupied Iraq and the way that this is reported through the Brand USA script. "Whenever Bremer needed a good-news hit," she wrote, "he had his picture taken at a newly opened women's centre, handily equating feminism with the hated occupation. (The women's centres are now mostly closed, and hundreds of Iraqis who worked with the coalition in local councils have been executed.)" Secularism, and the related issue of women's rights, becomes associated with the notion of liberation by the allied forces, with predictable results, and thus the democratic forces in Iraq are robbed of their most potent tools.[18]

The equation of the U.S. government's alleged feminist agenda with the aims of the occupation is further underlined by the fulsome support accorded to the principle of women's rights on the government's own Web sites. A quick search of the official White House policy statements reveals that

> Global respect for women is a Bush Administration foreign policy priority. The United States is in the forefront of advancing women's causes around the world, helping them become full participants in their societies through various initiatives and programs that help increase women's political participation and economic opportunities and support women and girls' access to education and health care.

This policy statement clearly echoes the rhetoric surrounding the invasion of Afghanistan in 2001 when the visibility of the Taliban's brutal repression of women briefly took center stage. While no one is arguing that feminists should be any less concerned about Afghan women simply because the Bush administration appears to have hijacked the issue for its own ends, the notion that women's rights could be delivered through the use of stealth bombers and through the funding of high-profile initiatives requires extra careful scrutiny. I was grateful to an observant student who drew my attention to a photograph of Laura Bush laughing and chatting to a group of Afghan women who were her personal guests in the august corridors of the White House.[19] The image had been posted on an official White House Web site during the final months of the first Bush administration and was easily recoverable through Google images. The caption read:

> After the Taliban regime was overthrown by U.S. and coalition forces following the September 11, 2001, terrorist attacks, the United States launched a historic initiative to elevate the status of women in Afghanistan. Toward that end, President Bush and Afghan President Hamid Karzai on January 28, 2002, announced the creation of

USAWC (U.S.-Afghan Women's Council). Education of Afghan women and their rehabilitation in society through small business income have become the top priorities of USAWC.

A second image showed the same group standing with Condoleezza Rice. Again the caption explained: "Here 12 women teachers are greeted by the First Lady on November 8, following which they had meetings with Paula Dobriansky, Under Secretary of State for Global Issues, and ECA assistant secretary Patricia Harrison."[20] A brief investigation into the composition of USAWC revealed that the council also included Karen Hughes, President Bush's closest adviser during his first administration, who resigned in 2002 to spend more time with her family in Texas.[21] The dubious extent of her commitment to women's rights was revealed when she was asked by CNN journalist Wolf Blitzer how big the issue of abortion would be in the 2004 presidential election. Hughes, who returned temporarily to help orchestrate the campaign, responded by linking abortion rights activists to terrorists, saying that

> The fundamental difference between us and the terror network we fight is that we value every life . . . Unfortunately our enemies in the terror network, as we're seeing repeatedly in the headlines these days, don't value any life, not even the innocent and not even their own.[22]

Further investigation revealed that the USAWC has various programs that ostensibly address women's issues within Afghanistan, mostly in the areas of education and health. One example is the Adopt-a-school Program, which gets church communities in Texas to provide their adopted school with supplies, textbooks, and training. The official White House Web sites carry updated information on the successes of different reconstruction and humanitarian projects in Afghanistan, all funded directly by U.S. aid. There seem to be no problems, no complications, no failures, no deviation from the line that this was a liberation that rescued a persecuted people from tyranny, and definitely no hint of recognition that development programs in war-torn countries might draw on decades of feminist and postcolonial expertise. When Laura Bush announced the creation of USAWC in 2002 in the presence of the interim chairman of the Afghan authority, Hamid Karzai, she adroitly gave him official endorsement as the White House candidate for the presidency. In addition, her speech neatly compressed the notion that Afghan women's rights were a priority for the freedom-loving Americans, and that they all shared a common enemy in the form of Al-Qaeda.

> I am delighted to be here to highlight our nation's commitment to the people of Afghanistan, especially our support for the education of women and children. Last November I joined Americans in focusing on the brutality against Afghan women by the al-Qaeda terrorist network and the Taliban regime in Afghanistan. And today we continue to speak out on behalf of the women and children—especially girls—who, for years, were denied their basic human rights of health and education.[23]

The Web sites showcasing the achievements of the Bush administration provide a means of scrutinising the "reality" of empire at this time of war. The issue of women's rights is used both as a stick to beat Islam with, and also as a pious and intermittent justification for invading countries and installing cooperative governments in the name of democracy.

The appointment of powerful women such as Karen Hughes to the U.S. Afghan Women's Council is proof that this enterprise has a mission that extends far beyond the provision of grants for Afghan women. Hughes's speciality as the architect of the Bush message is a sure sign that the strategic attention to women's rights is an effective weapon in a global info-war that is being fought on many levels. My argument has been that this battle demands a particular form of feminist response, one that might effectively counter militaristic propaganda that diverts attention from the human costs of war and occupation.

Paying attention to what is happening in Afghanistan is important for many reasons, not least because it is extremely hard to gauge how far women's access to gender justice and equality have improved since the fall of the Taliban.[24] International feminists may have been vocal in their demand for women's rights in Afghanistan before and after the invasion in 2001, but there has been a great deal of confusion and divisiveness about what to do by way of support. Asked to provide a reference for a student applying to intern with the Feminist Majority's campaign for Afghan women and girls, I checked out their Web site. I found a page headed with the words "Help Afghan Women" under which there was information on how to send money or even make contact with various projects set up there with donated funds.[25] A factsheet with the title "Freeing Afghan women—unfinished work" asked readers, among other things, to write to President Bush to increase the international peacekeeping force in Afghanistan. The features of this work, which started in 1987 as a campaign to publicize and bring an end to gender apartheid in the country, were admirable, but I found myself reacting against words such as "Freeing" and "Help," and certainly the combination of the two. I compared this site with one dedicated to the Revolutionary Association of Women in Afghanistan

(RAWA), looking for alternative ways to imagine a connection to women in Afghanistan. I discovered that RAWA, which describes itself as the "oldest political/social organization of Afghan women struggling for peace, freedom, democracy and women's rights in fundamentalism-blighted Afghanistan since 1977," was in danger of collapsing due to lack of funds as media attention turned away to other regions. Working closely with the Afghan Women's Mission (AWM), RAWA members are trying to set up and support hundreds of humanitarian schemes in Afghanistan and among refugees in Pakistan.[26] Their Web sites testify to the immense problems that women face in a country increasingly ignored by global media, but there are no words such as "help" and "free" on these pages. In fact an article written by Sonali Kolhatkar, a founding member and vice president of AWM, explained some of the misconceptions that arose from the idea that the U.S. invasion has liberated Afghan women from their oppressors:

> The struggle of Afghan women has been reduced here in the United States to a simplistic discussion about the burqa. Don the burqa and you're oppressed, take it off and, lo and behold, you're free. But what does this really mean? It means that to constantly portray Afghan women as weak, covered up, defenseless, needing our help, makes us feel good about helping Afghan women, about saving them. To express solidarity with Afghan women, we need to understand what affects them, starting with what we are responsible for and have the power to change—the use of bombs and warlords as tools of US policy. We need to begin treating Afghan women with dignity and not reduce them to a piece of clothing. Afghan women's rights are a crucial part of the equation of Afghanistan. One year later, it is clear that Afghan women are not "free"—they are simply enduring American freedom.[27]

Another article written by Kolhatkar, entitled "Saving Afghan Women," detailed various encounters with American and British feminists who demonstrated a patronizing disregard for the political priorities of Afghan women, even to the extent of lecturing them on the barbarities of female genital mutilation, not incidentally practiced in Afghanistan. This reminded me of a section in Lazreg's essay, quoted earlier, where she referred to feminists' search for the disreputable and the uncouth: "Local customs such as polygamy and/or veiling, wherever they take place, appear decontextualized and are posited as normative absolutes."[28]

Again I hear the question: what other way to speak? What other way to speak about Afghan or Arab women? What other way to speak about Islam that does not demonize, universalize, homogenize?

SELLING CULTURE TALK

Looking beyond the government's own publicity machine, there are plenty of indications that the subjection of Oriental women means big business. A case in point is this snap-shot I took in a bookshop in London's Heathrow airport in November 2004 (Figure 8.1). At the time, my discovery of this new special section, "Eastern Studies,"

Figure 8.1   The Faces or Orientalism.

Figure 8.1 (Continued) The faces of Orientalism.

reinforced my belief that feminists had to deal with the circulation of information and ideas about Islam on many different levels.

On close inspection, one notices that Eastern Studies consists largely of autobiographical books by women from east Istanbul, often in the form of survivors' testimonies, or success stories in the face of cultural and/or patriarchal restrictions. The "Eastern" women gracing the covers of these books are exotic, Oriental, definitely Other. The majority wear head coverings of varying degrees, and one simply displays her jewelry-bedecked cleavage. Among the few books written by men, are two by the Orientalist scholar Bernard Lewis, including one entitled *What Went Wrong?* The juxtaposition of this title alongside images of Japanese geishas, abducted British schoolgirls, and stoic Arabian princesses speaks volumes.

The subject of the veil, whether it implies a nominal headscarf or a garment covering the whole head and body, has achieved more notoriety than any other single piece of clothing worn by humans—only when worn by women. It stubbornly remains the index of an alternative mode of femininity that seems to declare itself to be utterly opposed to everything that American and European feminists have fought for. The heat it generates leaves little room for a more complex reading of cultural practice rooted in geographical, historical, social, economic factors. The idea that the hijab might, in some contexts, represent a determination to become an active citizen is often unfathomable for secular women and men. In her study *Politics of Piety*, Saba Mahmood notes that "Women's participation in, and support for, the Islamist movement provokes strong responses from feminists across a broad range of the political spectrum."[29] In an essay entitled "The Language of the Veil," commissioned by the *Guardian* after September 11, 2001, Ahdaf Soueif voices impatience at the British obsession with the hijab as an index of muslim alterity. She writes: "How odd that we don't have one word in Arabic equivalent to 'the veil.'" She continues:

> But perhaps not odd at all, for doesn't English have bowler hats and top hats and trilbys and cloth caps and boaters and Stetsons, while Arabic only has *qubba'ah*, "hat"? . . . To the West, "the veil," like Islam itself, is both sensual and puritanical, is contradictory, is to be feared. It is also concrete, and is to do with women, and since cultural battles are so often fought through the bodies of women, it is seized upon by politicians, columnists, feminists.[30]

Soueif's reminder that cultural conflict frequently focuses on women's bodies helps to explain the predominance of women's texts on the Eastern Studies bookstand. But those books would not be there unless they were capable of earning serious money. One of the best sellers on this Eastern Studies stand, lodged between *The Good Women of China* and *Star of India* is *The Bookseller of Kabul* by Åsne Seierstad, Norway's best known war reporter. She wrote this book after spending six weeks with the Northern Alliance foot soldiers during the war against the Taliban, living alongside them as they traversed the harsh landscapes of Afghanistan. After the Taliban had fled Kabul, Seierstad traveled to the capital to document the ways that ordinary people were adjusting to the Post-Taliban period. Here she seized an opportunity to experience living in an Afghan family at the home of a bookseller whose acquaintance she made shortly after she arrived. From this she wrote a book that attempted to describe the inner life of women and men in Afghanistan for the edification of readers outside that blighted country. Fascinated by the bookseller's stories and the hospitality provided by his family—two wives, five children, and several other relatives—Seierstad extended the fatal Orientalist gaze, past the visible signs of difference indicated by the infamous burka, right inside the heads of her hosts:

> I was a guest but soon felt at home. I was incredibly well treated; the family was generous and open. We shared may good times, but I have

rarely been as angry as I was with the Khan family, and I have rarely quarrelled as much as I did there. Nor have I had the urge to hit anyone as much as I did there. The same thing was continually provoking me: the manner in which men treated women. The belief in male superiority was so ingrained that it was seldom questioned.[31]

Her book has been the best-selling Norwegian nonfiction of all time, subsequently translated into thirty languages. It became more famous when the patriarch of the family, bookseller Mohammed Shah Rais—Sultan Khan in the book—flew to Norway to sue her for defamation. In an interview in the *Observer* she said, "It is a total clash of civilisations. I'm very surprised. I knew and told them in advance that they might not like the book but I think it is important to write about real life in Afghanistan. I'm not saying there is abuse particularly in this family, but this is still a society where women have almost no human rights."[32]

Seierstad is evidently a well-intentioned and courageous reporter, and like most authors she was not necessarily responsible for the copy on the dustjacket. By emphasising that she was able to use her skills as a female journalist to bring the truth out from under the burkas, those charged with the marketing of her book fell for every cliché of "culture talk":

> Stepping back from the page, award-winning journalist Åsne Seierstad allows the Khans to speak for themselves about their joys, sorrows, rivalries, loves, dreams, and temptations. Through this close-knit household, we gain an intimate view-as few outsiders have seen it-of life in an Islamic country just beginning to find its way between the forces of modernity and tradition.[33]

One of the other titles on the airport stand is evocatively titled *Sold*, the word scripted in red capitals over the head of a young woman whose face and hair is almost completely covered by black scarves. Only her eyes are visible, her gaze turned upward and away from the viewer in an expression of desperate supplication. This famous image of Nadia Muhsen, a schoolgirl from Birmingham, England, has been circulating throughout the world since the 1980s when her case first began to gain publicity. Together with her older sister Zana, she was taken to Yemen by their father and married off to a son of a family friend without her knowledge. Her sister, who was fifteen at the time, suffered the same fate but managed to extract herself eight years later after substantial media coverage and diplomatic intervention, mostly orchestrated by the girls' mother, Miriam Ali, who had remained in

England, initially unaware of their situation. Alongside *Sold*, Zana Muhsen's account of her ordeal (a book that was translated into eighteen languages and was a best seller within Europe) sits their mother's testimony *Without Mercy: A Mother's Struggle against Modern Slavery*, published in 1995. The same harrowing image is used for this book, back and front, although the front is overlaid with text and a small insert showing a snap of Nadia wearing her English clothes when her mother first managed to track her down in Yemen.

Browsing these bookshelves in November 2004, I recognized this story, which I had followed ever since it was first discovered that these two British teenagers had been held in Yemen against their will. I was not exactly surprised to see these books in this context, although it was interesting to discover that they had been given a fresh lease of life within this new marketing category. I will not return to this particular case study now, although I believe it would still yield many insights into the centrality of gender within discourses of civilizationism. In other words, it is a story that can be read in multiple ways: in terms of human duplicity, suffering, and familial love certainly, but also in relation to hundreds of years of Orientalist narratives in which Arab men are characterized as uniformly deceitful, conniving, and cruel and in which the West (often in the form of intrepid white woman) emerges as the champion of women's freedom from patriarchy. As the introduction to *Sold* makes clear: "This is a story of a terrible clash between some of the most primitive elements which still survive in our modern world, and some of the most sophisticated people on earth . . . This could be a tale from *The Arabian Nights*, except that it is happening now, and it turned out to be a living nightmare, not a dream at all."[34] The word "clash" here should alert us to the fact that this is also a story that is changed by the political context in which it is read, asking us to consider how else to understand what happened and also critiquing the racism entailed in its narration.

These examples, drawn from the literary world outside academia, return us to the question: if Women's Studies programs are to provide alternative readings of this Orientalizing genre, and to alert students of its dangers, does it relinquish the task to Area Studies specialists whose job it is to deliver courses on women in the Arab world, or on gender and Islam, thereby explaining what appears to be incomprehensible from the outside? This inquiry reminds me of patterns of thinking in the old days: race and racism were seen as issues best left to those who identified as black, whether inside or outside academia, and who were often asked to act as teachers or guides on issues of racism or African American culture that were considered peripheral to feminist agendas. Today, I suspect many women who are from Muslim-majority countries or who are identified with Islam and/or the Middle East find themselves placed in similar positions as "experts" by virtue of their ethnic or national identity. Just as "race" was regarded as the cultural and intellectual property of those who suffered from racism, so the ignorance and misinformation about Islam and the Middle East becomes the responsibility of those who are inherently connected either/both by birth or origin. The recent past of the feminist movement contains many guidelines and lessons about ways to incorporate antiracism into pedagogy and activism that are forgotten at its peril.

WHITENESS AS A GLOBAL BRAND

My interest in these issues arises from research into the social construction of whiteness as a relational category, in particular the tropes of white womanhood that circulated during the history of racial slavery and colonialism.[35] A feminist perspective on whiteness can enable alternative readings of Orientalist texts, especially if attention is paid to the changing context in which these texts are produced and read. I would also add, however, that since I began my own work in this area, there has been an exponential growth in what is sometimes known as Critical Whiteness Studies that has some bearing on this claim.

It hardly needs repeating that this focus on whiteness is a phenomenon that has emerged rapidly and, in some cases, with great effect, across the Humanities and Social Sciences, representing many political and cultural perspectives. Speaking now from a transatlantic standpoint, one of the problems within this field is the way that the debate is framed almost exclusively within North American terms.[36] This criticism is not an attempt to sidestep the work that needs to be done within the Unites States. The local context is extremely important in tracking the shifting currency of whiteness in relation to domestic politics: for example, the influence of the fundamentalist Christian Right, the impact of new laws and practices designed to improve surveillance in the name of homeland security, and the increased levels of militarization resulting from wars in Afghanistan and Iraq, these are among many factors affecting the politics of racism within national borders. The appointment of "minorities" to top government positions—Condaleezza Rice as secretary of state and Alberto Gonzales as attorney general—is another complicating factor that needs to be taken into account.

But the inability or refusal to recognize how this shifting currency of whiteness also operates within wider geopolitical circuits can undermine the work designed to expose it. It suggests that the forms of white supremacy that have operated historically in the United States are somehow isolated from and not connected to the rest of the world; alternatively it can imply that the rest of the world is like the United States, or, worse still, that it ought to be. A holistic analysis of whiteness needs to ask that if the values and meanings attributed to whiteness are so salient within U.S. borders, what happens when American racial cosmology is exported as an integral component of global culture, through Hollywood, MTV, CNN, McDonalds, or Britney Spears?

Clearly these are not questions intended for Americans alone, and it is hard to overemphasize the need for international dialogue and collaboration that are sensitive to the local politics of racism. An analysis of whiteness that is able to recognize its fluidity as a global category is all the more potent. To take one example, it is useful to refer back to the image of Lynch, Johnson, and Spears that I mentioned earlier, as the story of Lynch's "rescue" and promotion to war heroine is widely known. The presence of Johnson along with Lynch testifies to the fact that the U.S. armed forces not only include women in their ranks—surely the greatest symbol of female equality within a democratic society—but they also promote racial equality as well. These uniformed women who both suffered injuries during the course of their service in Iraq show a "soft" side of the military in contrast to the "hard," misogynist, nature of the male, Muslim enemy. At the same time Lynch's whiteness carries a special historical burden of victimhood as stories circulated about her rumoured mistreatment at the hands of Iraqi men, making her gallant "rescue" all the more heroic.

So far these observations are hardly contentious, and it is important to recall that many people were aware that the story of Jessica Lynch was an outrageous example of war propaganda. By chance, during the week of her recovery in the Iraqi hospital where she was being treated, I had organized a videoconferencing session linking my students at Yale to a Women's Studies class in London. One of the British students was so incensed by the local media version of the dramatic rescue that she brought along with her a copy of the newspaper to share with the class the article that had offended her. The students in both locations expressed their anger that this was little more than a publicity stunt concocted to make the allied forces look good as they tried to justify their illegal invasion.

While this was a reminder that the episode (including the subsequent publicity surrounding the publication of Lynch's book) had effects outside the United States, it also demonstrated the way that this postmodern form of info-war was able to rely on some pretty old themes. It was Lynch who was celebrated as heroine, not her roommate Lori Piestewa who was killed when their convoy—a support unit of "clerks, repairmen and cooks"—took a wrong turn.[37] Her death brought her the distinction of being the first Native American to die in combat on foreign soil, and the first American woman to die in the Iraq war. If it had not been for Lynch's determination to remember her friend publicly, and to contrast her friend's bravery with her own good fortune, Piestewa's name would scarcely have surfaced in the media at all. The fact that Johnson, who was also among the convoy but was released ten days after Lynch's rescue, and who also suffered injuries, was awarded 30 percent pension in contrast to Lynch's 80 percent is another sign that racism is an enduring factor in the military-media complex in spite of the veneer of equality.[38]

The Abu Ghraib scandal offered opportunities to interpret a version of white femininity completely at odds with the portrayal of Jessica Lynch. Although both women came from the same state, the wretched figure of Lynndie England abusing Iraqi prisoners provided a convenient cipher for the articulation of a different variant of whiteness fractured by class. Her behavior was too easily dismissed as "white trash," passed off by the president himself as "not the America" that he knew. Ann Coulter even used England's deviancy to argue against women joining the armed forces, on the grounds that they were too vicious. Investigating this episode further in the context of the Women's Studies classroom can provide a rich topical site for exploring and demonstrating the interconnected themes of race, class, and gender within an increasingly militarized culture at a time when the armed forces are stretched to the limit. There are important sociological questions too concerning recruitment practices, rates of desertion, the fate of veterans, and the adjustment of policies aimed at military spouses and families, as scholars such as Cynthia Enloe have painstakingly shown over the past two decades.

THE POLITICS OF IMAGINATION

Earlier on I cited the symposium conveners, in asking what other way have we to speak about women in Afghanistan, in the Middle East, in the Arabic-speaking world, without being drawn into the pitfalls of Orientalism, cultural imperialism, and civilizationism? This was the wrong question in many ways, because it is the act of speaking *about* that so often constitutes the problem. Instead of objectifying women on the basis of nationality, geography, religion, or ethnicity, it is crucial to remember that what is really required is a form of dialogue that depends on a readiness to speak *to* as well as an ability to listen.

The feminism of an earlier cold war era has taught that a politics of location is needed in order to anchor our critique of the world, wherever we are situated. Just as it is impossible to have a fruitful conversation with someone if you have already determined—and judged—what they are going to say, so the art of dialogue depends on being aware not just of where one stands, but also of how one's location might look from a distance. This demands qualities such as openness, imagination, self-reflexivity, and a willingness to take in what might sound strange and even counterintuitive to a feminist ear. The bitter experience of decades of struggle for women's liberation might have taught the folly of global sisterhood as a rallying ideal, but the dream of a feminist public sphere that is open to women from all over the world is today more appropriate than ever.

NOTES

1. *Beyond Rights Talk and Culture Talk*, ed. Mahmood Mamdani (New York: St. Martin's Press, 2000).
2. Susan Hawthorne and Bronwyn Winter, eds., *September 11th 2001, Feminist Perspectives* (North Melbourne: Spinifex Press, 2002); Zillah Eisenstein, *Against Empire: Feminisms, Racism, and the West* (London: Zed Books, 2004).
3. Recent research on gender and imperialism, slow in starting but increasing exponentially, provides an important baseline for the genealogical work that picks at the roots of European and American feminism. This can be read in dialogue with postcolonial feminism, a loose term defined by Robert Young as involving "any challenge to dominant patriarchal ideologies by women of the third world." Young, who has compiled a history of postcolonial movements, defines postcolonialism as a political philosophy that means "first and foremost the right to an autonomous self-government of those who still find themselves in a situation of being controlled politically and administratively by a foreign power." Robert Young *Postcolonialism: A Very Short Introduction* (Oxford: Oxford University Press, 2003), 109, 113.
4. The image can be found in *The Telegraph*, Calcutta, India. Wednesday, November 12, 2003. http://images.google.com/imgres?imgurl= http://www.telegraphindia.com/1031112/images/12britney.jpg& imgrefurl=http://www.telegraphindia.com/1031112/asp/foreign/

index.asp&h=115&w=170&sz=4&tbnid=lfdJf9q2rKEJ:&tbnh=
63&tbnw=93&start=3&prev=/images%3Fq%3DJessica%2BLynch%
2Band%2BBritney%2BSpears%26hl%3Den%26lr%3D%26sa%3DG.

5. Hawthorne and Winter, eds., *September 11th 2001.*

6. Ammu Joseph and Kalpana Sharma, eds., *Terror, Counter Terror: Women Speak Out* (London and New York: Zed Books, 2003).

7. Martin Chanock, "'Culture' and Human Rights: Orientalising, Occidentalising and Authenticity" in *Beyond Rights Talk*, ed. Mamdani (New York: St. Martin's Press, 2000).

8. *Women's Studies on its Own: A Next Wave Reader in Institutional Change*, ed. Robyn Wiegman (Durham, NC and London: Duke University Press, 2002).

9. Ibid., 368.

10. Ibid., 373.

11. Marnia Lazreg, *The Eloquence of Silence: Algerian Women in Question* (New York: Routledge, 1994).

12. Ibid., 7–8.

13. Ibid., 10.

14. Ibid., 8.

15. Phillip Knightley, "Fighting Dirty," *Guardian Weekly*, Monday, March 20, 2000 (http://www.guardian.co.uk/print/0,3858,3975978–103412,00.html).

16. Ron Suskind, *New York Times* magazine, Sunday, October 17, 2004.

17. Julian Borger, "Facts Fail to Bother Bush." *Guardian Weekly*, March 18–24, 2005.

18. Naomi Klein, "Brand USA Is in Trouble," *Guardian Weekly*, Tuesday, March 15, 2005.

19. Thanks to Caitlin Mitchell for this.

20. http://usinfo.state.gov/sa/Archive/2004/Nov/23–13202.html

21. (http://archives.cnn.com/2002/ALLPOLITICS/04/23/hughes. resigning/Karen Hughes's bio on the USAWC Web site reads: "Karen Hughes has been described as 'the most powerful woman ever to serve in the White House'" (*Dallas Morning News*) and President George W. Bush's "most essential advisor" (ABC News). As Counselor to the President for his first 18 months in office and as his communications director since he first ran for Governor of Texas in 1994, Mrs. Hughes has been a crucial influence in President Bush's inner circle. http:// usawc.state.gov/c10666.htm

22. http://www.cnn.com/2004/ALLPOLITICS/04/29/hughes.criticism/

23. This speech can be found on http://www.whitehouse.gov/firstlady/ news-speeches/speeches/fl20020129.html

24. Deniz Kandiyoti "The Politics of Gender and Reconstruction in Afghanistan," United Nations Research Institute for Social Development, Occasional Paper No. 4. Free download available at www.unrisd.org/ publications/opgp4.

25. Helpafghanwomen.com is a project run by the Feminist Majority.

26. See RAWA's Web site at http://www.rawa.org/malalai4.htm; and Afghan Women's Mission at http://afghanwomensmission.org/index.php

27. Sonali Kolhatkar, "Afghan Women: Enduring American 'Freedom'" November 2002. Based on Conference Presentation at Afghan Women's Mission Conference, October 2002. Published in Frontline magazine (India), Z magazine, and Foreign Policy in Focus. http://www.sonaliandjim.net/politics/index.html

28. Lazreg, *The Eloquence of Silence*, 10.

29. Saba Mahmood *Politics of Piety: The Islamic Revival and the Feminist Subject* (Princeton and Oxford: Princeton University Press, 2005), 1.

30. Ahdaf Soueif, *Mezzaterra: Fragments from the Common Ground* (London: Bloomsbury, 2004), 266–67.

31. Åsne Seierstad *The Bookseller of Kabul* (Boston, New York and London: Little, Brown, 2003).

32. Tim Judah "The Kabul Bookseller, the Famous Reporter, and a 'Defamation' of a Nation," *Observer*, London, Sunday, September 21, 2003, 3.

33. (http://www.bookbrowse.com/dyn_/title/titleID/1335.htm)

34. Zana Muhsen with Andrew Crofts *Sold: One Women's True Account of Modern Slavery* (London: Little, Brown, 1994), vii.

35. I have explored this case in further detail in "Defining Forces: Race, Gender and Memories of Empire," in Iain Chambers and Lidia Curti, eds. *The Post-colonial Question: Common Skies, Divided Horizons* (London and New York: Routledge, 1996), 150–54.

36. I have discussed this at greater length in *Out of Whiteness: Color, Politics and Culture* (Chicago: University of Chicago Press, 2002) coauthored with Les Back.

37. http://www.oshadavidson.com/Piestewa.htm

38. http://www.snopes.com/politics/military/shoshana.asp

LIST OF ABBREVIATIONS

AME	African Methodist Episcopal
AAR	American Academy of Religion
AIM	American Indian Movement
CBA	Christian Booksellers Association
CBE	Christians for Biblical Equality
CWA	Concerned Women for America
CBMW	Council of Biblical Manhood and Womanhood
EWCI	Evangelical Women's Caucus International
GED	General Educational Development
NAE	National Association of Evangelicals
NBEA	National Black Evangelical Association
NOW	National Organization for Women
NIV	New International Version
PCCNA	Pentecostal and Charismatic Churches of North America
PK	Promise Keepers
SBC	Southern Baptist Convention
WCC	World Council of Churches